Daniel Worcester Faunce

A Young Man's Difficulties with His Bible

Daniel Worcester Faunce

A Young Man's Difficulties with His Bible

ISBN/EAN: 9783337171889

Printed in Europe, USA, Canada, Australia, Japan

Cover: Foto ©Lupo / pixelio.de

More available books at **www.hansebooks.com**

A YOUNG MAN'S
DIFFICULTIES WITH HIS BIBLE

BY
D. W. FAUNCE, D. D.

PHILADELPHIA
AMERICAN BAPTIST PUBLICATION SOCIETY
1420 Chestnut Street

Copyright 1898 by the
AMERICAN BAPTIST PUBLICATION SOCIETY

From the Society's own Press

PREFACE TO ENLARGED AND REVISED EDITION

THE repeated calls for a new edition of "A Young Man's Difficulties with His Bible" have induced the author to revise the work, bringing it, especially in Chapter V., fully up to date. Here and there substantial additions have been made to the original text, and the book cannot but be more valuable than before. The author records with gratitude to God the very many instances in which he has heard that these lectures have been greatly useful. Some young men occupying prominent places in foremost churches have been helped to hold fast to their faith. In some cases young men in college who had gone over to the ranks of an open infidelity have owned that, under God, this little book has changed all the ideas of their life by changing all their conceptions of the Bible. May God similarly bless the new edition.

D. W. F.

PAWTUCKET, R. I.

PREFACE.

THE author, on assuming the pastoral charge of a church in a thrifty and intelligent inland city of New England, found in the community a large number of young men not exactly sceptical but a good deal unsettled in their views of religion. They were graduates of Grammar and High schools; intelligent young men who, though employed as clerks or apprentices, found time to read the papers, the magazines, and occasionally a book. They had caught the drift of one section of popular thought. They asked for some book which should meet briefly and yet fairly the difficulties which they felt. There were plenty of scholarly volumes, suited to men who had received a liberal education and who were masters of their own time. But a small, popular and at the same time accurate volume, suited to this demand, the author could not find. It occurred to him to invite these young men to state to him frankly their perplexities, and then to give a course of lectures on the general subject of these "Difficulties." The lectures were given to crowded houses on Sunday evenings, one in each month, for two successive seasons. It has been thought that good might be done by publishing selections from these lectures. A few of them have been taken, and the style somewhat changed from the spoken to the written form. The aim has been to give the results of careful study without the processes, to be as accurate in the statement of facts as if the work were to be used as a text-book, and yet to keep in mind the class of young men for whom it is designed. Every chapter, without an exception, has grown out of an actual conversation held with some young friend or else out of some letter or message received from him. When delivered as lectures the author received repeated thanks from individuals to whom they were helpful. Given originally to his former charge at Concord, N. H., a portion of the lectures have been repeated to the congregation which he now serves in Lynn, Mass. It is his prayer that God may make this little volume a blessing to those who read it.

D. W. F.

Lynn, Mass

CONTENTS.

CHAPTER I.
THE YOUNG MAN'S BOOK.................................. 9

CHAPTER II.
IS THE BIBLE TRUE?.......... 37

CHAPTER III.
IS THE BIBLE INSPIRED?... 66

CHAPTER IV.
DIFFICULTIES AS TO MIRACLES AND TEACHINGS........... 95

CHAPTER V.
DIFFICULTIES AS TO GEOLOGY............................ 123

CHAPTER VI.
DIFFICULTIES FROM ASTRONOMY.......................... 149

CHAPTER VII.
DIFFICULTIES ABOUT HISTORIC FACTS.................... 163

A YOUNG MAN'S
DIFFICULTIES WITH HIS BIBLE.

CHAPTER I.

THE YOUNG MAN'S BOOK.

IT is told of a certain publisher that he was in despair because a rival firm had issued so many excellent and successful books of advice to the young. He confided his perplexity to a friend. That friend advised him to select the finest paper and the clearest type, and then to reprint that book of the Bible known as "The Proverbs of Solomon" under the new and startling title of "Counsels for Young Men by a King." Whether the advice was followed, and whether if followed the venture was successful as a business speculation, is not known. But this is certain; that if some would be disappointed at their first opening of such a volume, on further reading they would be compelled to admit that the old book was new, and that the new book was the freshest and richest of all the many volumes addressed to young men.

Solomon had the advantage of knowing thoroughly

of the things about which he wrote. The son of a king, inheriting wealth, with princely tastes, with a love for learning, and a natural shrewdness in dealing with men, with manners courtly, elegant in person, a close observer of all the things and all the men about him, he gathered up the wise sayings of the ages, and passing them through the mint of his own mind, he issued them, newly coined, for the moral and social and spiritual currency of all the world. The Psalms of David his father were for closet use and for temple service on the Sabbath. The Proverbs of Solomon, the son, were for out of door life on all the week days of the year. David helps us sing and pray, but Solomon tells us how to live wisely when the prayer and the worship are ended. His proverbs are the condensed and portable wisdom of the ages. The versatility of the author is amazing. He seems to have listened to the prattling of childhood, and to the whispered accents of youthful lovers, to have put himself into sympathy with the trader in his store and the wife in her home, with the priest at the temple altar and the beggar at the temple gate, to have heard the grumble of the disappointed man and the chuckle of the man who has just seized on worldly success, to have heard all the haughty tones of the prince and the lowly words of the peasant, to have stood by manhood in its developed strength and by age tottering under the load of buried hopes towards a willing grave; and to each one of all these classes he interprets, better than the man himself could do it, the peculiarity of his wants, and the needs of his life, and then he offers by way of practical commentary, some quick pithy sentence of sanctified wisdom. He fused the older proverbs of the world, extracted the dross and retained the gold. He took up the selfish shrewdness of mere worldly wisdom, and where the proverb was wrong he made it right, and where it needed the salt of religion he always added it, as a power to purify and save. One idea, that of *godliness*, runs through the book. Wisdom is godliness; and by godliness he means "the love of God," and "the fear of God," the sense of the "eyes of the Lord as in every place," and of God as one who "will bring every work into judgment whether it be good or whether it be evil." This intense godliness is the golden thread on which all these pearls of proverb are carefully strung.

Nor was his Encyclopedia, for the book is really such in its character, the result alone of observation and learning. The author had known the *experience* of life. Written near the close of a singularly varied and extensive career, in which he touched heights and depths seldom visited by one and the same human soul, with memories of the widest possible contrasts of physical mental and moral position, an outcast at one time a king at another, here heading a rebellion and there the most loyal of men, at one time fascinated by philosophical speculations, next tossed to and fro by the dreariest scepticism as to God and the immortality of the soul, and again bedraggled in the mire of heathenism through the persuasions of his idolatrous friend, Hiram, king of Tyre, and then leaving his thin philosophy, coming out of his scepticism, and up from the slough of the lowest idolatry, we see him emerge upon the high ground of religion, humbled by his fall, penitent for his guilt, and resting, at length, as the result of the broadest experiences and as the climax of all his wisdom and knowledge, in the conclusion of the whole matter, that to fear God and keep his commandments is the whole duty of man.

His fall was indeed a sad one. For only one who stands so high can fall so low. Another has said of him that "He sinned with a high hand on a large scale and with a certain royal gusto. He drank of the cup of corruption deep and large; emptying it to the very dregs. His fall is instructive. The pinnacle overhangs the precipice. And any great proportion between gifts and graces renders the former fatal as is a knife in the hands of a suicide, or handwriting to a forger. His misery became something wonderful. And thus on all sides, bright or black, he was equally and soundly great. Like a pyramid, the shadow he cast in one direction was as great as the light he received in the other." In the Ecclesiastes we have his spiritual biography. We go with him through the changes of his infidelity, of his sensualism, of his ambition, of his disappointment in them all, and we see him in his return to God. And then, revising all his former work, recasting his maxims in the crucible of his own experience, and setting, in the purified wisdom of his later days, the seal of a divine inspiration upon them, he writes in his maturest years this book of "The Proverbs" which is addressed to the thoughtful and earnest men of the world.

Such is the book which commends itself to the study of young men. On further, we are to take up the matter of a young man's difficulties with his Bible. Objections are to be considered. The gravest questions about the volume which is popularly called by those who know it best and love it most "the Word of God," are presently to be discussed with what of fairness and candor we can bring to the consideration of them. But as every building must be in some way approached, as the architect plans always a portico to his edifice, so we will enter upon our work, through this royal gateway of ancient wisdom, by our study of Solomon—the wise man of the olden time.

Let us be sure that we get clearly before our minds the object of the author in this book, of "The Proverbs." There is indeed one general design running through all these books of the Bible. And yet under this general purpose, there are as many subdivisions as there are books. No two cover the same ground. For we have here a history and there a biography, in one book a direction as to what to believe, in another as to what to practice, now a collection of devotional psalms, and then an epistle to a church or a letter to a prominent man. But in each of these books there is a specific design to be accomplished.

What then, is the aim of the author in the Proverbs? A very brief examination of the book will convince us that its specific purpose is to show men their *duty in practical life*. It ferrets out men. It shows the eye of God's omniscience to be upon all the minutest thoughts and feelings and acts of our mortal existence. If other books concern themselves with the questions of our immortal life, this has to do chiefly with our present conduct as citizens of God's world. If any man says the Bible talks as if we had nothing to do but to die, talks as if "our life were all to be passed in a monastery or a church," we say to him, here, at least, is a book which follows you to your business, goes into the shop, comes behind your counter, sees the weights as true or false, looks over your shoulder at the ledger, goes back to your family, has a home thrust at every part of your daily life. There are no metaphysics here; for all is intensely practical.

If a young man with earnest heart comes to ask how he can gain the earlier inward experiences of religion, we would not point him to this book; unless we knew that some outward wrong had kept him from right feeling. It is true that we find the elements of every truth in this book of Proverbs. But who would go into a well that he might read by the starlight that penetrates to its depths, when he can have the full sunlight without that trouble? To the gospels, to that especially of John, would we send him; to the Acts of the Apostles he should go and see how inspired men answer the great question of the ages, "What must I do to be saved?"

But if a man is already a Christian and would know how on that foundation to build a noble structure; if he would do the best with himself, and make the utmost out of life, we would point him to the Book of Proverbs.

So, too, if there be any young man who has supposed that the ordinary social virtues are all the religion a man needs, and if he has an impression that the Book of Proverbs favors this idea, let him come and study these pages. He will find that no book is so at war with the idea of the merely ornamental virtues when not attached to a holy heart. God is in this Book of Proverbs. It insists in its opening chapters that sooner or later, in time or eternity, utter ruin will overtake the character that is not built upon "the fear and the love of God." Wisdom, moral wisdom, that which takes God's claims into account—is the basis of the morality it enjoins. This, the foundation stone, once laid, the book shows how every stone is to be hewn and every course to be placed as we build the edifice. And so all private life, and public life, all social, domestic, and political relations, all moralities and courtesies and charities are here separated and then combined and illustrated, their shape and color all given, and the whole commended and commanded to the young men of all ages and climes. Or, it may be, that one has imbibed notions which he thinks more especially broad and free. He cares less for the right ordering of outward life, thinking it more a matter of custom, convenience or education. He has become interested in the speculations of the hour as to the origin of all these things about us, and as to the laws of this wondrous nature that is engaging the attention and awakening the keen interest of the thoughtful and intelligent young men of the day. He is becoming less stout in his assertion of what man can do, and more aware of the mighty forces of the world. He is smitten by the majesty of law. He comes to think of this force, compared with which man's power is so feeble, as impersonal. Solomon became at one period absorbed in the thought of the objects of the natural world, as a modern young man is in danger of becoming absorbed in the thought of its laws. As the one found himself drawn to be an idolator, so the other is drawn towards fatalism in the presence of the vast powers of the universe. But there comes a time when a man sees the tendency of things. He has to own an impersonal Nature, or else a personal Creator and Sovereign. Fatalism says It, exactly as religion says God.

Each of these excludes the other. If there be a *God* who rules his universe, there is no room for the fatalistic *it*. If there be, in the smallest event, anything outside the divine control, then there is no more an infinite God. Fatalism, a century ago, loved to talk of all things as coming by chance, as if everything were too loose for a God. To-day it would insist that everything is so fixed, so bound by law, that there is no place nor need for God in the working of events. They work themselves out in definite ways. Buckle, with scholarly phrase, will have it that even moral actions are as fixed as physical events. And, in social life, a frivolous fatalism is constantly heard, saying, "It is all fixed, all fated. It happens so. It can't be helped. It is a thing of destiny. What is to be will be."

Now how is this fatalism to be met? By asserting the truth of man's free will? But that is simply meeting the vastly lengthened line of fatalism at one point. It is opposing an avalanche, by the brandishing of a pin. Within certain limits man is free. But his circle is as that of a peck-measure to the orbit of the most distant planet. A thousand things touch every man, over which he has no control. His birth, in its time, place, manner, circumstances, and, usually, his death also, are not matters of his own will. First and last and midst and always through his life, he encounters powers and events that are beyond his control. There is then no sufficient answer to fatalism in the undoubted truth of man's free will. There is one and only one answer broad enough to meet all the facts. It is the answer of religion. Religion insists upon a God, all-wise, all-just, who, through fixed law, and, if need be, over fixed law; who, through man's freedom, and if need be, over that freedom, can and does control all things according to the counsel and purpose of his own eternal intelligence and will. Strangely enough, some men always confound these two things—fatalism and the divine election. But they are as far apart as the poles. They exclude each other. Both cannot be true. One of them must be. And the only reply to the fatalistic *it*, is that furnished by the being and rule of a personal *God*.

Fatalism may be compared to a vast revolving iron wheel. It goes round remorselessly, pitilessly, crushing all before it. It can have neither intelligence nor purpose, neither justice nor compassion. It shrieks with every revolution, "It can't be helped. It must be endured. It is all fixed and fated. There is no purpose, no reason, no result. *It* is the only God." Before these awful revolutions of this terrible and monstrous lawless law—for law without a God is really lawless—all the light and love and joy of the divine Paternity are crushed out, and man seems to be the mere mote imprisoned in the mountain. Oh, how widely different in all its power on human life, is that great solar fact that "the Lord God Omnipotent reigneth!"

There is an ante-war incident that shows the power for despair of the one, and for hope of the other view. A dark cloud hung over the interests of the African race in our land. There seemed no way of deliverance.

Frederick Douglass, at a crowded meeting, depicted the terrible condition. Everything was against his people. One political party had gone down on its knees to slavery. The other proposed not to abolish it anywhere but only to restrict it. The Supreme Court had given judgment against black men as such. He drew a picture of his race writhing under the lash of the overseer and trampled upon by brutal and lascivious men. As he went on with his despairing words, a great horror of darkness seemed to settle down upon the audience. The orator even uttered the cry for blood. There was no other relief. And then he showed that there was no relief even in that. Every thing, every influence, every event was gathering not for good but for evil about the doomed race. It seemed as if they were fated to destruction. Just at the instant when the cloud was most heavy over the audience, there slowly rose, in the front seat, an old black woman. Her name, "Sojourner Truth." She had given it to herself. Far and wide, she was known as an African prophetess. Every eye was on her. The orator paused. Reaching out towards him her long bony finger, as every eye followed her pointing, she cried out, "*Frederick, is God dead?*" It was a lightning-flash upon that darkness. The cloud began to break, and faith and hope and patience returned with the idea of a personal and ever-living God. Such is always the result, whether we look out on the broad scenes of human history, or in upon the lowering events of any one human life. Everywhere *it* is the word of despair, and *God* is the word of faith and hope.

And as the divine plan of things is the true view of them, so there must be, unto the complete answer of all fatalism, an emphasis put upon the *eternity* of this divine plan of things. For are not all our thinkers pushing their inquiries backward? Are they not asking whence and when this established order of things? They go back before man to find his origin in some vast process of development. They push back their fatalistic *it* until they come virtually to make an *eternal* it. And the only answer possible is that furnished by the Scripture doctrine of an eternal God who from " before the foundation of the world hath chosen" the things that shall be. It is Solomon's doctrine that the recognition of the Lord is the beginning of all wisdom, and the sum of all knowledge. And Christian thinkers are being driven anew to assert this doctrine by the fatalistic tendency of certain lines of modern thought. As nothing less than the thought of an eternal and personal God meets the demands of the intellect, so nothing less than this meets the yearnings of the heart. How justly and beautifully has Faber said :

> "O Majesty, unspeakable and dread!
> Wert thou less mighty than thou art,
> Thou wert, O Lord, too great for our belief,
> Too little for our heart.

> But greatness which is infinite, makes room
> For all things in its lap to lie;
> We should be crushed by a magnificence
> Short of infinity.
>
> Great God! our lowliness takes heart to play
> Beneath the shadow of thy state;
> The only comfort of our littleness
> Is that thou art so great."

And when an inquiring young man is driven to this recognition of God, as a logical necessity of all thought, as a demand alike of brain and soul, of the outward nature that surrounds us and of the inward nature that is made to know and judge of these outward things and to trace back facts and laws to their only possible origin in the personal thought and personal act of a personal God, he has come to stand not only upon a broad and lofty ground, but beside all the best thinkers of the world. For some of those thinkers whose philosophic theories are often regarded as tending towards the denial of a personal God, make haste to deny the inference. Herbert Spencer claims that the doctrine of the correlation of forces does not exclude that of God, and Tyndall hastens to correct the inferable Atheism of his Belfast address.

And so the world's experience of philosophy and even of speculation leads a man back to the place where Solomon was brought—the place, beneath the fear, love and service of God, from which he never should have wandered, and which he entreats every young man never to leave.

Or, if one has been tempted to think it brave to doubt about God and the soul and immortality, this book will serve as a tonic for his faith. One book of Solomon, the Ecclesiastes, is the book of doubts; or rather the book of doubts solved. In that book, Solomon recounts the old arguments used when he was a sceptic, when he was a pleasure seeker, when he was astray in idolatry. We see him, hear him at his worst; and then, with him, go back to the "conclusion of the whole matter," in the devout recognition and the earnest service of God. But in the "Proverbs" there is a strong joyous faith which the writer not only possesses but commends to the young men of the world. The young man is addressed as *capable of faith*. God made man to believe. The great difference between him and the higher animals is very largely in the fact that he has the capacity for faith; the ability to believe upon testimony. The beast has no such power. The brutes can remember, can do many acts singularly like reasoning. But they cannot collect and compare evidence and believe and so act upon it. The men of fifty years ago collected various items of knowledge; and the boy of to-day starts where they ended; for he is able to believe. Not so the colts of to-day; for their sires collected no testimony. There is neither capacity to believe nor amassed material on which to exercise faith. Something can be done by interbreeding to develop other powers. But no capacity for faith in testimony can be developed in the brute creation. Hence progress for them is impossible. They have no faculties adapted to faith in others' testimony. They are made to know what they can through eye and through ear, by touch and by taste. Man alone is *capable of faith.* He receives most of his knowledge by credence. He believes it on the testimony of others. Man, unlike the brutes, is by his nature a believing animal. When he has no faith in testimony he is no better than a brute. A man's great characteristic is power to believe —to believe the testimony of his fellow-man and the revelation of his God.

Some young men are tempted to think that, since we have the power of doubting as well as the power of believing, we are to work both by doubt and by belief. But we have the power of doubting just as we have the power of sinning. We sin by perverting our powers. They were given us not for sin but for service. So we have eyes for seeing, but we have power to put them out. Nevertheless God gave us eyes not that we might be blind with them, but see with them. Seeing is the legitimate use of the eyes, just as believing is the legitimate use of the faculties of the mind and soul. And what blindness is to eyes made for seeing, that doubting is to a mind made for believing. When shutting the eye and closing the ear are the best ways of seeing and hearing, then doubting will be the best way of gaining knowledge about truth and duty. That young man who supposes that if he is just a little sceptical, he shall be more likely to know what is truthful, makes a terrible mistake. The habit of doubting is the least reasonable of all habits. For a man was made to believe; and he had better believe wrongly on some subjects, than to believe nothing on any.

There can be no progress by doubt and negation except in error. But, says one, "Would you not have a man doubt an error, and is not such a doubt a help toward coming to the truth." We answer that if a man doubts an error because he is in the habit of doubting, he will doubt the truth for the same reason. We would have him see and believe the truth, and then whether he doubts or does anything else with the error, is of no consequence. Let any young man see that the believing and not the doubting spirit is the guide to truth. For God made us and Jesus commands us to believe. So, too, if we are made to believe, there is *something to be believed*. God made the eyes to see something. If the feet are to stand, there is provided an earth to stand upon. If man is a believing animal there is somewhere truth to be believed. Truth must be a positive thing. It is of God. For God is the "God of truth." It is sometimes said that the truth to any man is what he honestly believes it to be. "It is truth to him, though error to another." If that were so, truth would not be truth, but only each man's fancy. But God made the mind to believe, and the truth to be believed. When a young man says "I cannot decide among so many religions," he says either that God has not given him brains enough to believe, or else has withheld the truth, so that he cannot know it. If he says the first he denies his own manhood; if he says the second he condemns his God for so making the mind and not making the truth which the mind was made to believe.

In dealing with his doubts a young man should also be careful not to deem doubting the sign of a stronger intellect. It is far from that. Anybody can doubt. And a man who is floundering in a sea of doubts has no right to call out to others to come and see how brave and strong a swimmer he is. The strong and brave swimmer is he who gets through and gains the other shore, and stands firmly on the rock. He who can never quite make up his mind on any subject is not usually praised for vigor of intellect. The young man who begins a trade, a business, a profession, and then, speedily doubting his ability or taste for it, turns to another only again to doubt his ability, is a young man who awakens only pity for his want of perception or of purpose. He who cannot make up his mind on any public question, who always doubts how to vote, gets no praise for manliness. Doubt and indecision are marks of weakness rather than strength, and this book of the " Proverbs " breathes all through it a bracing atmosphere of faith in truth, in right, in manhood and in God. It shows on every page the native nobility of the man who is strong alike in the integrity of his outward virtue and his inward faith.

The *plan* of the book of the Proverbs is in harmony with the design of its author. Its sayings are often used by us in disjointed fragments. For it is portable wisdom. But then any separate part is richer when seen in its connection with the scope of the entire book. It is not a chance medley of miscellaneous remarks. It is no mere scrap-book. It is far from being a confused mass of apothegm and epigram. The casual observer of the heavens on a winter's night might at first think the skies were full of bright disorder. To him it might seem as if God had scattered here and there the dust of stars carelessly over the firmament. But his friend bids him observe the lines of gigantic boundary, tells him of the order and place of each constellation and shows him that instead of chaos, there is plan in the skies. So it is with these proverbs. They seem like a whole firmament of gems. Such is their point and brilliancy that the very things that make them proverbs give them also their seeming abruptness and lack of connection. But the plan is there, and study will bring it out, until we admire the setting as much as the gems themselves.

The first part of the book comprises nine chapters. In these the importance of a well grounded and firmly settled piety is insisted upon for every young man. The dangers and duties of early life are pointed out so clearly that this portion of the book has been called the "Young Man's Directory." The second part, comprising the next fourteen chapters, supposes that the clerk or apprentice or student has acquired his business, his trade or his profession, and is ready to step forth into actual life. It tells him how to deal with men in such a way as to be prosperous and at the same time please the Lord. This second part may be called the "Merchant's Directory." The third division, though endorsed by Solomon, is the work of the son of a noble mother, who, with that mother in mind, sets forth the glories of true womanhood. It is the finest word painting in literature; and that too in a line where the poets of the world have woven their choicest garlands and sung their sweetest songs. But if these are the main divisions of the book, it comports well with its plan, that all through it, there should be delightful episodes; the bowers of fancy where the poet may sing his verses, and the gardens where the philosopher may walk without interruption while talking to the admiring disciples, who, after the manner of eastern scholars, love to call some veteran in wisdom by the name of master.

In a gallery of art there are large and even colossal objects in one picture, while another is a miniature of not more than a hand's breadth. And here in this gallery are pictures with a solitary figure—a single proverb; and there are also pictures of broadest artistic grouping. Here is a brief sentence, and there a long allegory. At one turn, we see the gilded coverings stripped from some sin, and at the next, the polished and barbed arrow goes home to the heart of a cherished wrong. And the whole is so condensed and pithy, so full and yet so keen, with outward duty mentioned and yet the right heart so insisted upon, piety blended with morality and morality so enforced by piety, that the book is always venerable but never stale, can always be consulted yet never exhausted. The oldest finds in it food for thought and the youngest a diversion and a delight. Those who enjoy the sketches of character and those equally who love to see a condensed argument in a single sentence, can find in this book the thing that suits their taste. Will that single proverb ever grow obsolete while men love their holy dead—the proverb that says, "The memory of the just is blessed;" or will men ever cease to own the aptness of the saying "The heart knoweth its own bitterness and a stranger intermeddleth not with its joys?" And who has not been compelled to say as he has met the experiences of life, "Faithful are the wounds of a friend, but the kisses of an enemy are deceitful?" And how pertinent the sentence, "The beginning of strife is as the letting out of water; therefore leave off contention before it is meddled with." What convert coming into the peace of God's forgiveness has not repeated those words, "Wisdom's ways are ways of pleasantness and all her paths are peace." Lord Bacon has been applauded for his saying "Knowledge is power." But put the word wisdom for the word knowledge, and Solomon had said the same thing ages before.

Observe also that many of these proverbs get their power from some picture in them. A comparison of a single word in the heart of a pithy sentence has made it easy to remember, and pertinent for quotation. "There is that scattereth and yet increaseth;" "He that watereth shall be watered;" "He that ruleth his spirit is better than he that taketh a city;" "The slothful man saith there is a lion without;" "A word fitly spoken is like apples of gold in pictures of silver." And if any man thinks these proverbs are mere truisms, let him pause over them and study them till they reveal themselves. He will find that there is a heart behind them. For they rise higher and strike deeper than the mere surface of our ordinary life. I never knew a man of sagacity, of practical skill in dealing with men, who was not fond of this Book of Proverbs. Such men have often these proverbs close at hand, an exhaustless treasure for daily use.

The moral sketches that are scattered through the book are worthy of our study. They are exceedingly graphic. Perhaps there is no more terrible sketch in the Bible than that given in the opening chapter. A young man is warned not to go out into actual life without true piety. If he shall do it, all will go wrong. If he shall do it, God will be angry. God against him, calamities will sooner or later gather about him, and destruction come like an armed man and there be none to deliver. "They shall call but I will not answer. They shall seek but not find." To the young man that laughs at religion and mocks at pity, who goes the voyage without the chart that God has given, he saith, "I will laugh at your calamity and I will mock when your fear cometh; when distress and anguish come upon you." And the reason for all this is given, in these words, "*because they did not choose the fear of the Lord.*" So that in the opening chapters we have the key note of the whole book, and no where is there any declining from this grand and lofty tone with which the book begins, viz: that the fear and love, the trust and the joy of the Lord are the essential things in a true and noble life. The high and beautiful severities of morality and religion stand forth, the glorious mountain summits that are never to be lost sight of in all our climbing. The air grows purer, the vision broader. The very precipices of doom are for a salutary warning that we venture not too near the shelving edge of any evil, lest we provoke God to leave us. And thus alike by warning and by wooing, by words that startle and those that encourage, by the fear of God and by the love of God, we are instructed, admonished, profited. The ruin of the godless man is made in this opening chapter a minister of salvation to all who propose to "walk not in the way of the wicked and refrain the foot from their path."

Another of these character-sketches is peculiar to eastern life as seen to-day among the unaltered customs of the Orient. There, enervated by the climate, by lack of general enterprise, by the ease with which the few necessities of life are gained, men will doze away a lifetime in an idleness that has no prosperity to excuse it. The idle man in the East is not a retired rich man, but often one who has need of daily labor. And Solomon's picture of the idler is drawn so sharply that we can almost see him in his sloth. There he is, prone on his bed, though the sun has risen, and others are at work. His fields are grown over with weeds. "Yet a little more sleep," he says drowsily when one would rouse him, —"Yet a little more sleep, and a little more slumber, and a little more folding of the hands to sleep"—and he has gone again. Roused once more, he turns lazily on his bed and says, "There is a lion without in the way; yet a little more sleep." Do *we* need to study this picture? If we had lived in the former ages before industry had become a passion of the nations, some exhortation towards worldly thrift might have been needful for us. But industry is the New England virtue, and a lazy man is the contempt of the community. And yet this outward thrift is often unattended with any inward aspiration. "To get on in the world" becomes the great aim. The intellect is often untilled, and the soul is a luxuriant wilderness of weeds, the chance growth of accident on a soil that needs to be reclaimed and redeemed for God. Idlers on one field we despise. Then must there be care lest, looking on the picture which Solomon has placed before us, we should fail to see his two-fold meaning; fail also to see that we may have escaped from the one to be ensnared in the other and the sadder peril.

And the drunkard is also sketched by our royal artist. The twenty-third of Proverbs has been called the "drunkard's looking-glass." "*Look not* upon the wine when it is red; when it giveth his color in the cup; when it moveth itself aright." Do you see the man in the picture as he balances daintily the cup, as he looks lovingly upon it, lifts it carefully, then drains it off deliberately with the gusto of the finished drinker. He does not look within. He does not see the bottom of the cup. But Solomon—and he had seen it in a sad experience—will allow us to look through his eyes. And now looking closely at the picture, you will see that Solomon has painted a *serpent* in the cup. How plain it is. It is visible to every one except to the drinker himself. And as he drinks "it biteth like a serpent and stingeth like an adder." The deadly wine begins to circulate. Through every part of the system it is borne. And now comes the result. "Who hath woe? Who hath sorrow?" "Who hath contentions,"—is ever quarrelsome? "Who hath babbling?"—that word "babbling," is the very word; for the silly besotted man has now become a creature to whom blasphemy is wit and nonsense wisdom. " Who hath wounds without cause?"—received of course in some low drunken brawl. " Who hath redness of eyes?" "*Those that tarry long at the wine.*" It seems then that a man may become wretchedly, boisterously, filthily drunk, though he may only drink wine." He continues,—"Thine eyes shall behold strange women." Strong drink feeds the flames of a raging lust. "Thine heart shall utter perverse things. Yea; thou shalt be as one that lieth down in the midst of the sea, or as he that lieth upon the top of a mast." Is not that an exact description of the staggering gait of a drunkard? "They have stricken me, thou shalt say, and I was not sick; they have beaten me, and I felt it not." The poor inebriate has been kicked and bruised by the men who induced him to drink, and he did not know it at the time. And when he comes to understand it, instead of resolving never again to touch the maddening draught, he cries out, " When shall I awake? I will seek it yet again."

Such is Solomon's picture. And, if I could get every young man who reads this volume to look fairly upon that picture in its faithful lines and its terrible colors, and then could show him that there was the remotest possible danger of such a fall for himself; or that some friend might thus fall; or that there is one solitary man on earth who might come down into this misery;

C

and if, on the other hand, I could show him that by total abstinence he could certainly preserve himself, could prevent his friend, could hinder even an *enemy* from this result, I should have an argument of no small force to press upon him for signing at once the most stringent of pledges to avoid all that intoxicates.

And surely there never was a more strict pledge than this of Solomon. "*Look not,*" he says. We think it enough to say, drink not. But he knew the force of the temptation. The color, the sparkle, the very sight may awake the demon of appetite that is never allayed. "Look not on the wine."

There is also, in these Proverbs a picture of true and noble *womanhood*. And it stands right over against a vivid portraiture of her whose house goes down to death. In the latter sketch, the wiles, the tempting words, the whole process of allurement are described; and then the folly, the wretchedness, the miserable and accursed end of him " Who goeth after her straitway as an ox goeth to the slaughter." " Her house is the way to hell going down to the chambers of death." But the other portrait, how beautiful—beautiful in itself and beautiful in contrast. It is the portrait of a noble woman—the picture of a mother by her son. " The heart of her husband doth safely trust her so that he shall have no need of spoil." " She worketh with her hands." The writer had no idea of a human doll too dainty for labor and fit only for show. " She riseth and giveth meat to her household." She is domestic, and yet while domestic when there is need for it, she is skilful in trade. "She considereth and buyeth a field." She is industrious—for it is said, "her hands hold the distaff." She is charitable. "She stretcheth out her hands to the poor." But mind and heart are not neglected. "She openeth her mouth with wisdom." "Her children rise up and call her blessed." She has helped and not hindered her husband's prosperity; for it is said "Her husband is known in the gates, when he sitteth among the elders of the land."

I would have a young man believe in God with a practical daily faith. I would have him believe in good men, and keep company with them. But next to this, I would have him believe in a pure, noble womanhood. There are doubtless base women. There are frivolous creatures, who live with no plan but to see and to be seen. And such women a young man should avoid as he would the plague. But there are those whom God sends for a man's help and guidance. He who believes in noble womanhood can find it. He who sneers at woman's virtue only proves himself to be base. A true man shows the nobility of his nature by his high ideal of womanhood; and in turn they who are to meet that ideal have need to be careful of purity, honor, intelligence and religion.

Enough has been said to show the general spirit and tone of this book of the Proverbs. Its peculiarity above any other one book of the Bible, is in the fact that it is directly addressed to young men. And this sketch of its contents is placed here at the beginning of the discussion as a sort of a portico, royal in its origin, attractive in its form, through which we may enter the temple of revelation, and mark certain mysteries, certain wonders, even certain difficulties that have perplexed many a young man and kept him from joining in the worship.

It may be too, that going through this open door we shall discern more clearly the general plan of the Bible, and see how that in adopting each of all the forms that Hebrew literature took upon itself, we are specially privileged with that variety of literary method which enables us to behold truth in its many-sided attractiveness. Proverb and psalm, history and song, law and prophecy, are all seized upon and built into the wonderful edifice. The book is thus the "Young Man's Book," not only as addressed in many parts of it to young men, but as opening before them a life-long study; so that they can be sure of a line of thought and a theme of interest that will never clog. Age will not wither these inquiries; for man shall never outgrow these questionings and answerings that are at once stimulated and gratified in this book.

CHAPTER II.

Is the Bible true?

"You believe in the Bible, I presume," said a man to his fellow passenger in the railway car. "Certainly, I do," was the instant reply. "I presume you believe in it because of your mother's teaching," said the first man, in a sneering tone. "Precisely so," was the answer, "I do believe in the Bible for that among other good reasons." "I don't see," was the reply, "how that can be a good reason. Suppose your mother had been born a Hottentot, you would then have believed in idolatry, or, if she had been an Indian woman, you would have had faith in Juggernaut." "I probably should," replied the other. "I am surprised to hear you own it. Nine-tenths of the people who believe in the Bible have no better reason for their faith than just this; their fathers taught it to them, and their mothers made them say their prayers, and so they believe in religion. I am independent. I don't mean to believe any thing because somebody else does so." "Stop," said the other, "Stop right there and hear me a moment. I was taught the Bible by my mother, by her life as well as her lips. The Bible made my mother the best, the sweetest, the noblest woman I ever knew. It was her strength in life; her comfort in sickness, her all in death. I saw what it did for her, and I started with every presumption in its favor. I have other, and perhaps to you, they would be stronger, reasons for believing in my Bible. But let me tell you that for myself the strongest of all reasons is that my mother, and she was such a mother, taught me its truths. I had a Christian home. I have travelled some; and I know that there is not a Christian home on the continent of Africa; there is not one in Asia, aside from what this religion of the Bible has done within a few years just past. In the hut of a Hottentot, or in the tent of a Bedouin Arab, I should have been taught in another religion, exactly as I should have been taught in another kind of astronomy, and natural philosophy and geology. What then? Shall I think less of the true system of astronomy because I was educated to believe it in Christian New England, or doubt the facts of natural history because Agassiz taught them to me in America? Shall I believe less firmly the facts of science because I learned them under circumstances most advantageous, in places where they could best be learned, and from the best of teachers? And as for you, sir," turning to the other, " let me say just this; either you had or did not have an early Christian home. If you had a pious father and a praying mother, and were taught the Biblical truths, and now have turned away from the Holy Book, you are,

I am certain, far less of a man morally for it. For you have not the sanctions of that book when you do right; nor its warnings when tempted to do wrong. You are not so pure, so strong in principle. Right and wrong, good and evil are not words with so much meaning as they would have had if you had read your Bible and striven to shape your life by its directions. Or, if you had no Christian home, if your parents were not devout people, then you started in life under a terrible disadvantage, a disadvantage to your moral nature as great as it would have been to your physical nature if you had been born without feet or without hands. And instead of you reproaching me for my mother's religion, I am the one who should pity you for the terrible calamity under which you commenced life—the calamity of not having a Christian home." "Yes," continued the young man, "I do believe in the Bible, in part at least, because my mother did. And it is dearer because it was *her* Bible, and my God is more reverenced because he was my mother's God, and Christ is loved because he was my mother's Saviour, and heaven is more precious because the heaven of the Bible is my mother's heaven."

And the sceptic was silent. What was there for him to say?

Many a young man educated to believe the Bible is entirely satisfied for himself. He knows that the book, which, universally obeyed, would bring universal joy— for that is its result as far as its precepts are followed—

must be God's book. His Bible is true. And yet, he is disturbed sometimes by the objections brought against it. He wishes to be more familiar with the outward evidences of the integrity of the Bible, that he may answer the sneers of opposers, and also that he may feel sure, on other and independent grounds, of the truthfulness of the Scriptures. And there are some young men about whom, early in life, were thrown hosts of difficulties and perplexities; and these were accompanied with sneers and innuendoes against Christians. Such young men have no appreciation of the moral agument from the elevation of a Christian home, nor can they understand the moral power of those benign influences which make up the moral atmosphere into which the more favored young men of this country were born. So that the argument to be presented in this chapter, having these two classes of young men in mind, must needs be both historical and moral.

We will ask two questions. One of them is this: "*Is the Bible true?*" The other, immediately following it in logical order, shall be: "Is *the Bible inspired?*"

In asking whether the Bible be true, the question is of the same kind as that raised when we inquire whether Macaulay's or Motley's or Bancroft's histories are true. It is an inquiry whether the persons who wrote these books of the Bible were eye-witness of the facts, or, if not, whether they had access to documents which they used so fairly that we can trust them as we do other historians. When they state facts in their narrative, we propose to ask first as we do about any other writers of history, *Are they credible men?* Are they men whose character, opportunities for knowledge, whose presumed motives and whose conduct in life warrant our confidence? Finding them reliable historians, men who state actual historic facts, it is indeed possible that we shall be compelled to go further. It may be that if true, they are true about such things, and in such a way true, that we shall be obliged to go on and to own their inspiration. But the inquiries before us now are with reference to their truthfulness, their integrity, their credibility.

We cannot here take up in order the vast number of facts they state, and examine them in detail. That would be to write a commentary on the Bible. Nor can we quote at length the testimony of travellers in the lands of the Bible, nor recite the evidence accumulating every year from Assyrian, Babylonian, Judean and Egyptian tombs and monuments—that vast mass of corroboration of many of the more important statements which are given in the scriptures. This is a field of unspeakable richness and of unfailing interest. No one can spend an hour with such a book as Rawlinson's " Historical Illustrations of the Old Testament" without wonder at the new evidence, reserved for the investigations of the present generation, of the minute accuracy of many portions of our historical scriptures. To enter on this field is impossible for us in this volume. Nor is it needed. For the strictly historical argument is really very simple; is narrowed down to the establishment of a very few facts which any man of ordinary judgment can easily understand, and about which he can easily make up his mind. The whole inquiry concerns the New Testament. And of the New Testament we need only to consider the integrity of the four Gospels. For if these biographers of Jesus are to be trusted, our Lord indorsed the Old Testament and *promised* subsequent books of the New Testament similar to those which we have now in the Epistles and the Revelation. So that the whole inquiry for us is just this; have we reason to believe, that Matthew, Mark, Luke and John have given us a fair and correct account of what Jesus Christ said and did ? To this inquiry the whole matter comes at length ; and on this thing depends the historic argument.

Nobody doubts the existence of just these sacred books which we call the Old Testament in the days of Jesus. He quoted that volume, citing those very facts to which most objection is made, viz.: the fall, the flood, the attempted sacrifice of Isaac by Abraham, the manna, the lifted serpent and the story of Jonah. Sometimes he quotes the volume itself; sometimes he gives the name of the special book from which he quotes. To a people venerating their sacred writings to the verge of bibliolatry he said "search the Scriptures," and he continually was saying that certain things were done, " that the Scriptures might be fulfilled."

So that the whole question of the integrity of the Old Testament, though abundantly capable of defence on independent grounds, for us, in our present argument, may be said to be involved in that of the truthfulness of the New Testament. And as the Gospels indorse the Old Testament, so they also carry with them the integrity of the Acts, the Epistles and the Revelation. Assured that we have a fair record of what Jesus did and said, we find among his undoubted discourses direct promises of a superhuman guidance, not only in bringing to mind what he had said to his disciples, but in guiding them into all truth ; even that which he could not tell them while he was in the body. He had more truth to reveal when the Holy Spirit should be given and they were to be shown the things to come. And assuming that these Gospels accurately report him, where shall we find the fulfillment of his promise except in these later New Testament books ? These later writers make the claim, and they are the only serious claimants to-day. If Jesus spoke truly in the promise as recorded in the Gospels, then these other New Testament books are the fulfillment of his words.

The whole matter comes down to very narrow limits. A thousand incidental questions may be raised which have only an incidental bearing. The decision as to *three vital questions* will decide the whole case. They are these. *First:* did books substantially like our four Gospels exist in the earliest Christian centuries?

Second: did the authors of them enjoy opportunities for knowing what they affirmed; and were they such persons that we can trust them to tell us the truth? And *Third:* have these four histories of Christ been preserved with as reasonable a degree of integrity, and have they been as fairly transmitted to us as have the works of other ancient historians?

As to the first of these inquiries, viz: the early existence of the books, little need be said; for the unanimous verdict of scholars is well known.[1] Volney and his school, in an unfortunate hour, ventured to utter doubts as to whether Jesus and his apostles had ever lived. It was instantly shown that heathen and Jewish, as well as Christian *historians* testified to the existence and influence of him and his religion. And in the face of the fact that Christ's religion, as recorded in these books, had named an era in human history, this class of sceptics saw that they had blundered. And no decently informed man repeats these absurdities to-day. Rosseau, himself belonging to another school of scepticism, published an answer to Volney, in which he insists, that if Jesus did not live, those who invented such a character as that given in the four Gospels, putting

---

[1] Those who desire a full discussion of this matter can find it in the elaborate work of Tischendorf, "When were our Gospels Written." See also Westcott's, "Introduction to Gospels." In these lectures, I have endeavored to give the results reached in the present state of Biblical scholarship, without entering at all 'nto the processes by which those results have been gained. This is true both of this and the following chapter.

such words into the lips of an imaginary being—have performed, in so doing, a greater miracle than any that they ascribed to Jesus. To-day the assent is uniform as to the existence of these biographies in the earliest Christian centuries—a fact allowed by Strauss and Renan. No matter, here and now, for the way in which these two distinguished authors account for the fact. No matter for any theory, once attracting some notice and now vanishing, of myth as mingled with historic truth. No matter, so far as the present part of our inquiry is concerned as to whether the books contain only a mere substratum of truth ; no matter if any one should have the hardihood to venture again the absurdity of Volney that the very basis was false. The argument now is about the early *existence* of these books,[1] the Gospels. And here there is an absolute unanimity ; all admitting that such documents, the basis of appeal for both friends and foes as to the alleged facts, did exist in the earliest Christian centuries.[2]

[1] "The strictest historical investigations bring this compilation—even by the admission of Strauss himself—within thirty or forty years of the time when the alleged wonders they relate are said to have occurred."—*Henry Rogers* in " *Reason and Faith.*"

[2] On this point see the exhaustive treatment of Westcott in "Introduction to the Study of the Gospels." He shows that the " Oral Gospel," was the first Gospel—the story of the facts as told by word of mouth ; the apostles repeating the facts. And he shows why t was so for years in Palestine ; and how, at length, out of this, came the Four Written Gospels ; the apostles committing their facts to writing when in the course of nature they must leave their work—a work in which they could have no

These four histories of Jesus Christ began to be read in churches as they became known; John's Gospel being thus indorsed and employed last, because last written, and because one early sect deemed the teaching of John's Gospel to be in opposition to their peculiar views.[1] But these objections were soon removed, and the Chris-

successors. Jesus himself wrote no line. Not that he was unable so to do; for his knowledge of "letters," *i.-e.*, languages, amazed some of his hearers. He knew the Aramaic, his native speech; he quoted the Hebrew; he used Latin words, again and again, with the precision as to derivation which marks the scholar; he quoted from the Greek language the very words of the Septuagint. In adopting the oral method rather than the written, he did exactly what other teachers of his age were wont to do. And so far from an objection, it is a confirmation of Christianity, that it represents our Lord as adopting at the outset the usual oral method.

[1] For an account of this sect, the Alogi, see Westcott's "Introduction, etc."; in which there is shown the reason why this heretical sect hesitated for a time to acknowledge this Gospel *as inspired*. But the point *here* made in my argument is not the inspiration but the *existence* of the book. And as to its genuineness as history, it is perhaps a stronger proof of the carefulness of the early churches, that while there was the least doubt, they hesitated But doubt for the reason given by the Alogi—that it condemned their doctrine—is a doubt which is an evidence of the integrity as well as the existence of the Fourth Gospel. Not one solitary fact was ever alleged against the genuineness of the book, save this that I have named. The hint which was thus furnished 1700 years ago has been taken up and used by unbelievers within the last fifty years. And the decision of 1700 years ago is now reaffirmed. Ewald, the great German critic, who has devoted immense labor to the matter, sums up the whole discussion as follows: "Every argument, from every quarter to which we can look, every trace and record combine to render any serious doubt upon the question *absolutely impossible.*"

tians of the early Christian centuries received the books of Matthew, Mark, Luke, John as the authentic documents of the new religion.

The second inquiry is as to the authorship of these books. All accounts represent the authors of them as once residents of Palestine. All accounts represent them as plain men; in part Galilean fishermen; with one only of them, Luke, the physician, a man of professional education. The writers were plainly not scribes of the law; they were not ecclesiastically educated men. But it is equally sure that they were not untutored peasants. They show a peculiar but an untrained ability. They see things clearly, and have the mastery of a style of description that in its simplicity is at a world-wide remove from that of the elaborate historians of the age. They had just keenness and culture enough to make the very best class of witnesses to a question of fact, and to enable them to state that fact in honest, unadorned, but accurate language. That they were men of either the ability or training required to *originate* such a character as that of Jesus Christ, is too absurd for any man's belief! What! Galilean fishermen describing such a character, putting him into the most trying positions, in which he never once failed, placing words in his mouth that have led the wisdom of the ages,—*they* giving us the only ideal of perfect manhood that is found in all the literature of the world— and doing this out of their own brain—mere novelists depicting an imaginary hero! To believe *this* is a far greater demand upon our faith than to believe any or all the miracles that are found in the Bible. Our Lord must have lived, and these men must have been with him in the intimacies of social life as well as in his public teachings. They must have been witness of his miracles and so his historians[1]. An actual life, and the historians of that life his friends, intimates, disciples— these two things are demanded by the whole scope and the entire detail of the books themselves. Nor is there another claimant to the authorship of them. It is they, or the authors of books that would have made a world-wide reputation for any body, are unknown. The verdict of the world is given in favor of Matthew, Mark, Luke and John as the writers of the respective books which are everywhere known under their names.

As to the theory once defended, but now entirely abandoned, that they were impostors, it is enough to remark that the ordinary motives to imposition are wanting, and that it is not possible to imagine motives for such a kind of deception, much less that these men could have done it, and then could have succeeded in foisting their imposition upon the keenest age—the Augustan age—

---

[1] Mark's Gospel is an exception only in appearance. For, (1,) the *internal* evidence that it is the work of an eye witness is stronger in Mark than in any other Gospel. And (2,) the Gospel is Peter's Gospel as to facts, while it is Mark's as to arrangement and verbal authorship.

which the world has ever seen. Impostors could not if they would and would not if they could invent such a character as that of Christ.

The theory of imposture surrendered, is that of *self-deception* any more plausible ? Enthusiasts with fancies for facts would have fared ill in publishing their pretended histories to a keen generation in which not a single false or even exaggerated statement could have passed unquestioned. Names, dates, places, references to streets and to persons, to public facts and private details, are scattered through these Gospels with lavish hand. And with such means of detecting the error furnished to them in the very documents themselves, it is certain that the skilful opponents of Christianity would have seized upon any alleged fact, and have proved it false, if that could have been done ; and in this way they would have inflicted such a serious blow upon the new religion as to have crushed it at the outset. For in no way could they have so destroyed the force of the new faith as by showing an error in its authentic documents on a question of public fact. Had such error been detected it would have been at once published to the world ; and, once published, the work containing it would not have been allowed to perish. But no such work exists. Keen opponents there were, who, if Jews, ascribed the Gospel facts to Satan, and if Gentiles, ascribed them to magic; in either case owning the facts ; and always quoting the facts from these accepted narratives of the Evangelists.

D

And as to the theory that these Gospels *might have been* written and placed in their present form partly by good men and partly by bad men—a theory just now most popular with objectors, and a theory the most desperate and the least plausible of any—it is enough to say that what might have been is not a proper matter of historic inquiry. No absurdity can be greater than to imagine the doings of this singular conclave where pious saints and impious knaves have met for the purpose of foisting Christianity on the world,—one party supplying a miracle and the other furnishing the teaching to match it, and the two woven together so firmly in one narrative that, like the seamless robe of Jesus, no men may part it. Or, if the good men and the bad men are supposed to have worked separately, what more incredible than that bad men should retouch the draft of good men, and their patch-work of evil be undiscernible from the original fabric, unless it is the still more incredible supposition that good men should consent to retouch the draft of evil men, knowing it to be the evil work of such men, and yet indorsing it! Strange good men, those!

The *third* point of vital importance is as to whether there has been a fair transmission to us of these Four Gospels. They were at once earnestly sought and highly prized by the friends of the new religion. The doctrines founded upon these facts which they state were made instantly matters of controversy. Every one can see that it would be impossible to interpolate a new miracle or new sermon into these Gospels to-day. And for the same reason it would have been impossible fifty years after the books were written. Enemies were alert, and friends were already divided in their views of doctrine and duty. To have added any thing of importance, any new fact, favoring any particular school of belief, would not have been allowed any more than it would be to-day. In the second and third centuries, amid the divergence of beliefs, it was wished by some of the sects to obtain if possible the attestation of the apostles to the new doctrines and practices. But mark one universally conceded fact. The heretics, not daring to tamper with the recognized documents, invented others, *new Gospels*, to some of which the more bold ventured to affix the names of the apostles. But to all the Christian world by the close of the second century the fraud was as apparent as it is to us to-day. A few persons were deceived for a time. But the imposture is as evident as would be the interpolation of a sentence of Jefferson Davis' speech on secession into the Emancipation Proclamation of Abraham Lincoln. In a subsequent discussion this matter will be named again. It is mentioned here only to show that the very existence of such fraudulent books, is a positive proof that the accepted documents could not be then altered by the insertion of any new miracle or doctrine.[1] They could no more have

---

[1] Westcott, in his "Introduction, etc." has shown that in the

been purposely corrupted or changed then, than they can be to-day. Of course no miracle is claimed for the preservation of the Scriptures. In printing the Bible even with our splendid facilities there occur typographical errors. Indeed it has been claimed that no volume of the size of the Bible has ever been printed without some mistake. But these errors do not harm the substance of a volume. The most of these are of about the same importance as the omission to dot an *i* or cross a *t* on the written page. They are never alleged as against the integrity of an author's work. Changes in languages, differences caused by thousands of various readings as in other ancient works, have had their influence upon the text of the New Testament. But these things injure the integrity of the books just as little as they do the works of Cæsar and Sallust and Virgil and Demosthenes. These verbal variations are merely curious questions of nice scholarship, and do not affect any one of the great Christian facts.[1]

The Gospel writers are unimpeached. The records are fairly preserved. For the jealousy of friends as well

second century the *whole New Testament*, as now we have it, Epistles, and Acts and Revelation—the Gospels of course much earlier—was accepted with the same reverence with which Christians regard the Scriptures to-day.

[1] 'By all the omissions and all the additions contained in all the manuscripts no fact is rendered obscure or doubtful."—*Pres. Hopkins.* " By none of these variations etc., shall one be able to extinguish the light of a chapter or disguise Christianity but that every feature of it will be the same."—*Bentley.*

as the hostility of foes has combined to preserve these documents from any considerable error. They are trustworthy histories of actual events. And these true, as has been shown before, they carry with them the truth of the Old Testament which they indorse and the remaining portions of the New Testament which they promise.

It would be of interest to note how the Gospels once ascertained to be true and so the other parts of the scriptures also true, that they in turn yield their evidence to these four Gospels. Given the books that go before, given also those that follow, and somewhere there must be such books as these gospels; and it is these or none that can fill the conditions of the question. The Hebrew ritual obliges us to find somewhere the New Testament Christ. And the Acts are impossible apart from the christian facts which they indorse and out of which they grew. And Paul takes up every main fact, not by any special purpose, but incidentally, in his epistles, so that he has been called our fifth Gospel.[1] But all this is incidental proof, nor need it be entered upon.

The vital points of the historic argument have been presented, and the proof given that we have in the works of Matthew, Mark and Luke and John, trustworthy histories, and that in a fair degree of purity these books have come down to our own times. And it is clear that,

[1] See this idea developed in an article "Paul as an Argument for Christianity" in "Baptist Quarterly," October, 1873.

these points proven, we may turn a deaf ear to a hundred minor questions, even if they have difficulty in them. For these questions are of side issues, and they bear only remotely on the subject. The opponents of Christianity have skillfully raised many a discussion on these side issues ; and the friends of a historic religion have allowed themselves to be seduced from the main question to engage in controversy on points not vital to the main argument. Says Isaac Taylor, " The subjects of debate in the Christian Argument have come to us in inverted order. The logical order is this : Are the *principal facts* on the reality of which every thing rests, real or not ? If *they* are true, the conclusion carries with it all we need. If they are untrue, then a laborious discussion concerning such things will barely repay the few who abound in leisure and learning."

In a very simple way elsewhere we ascertain a question of common fact ; as for instance, of the sailing of a ship from Liverpool to New York. There are a thousand incidental questions that can be asked about that ship, all of them of interest, some of them highly important for other purposes, but none of them having the least bearing on the inquiry " did the ship actually make the alleged voyage from Liverpool to New York." Questions might be raised about her hull as wood or iron ; about her cordage and cable as wire or rope ; about her capacity as so many or not so many tons ; about her engines as American or English ; about her cargo and of what proportion was dry goods and what hardware; of her officers and her crew as capable or inefficient, and of her voyage as smooth or rough. And it is possible to conceive of men as exercising their ingenuity so sharply on these things about that ship, and raising thereby such a multitude of difficulties, that some would be inclined to express a doubt as to whether there was such a ship and such a voyage. And this is exactly what has been done about the Bible. Opponents have seized upon minor matters and pressed them. They have drawn off public attention from the very few vital facts, against which, once established, all objections are useless. They have discussed questions as to sails and hull and course and cargo. Meanwhile there are just a few facts which can easily be settled, as to the voyage of the ship, and which decide fully the whole matter. They are these three: Did she sail? And the record on the books of the Custom-House at Liverpool settles that inquiry. Did she arrive in New York? And the record on the books at New York is the evidence. Is the record correctly transcribed and faithfully forwarded? And this third inquiry can be easily made, and an exact answer be given. And this closes the evidence. Precisely so in the case before us. The three questions we have discussed as to the Four Gospels, cover all that is essential. Nor should any young man allow himself to be confused by inquiries not vital to the historic argument for the integrity of these books.

The argument stands unimpeached. And the religion of the Bible is able to make the high claim, that it is a *religion of facts*, and a religion that presents these facts as proof that it is from God.

2. To the *moral argument* we now turn. The general influence of the Bible on men is a fact that one cannot overlook. The question is not whether any perfectly obey it. But whether any are made better by it; whether its tone is healthful. Does it elevate society to have the Bible circulate in the homes of a community, to have the Sabbath it enjoins devoutly kept, to have the religion of the Bible studied and practiced in some fair degree? I need not ask these questions of any young man. They scarcely admit of being stated; for the whole thing is almost self-evident. There is not a piece of property that is not worth more, nor an industry that does not thrive the better, for the practice, however partial and imperfect, of the precepts of the religion of the Bible. The church building increases the value of the property in the town; and purely as a means of general thrift, of public virtue and moral education, in more than one New England community, men of sceptical views have given liberally towards the erection of the sanctuary and the support of the Sabbath School. It is true that some have insisted upon charging the wars and persecutions unfortunately too common in human history to the influence of the Bible. But this is to confound its pure teachings with man's perversions, mis-

takes and hypocrisies. As reasonably might an argument be constructed against all government on the ground that men had wrested it from its purpose and used it as an instrument of tyranny. If every ciime has been at some time perpetrated under the name of religion or of government, we are not to attribute that fact to any thing that belongs to pure religion or good government. Surely we are able to make the distinction between the Christianity of the Bible and man's corruption of it in human history. And the good influence of Christianity—good in exact proportion to its purity—is seen everywhere. It is the strength of law. It gives purity to public sentiment. It favors learning. It extends the domain and strengthens the motives of all sweetest and most blessed charities. It gives sacredness to social life. Everywhere it is the friend of truthfulness, of honesty, of purity, of every noble virtue. Could bad men have given the world such a volume as the Bible, even if they would; or would they if they could?

It is moreover a singular fact that those who *know this book best love it most.* They are best qualified to judge of it. The devoutest students of it are just those most thoroughly persuaded of the divine origin of the book. True, some persons of intellectual eminence have rejected Christianity. But in nearly every case, they have not known intimately the New Testament. For it by no means follows that because one is eminent as a naturalist, or as a mathematician, or as a historian, or as a literary critic, he is therefore a Biblical scholar. A mathematician and not a poet is the best judge of a question in the calculus. Indeed the poet's opinion may be worthless. And so on these questions of the integrity of the Bible, an array of great names is sometimes quoted on the side of unbelief. The eminence of these men in their own department, so far from qualifying them for authorities in such Biblical questions, is often the very thing that renders their opinions on this matter almost valueless. Hume's historical inquiries were confined to a certain secular line. Huxley's naturalistic studies are not of the slightest value in questions of religion. Large attention elsewhere, hinders necessarily large attention here. Hume gave himself to history and philosophy. His works would stand substantially as now if he had never seen a New Testament. For his arguments are directed against all religions, and indeed against all actual knowledge of every kind. He aimed to sever the relation of cause and effect. He needed no acquaintance with the New Testament to construct a metaphysical argument which strikes a blow equally at all religion and all science. Voltaire's name has been quoted among those whose scholarship has been arrayed against revelation. But he had no scholarship at all on *this* matter. He made blunders that would have disgraced a Sunday-school boy of a dozen years, in quoting Biblical incidents. He gave his life to other books, and did not know the Book he denied. And Gibbon at 22 years of age or thereabouts says, "Here I suspended my religious inquiries." And he confesses to an idle life before this time. Surely such a man, however eminent in other lines, has no weight at all as against the sentiment "they who know the Bible best love it most." There are men of majestic intellect, and of calm, careful, profound scholarship, men who have made this book their study for years— men like Newton and Pascal and Leibnitz and Edwards and Chalmers; and these are the men competent to testify in the domains of scholarship. Nor scholars only. There are tens of thousands of honest, careful, sound-minded men in every walk of life who have just lived mentally and morally on this book. They have thought of it on the week day and studied it on the Sabbath. *They know the Book.* If an imposture, they would be the first to discover it. If it did them harm to practice the directions of the book, they would long ago have renounced and denounced it. They are honest, trustworthy men, if there are any such on earth. And they say that they read it with more and more interest and admiration and love with every year of their life. Such evidence is not to be set aside.

There is also a wide difference between the *morality* taught by the writers of the Scriptures and that expressly taught by the leading sceptics of the century now ending. Some of these writers of the Bible were certainly men all of whose acts no one defends. And here is the thing to be noticed; they do not defend themselves. In wrong doing they do not go with but against their own teaching. They condemn their own mistakes and confess their own sins. We had not known those sins, but for their honest confession and condemnation. Their precepts and the vast preponderance of their personal conduct are certainly on the side of virtue. But what of the *teaching* of men like Herbert, who declared that lust and passion were no more blame-worthy than hunger or thirst; like Hobbs who maintained that right and wrong are but mere quibbles of imagination; like Bolingbroke who insisted that the chief end of man was to gratify his passions; like Hume who declared that humility is a vice rather than a virtue, and that adultery elevates human character. Paine was in his last days a drunkard, and Voltaire was found by his friends to be so often a liar that his word was worthless. Let a company of men believing these teachings organize themselves into a society for putting them into actual practice in any community, and that community would be compelled to rise and expel the foul plague from their borders. In short, let a company of men undertake to obey such teachings exactly as a church is organized to obey the teachings of Christ, and let them do it as far as Christians obey the precepts of the Bible, and who could or would endure it? And while the Biblical precepts perfectly obeyed would bring almost the old Eden days to our sorrowful earth, these precepts of sceptical writers perfectly obeyed would make a very pandemonium of wretchedness and abomination.

The moral argument for the Bible plants itself upon the substantial agreement of its different parts. Revelation is progressive. There is a progress of development from first to last. And truth is given in forms more crude in the earlier and more finished and comprehensive in the later books of the Bible. Hence here and there those merely verbal and temporary discords which serve, as musicians say, to heighten the whole effect. Those who would make capital of these things playing off a partially revealed truth of the Old Testament as in some sense antagonistic to the full-orbed truth of the New Testament, only show their lack of appreciating the breadth of God's plan in his Holy Word. And as to the slight discrepancies of the Evangelists, it is enough to say that they are just such and so many as a lawyer likes to have among the witnesses on the side of his client. For they prove that there was no collusion, no agreement to support a fraud. These little discrepancies are exactly in those things necessarily omitted in the mere sketches and fragmentary notices of Jesus Christ which these writers profess to give us. As between any two of them, often a single word supplied incidentally by the third gives us the missing link that was needed to make the story coherent. And some difficulties remain on the face of the narratives when we would make a perfect harmony of the order of the events, which doubtless one word would solve—a word that, needless then, would be helpful now. It was indeed no part of the work of either to indorse the others. When they do it, it is not of design. Each had his own work to do, and did it. Had they been careful of their own harmony, mutually indorsing each other, their evidence would have been terribly weakened. But their carelessness in that matter, their "abandon," to their work, by which they go each straight to his own mark, without one thought that Peter's facts may cross Matthew's, or John's narrative injure Luke's story—their perfect unconsciousness of any suspicion—these are among the evidences of their divine commission. And the agreement not only in the facts, but what is far more important, in those great ideas that run through the Bible as to God, as to immortality, as to the way of salvation, as to a judgment, as to future awards—the agreement as to the *ideal* of Jesus Christ shown by the four writers of our Gospels, shown also by the writer of the Acts, shown also by Paul, by Peter, by John in their Epistles—*this* is the highest and best possible agreement, an agreement deeper than that of mere words. We see the blended rays of the same great solar truth, whether beheld in the promise of its dawning, in its onward march up the sky, or in the full glory of its midday completeness.

There is a powerful moral argument in the *idea of*

Jesus Christ which the Scriptures present. Reference has been already made (See page 61) to the fact that the writers of the four Gospels are in substantial accord, as between each other, in their portraiture of the character of Jesus Christ. But here the argument is drawn from the *ideal* itself. Whence came the *thought* of such a person? If he is a fiction, existing only on these pages, somebody originated the fiction. And whoever that person or that company of persons, it is certain that the creation of such a character was too great an achievement for the party or parties to remain unknown. But where are the claimants of this greatest of honors? Who originated the idea? Even Rousseau, himself in some respects a sceptic, was struck with the moral majesty of the conception. He writes as follows:

"Is it possible that a book at once so simple and sublime should be the work of man? Is it possible that the sacred person whose history it contains could be a mere man. What purity, what sweetness! what sublimity in his maxims! What profound wisdom in his discourses! What truth in his replies! Shall we suppose the evangelic history a mere fiction. It bears not the marks of fiction. The history of Socrates, which nobody presumes to doubt, is not so well attested as that of Jesus Christ: the marks of truth are so striking that the inventor would be a more astonishing character than the hero."

Again I ask the question whence this idea of Christ ?

Did a knot of plebeians in Galilee, the most despised portion of a far-off Roman province, themselves unskilled in the grand conceptions of Grecian or Persian or Arabian poets and philosophers—did they *invent Christ?* Setting aside, now and here, the absolute impossibility that they should have perfectly depicted him —depicted him with just enough of diversity to give unity to our impression of him, where did they get the ideal perfect man. There is one, and only one explanation. *Jesus must have lived.* His disciples saw him, listened to him, reported him. The Roman hero was no such character. An educated Roman would have made Jesus say, Blessed are the brave, the heroic and the noble. A brutal Roman would have said, Blessed are they that can strike back; the men of nerve and muscle for the combat. But Jesus said, "Blessed are the meek." A Grecian would have made him say, Blessed are they who, wrapped in the contemplation of divine philosophy, forget the common herd of men, above whom they stand. But Jesus said, "Blessed are the poor in spirit." The Pharisee would have had him say, Blessed are the exact and careful in the ritual law. The Sadducee would have had him say, Blessed are they who care for this life, as the real life, and leave the future, if there be a future, to care for itself. The Essene would have had him declare, Blessed are they that conquer the body with stripes well laid on for righteousness' sake. But Jesus, turning from every form of Jewish ideal, said, "Blessed are the pure in heart, for they shall see God." Hillel, the first Rabbi of the age of Christ, would have said, Blessed are the educated in the Levitical law; "for no common person is pious."[1] But Jesus said, "Come unto me *all* ye who labor and are heavy laden, and I will give you rest." How is it that here we have a character absolutely perfect! Whence came the *idea* of Jesus? There is only one possible answer. And that answer owns that the one great miracle that of Christianity, its sun to which all other miracles are but the stars, is the *character of Jesus Christ!*

[1] His very words. And yet the Jews to avoid the force of the powerful argument in support of Christianity of the *character of Christ*, have intimated that some of his sayings might have come from their Rabbi Hillel; a hint not lost on Renan in the French novel which he has called "The Life of Jesus."

CHAPTER III.

Is the Bible Inspired?

PILATE'S question "What is truth," has been called the question of the ages. For we are made up in such a way as to believe in truth. And no matter how many wrong answers have been given, the fact remains that men will believe that truth is *real*, and that the *truth can be known*. This is so, of course, only about what can be proven. And we have seen how careful is the Bible to appeal to evidence. Christianity is a question of fact. It offers proof of its truthfulness in miracle, in prophecy, in peculiar teaching, in the person of Jesus Christ.

But every young man opening the pages of his Bible can see that, true at all, the book is peculiarly, grandly true—a kingly book among men's books. The tone of it is unlike anything else in all the literature of the world. It asserts. It speaks with authority. It does indeed give proofs. But it does it easily, incidentally; never with labor, as if men were hesitating and so it must hesitate; never as if doubting somewhat its right to the most direct and positive speech; never as if its absolute authority could be questioned. It is a book that, allowed to have any claim, must be allowed all it claims. True at all, it is true in such a way, and about such things, that there is not nor can there be any other such volume on earth. Nor is this claimed for the Bible simply on the ground of its literary character. It has indeed poetry that is sublime, history that is dramatic in its form and careful in its fact, and narrative that is unequalled in simplicity and dignity. These are the indubitable marks of human genius. It needs no proof that some of these writers—the claim is not made for all—were men of exalted ability. They have made a book that is without a peer. It stands up alone, apart, peculiar in its claims, giving evidences of its truthfulness, and compelling homage for the genius that irradiates its pages.

And now comes the further inquiry as to this Book, the truthfulness of which we have already ascertained, whether besides human genius, there is also divine guidance ; whether God had any thing to do with this book in a sense in which he has not had with any other ; whether the book has not only the human inspiration of exalted genius, but also the superhuman inspiration, not of angel or of seraph, but of God's Holy Spirit. And the inquiry is whether, obliged to admit as much as we have already seen with reference to the book, we are not compelled to go on, and to admit that the book is divinely inspired.

Let us ask what is meant by the *inspiration* of the

Scriptures; next consider some of the *objections* to this claim; and then let us attend to any direct *proof* that this human book is really a divine inspiration.

We are sometimes asked to define inspiration. Let it then be at once conceded that it is easier to describe than to define what we mean by that word. Even as to those sudden intuitions, discoveries, disclosures, those revelations of the mind to itself as to the way in which a given thing can best be done, that surprising insight which in some gifted moments enables us to see what was dark before, that quick flash of sunlight on the perplexity that had baffled our study for days and weeks, that unravelling and clearing of a tangled skein of things, that glad heart-throb when an idea is born, a thought struck out, an invention perfected—even as to these inspirations of human genius, it is not easy to offer any careful and exact definition. The great inventors and discoverers and poets and painters and orators cannot tell you what it is they feel. They can only give us some very general account of the state of mind in which they are when seized upon with the idea which they have given to the world. They say it must be felt in order to be understood.[1] But we have no man

---

[1] Mozart describing the state of mind in which musical composition was to him most lively and successful says; "Then, the thoughts come streaming in upon me most fluently, whence or how is more than I can tell. Then follows the clang of the different instruments; then if not *disturbed*, the thing grows greater, broader, clearer. I see the whole like a beautiful picture. This is delight."

living to-day who is under a *divine* inspiration; the inspiration not only of one's own genius, but of a divine guidance for the communication of new moral truth to the race. We have no man who has the peculiar consciousness of speaking "the words, not which man's wisdom teacheth but which the Holy Ghost teacheth." And only incidentally did those who once were thus inspired tell us of the state; nor do they inform us how they knew when they were and when they were not under the influence of this inspiring Spirit. Evidently it was not their ordinary and normal state as Christians. For they often distinguish between the sanctifying and the inspiring influence. But if they do not define they describe; and if they do not tell us specially of the state itself, they tell us of the results of that inspiration in the production of the volume which we call the Bible.

As we look upon these pages, we see that there must be a great variety in the forms and degrees and kinds of inspiration. The inspiration where a man is an eye-witness of events which he is to record must be very unlike that needed when a man is uttering prophecy, the full meaning of which it may or may not be needful for him to comprehend. And yet in all of it there may be needed that superintendence which preserves from actual error, even in the record in things that have fallen under the direct notice of the narrator himself. And besides the evidence furnished in the volume itself, as to the kind and degree of this guidance, we must take the testimony of the writers of a book which we have found to be truthful, with reference to the fact of their inspiration. They claim, and their work proves it as well as their words, that their work is twofold in its character. It is human, they say. And they say, just as distinctly, that it is the work of God's inspiring spirit.

Beginning, then, on the *human* side, in our description, we should say that we have here in the Bible a book written, not by angels, not by God, but by *men*. Their own description of the human element is given in the words of one of them as he speaks of his work and that of the others. It is this; "Holy men spake as they were moved by the Holy Ghost." Notice the recognition of the human element.

"*Holy men* spake." They were voluntary agents, using their own human language. But they "spake as *moved by the Holy Ghost.*"

And in this combination of a human element and a divine element, we have not partly the one and partly the other; not one text fallible and the next infallible. But all of it is of man, and all of it is of God. God penned not one word. Man wrote it. Man wrote not one word by himself unwatched, unassisted of God. So that it is both man's word and God's word. It is the work of Moses, Isaiah, John, Paul, and the rest of them. And yet at the same time it is God's inspiration of man's thought as he was "moved," and of man's word as he "spake."

Or, approaching this matter from the *divine* side, as do these men sometimes in their descriptions, we hear them say, "All Scripture is given by *inspiration of God.*" So that we have an instance in which God takes up frail and imperfect men and human language in order to come near and reveal himself in human *literature,* even as he has done in human nature by his Son Jesus Christ.

And just as a superior overworks and absorbs an inferior power, so God infuses his thought into men, and secures its accurate expression by them. And thus they become his voluntary or his involuntary instruments. When they are bad men, as in the case of Balaam, the inspiration is involuntary. These cases are few. And when they occurred, it was to confront and overwhelm evil prophets and evil men. But the Scriptures, it is claimed, were God's inspiration through good men to teach the world authoritatively the truth it needs to know. There is a human element; and so we see various styles and methods of writing. But there is, we claim, a divine element, and this overspreads and animates the human; the stronger using the weaker. As God is true, so his word is true. It is without admixture of error, and is thus a final authority in faith, in doctrine, in duty; and it contains all about religion that we need to know or can know on earth. "The word of the Lord is perfect."

Two men, intimate friends, are seated together at the same table. One of them will write a narrative of certain events on which he has a considerable degree of knowledge. It is necessary that the narrative should be accurate. The first shall write; but the second, whose knowledge is full, accurate, perfect, will help the first man. He names no new items of information. But he corrects the impressions of the first so far as they are imperfect. If a wrong word is about to be used by the first, the second man suggests the right one. If the preposition *to* will convey the thought to be expressed better than the preposition *of*, he suggests that word in place of the other. He writes not a word himself; yet on the other hand not a word is written but he weighs its meaning and indorses or corrects it. In the narrative, as corrected and published to the world, you have the style of the first man, his peculiar methods of expression. It is his book. But it has also all the accuracy, all the thoroughness, all the *inspiration* of the second man.

Given the Holy Spirit in the place of one of these men, and Matthew Mark or Luke, in the place of the other, and you have the very case before us. And the result is a human book, and a divine inspiration, a book all of man, and also a book all of God.

Let us consider, next, some of the popular *objections* to the divine inspiration of the Scriptures.

The *individualism* every where apparent in the

volume has been urged as antagonistic to its claims. Paul does not write like John, nor David like Moses. And this fact has been alleged to be inconsistent with a divine revelation. To which it is enough to reply that there is no reason why God's inspiration through a man should change his style of writing any more than it should alter the features of his face. Indeed, these peculiarities are fresh proofs of the divine wisdom in the selection of fitting instruments to do a given work. To know men is kingly. To know them so as to use them, each in the best way, is proof of superior genius. A wise general employs subordinates according to their gift. Grant had his Sheridan for the valley of the Shenandoah, and his Sherman for the march from Atlanta to the sea.

And when, in his providence, God has a work to be done, he has always a man to do it. In like manner when he has a revelation to give to men about matters touching eternal salvation, he selects not weak or unsuitable men. That would be to ignore his own infinite wisdom. But he has a Paul to write the epistle to the Romans, and a David to sing the songs of holy experience, and a Luke, the physician, to chronicle the life of Jesus, and a John to reason not through the brain like Paul, but to enwrap all truth in the roseate hues of his own loving heart. God makes no mistakes. Paul never has John's work to do. The inspiring spirit adapts means to ends.

Another objection is drawn from the scientific allusions of the Bible. "A perfect volume," it is said, "should be perfect in its science." Yes; we reply, if it attempts to teach exact science. But the Bible makes no such claim. It is a religious book; recording facts from a religious point of view, and teaching men about God and duty. When it alludes to science, it adopts the scientific language of its various eras. No other course was possible for such a volume. Had it used the terminology, had it declared the discoveries of the centuries since it was written, the book would have been loudly denounced in all former centuries as false. A volume claiming to be five hundred years old that described the modern steam engine and the telegraph would be likely to awaken not only suspicion but derision. Indeed, had these scientific truths been here stated, the fair inference would have been that the Bible was a forgery. Then, too, if it had used the words of exact science, the world would in many things have utterly failed to understand it. And as to "exact scientific accuracy," about which so much is said, who will pretend that we have come to the era of perfect science? We are, in our turn, to be laughed at a thousand years hence, for our mistakes in astronomy, in geology, in chemistry and in all the other sciences. Perhaps allusions to exact science, as it is to be in some coming time, would be riddles to us.

"But does the Bible teach scientific *error*," asks

one. No; it teaches nothing about science.¹ It names the facts of the physical world and the mental world as illustrations of moral truth. To-day we find, in the most careful writers even upon astronomy, allusions to the "rising and the setting" of the sun; to "the ends of the earth;" and to "the revolution of the heavens." To deny the accuracy of such writers because they employ the popular phraseology of their times is absurd. A revelation from God in our human language must use the modes of speech, scientific, literary, or even religious, which men commonly employ at the time when its writers are living. It can do nothing else. The attempt to do otherwise would awaken suspicion. And no course can be more unfair than to demand that a revelation from God shall tally with "the latest form of science," whatever that phrase may mean. For who

[1] What the writer would assert is, that science, in its classified and arranged form, is not distinctively taught. There are Biblical *facts* of Cosmogony, of Geography, and of Ethnology. The Bible goes not out of its way to state them. Some of our Christian scientists have been at great pains to show that when it is said, "He hangeth the earth upon nothing," there is the *scientific* statement of a fact; similarly some have dealt with the Mosaic account, which in advance of modern science, they say, has put the light before the sun, the plant before the seed, the period of fishes and plants before man. It is not intended, in the above, to assert that when the Bible teaches a *fact*, scientific, geographical, or ethnological, it is of no authority. Far from that. But as against objections, it is claimed that, in the mode of statement, its usual language is not that of scientific theory, deduction, and classification. "Science," says Webster, "is a collection of general principles or truths *arranged in systematic order.*"

shall tell us which of the conflicting theories of eminent geologists is to be taken as the standard on any question they have raised; say, if you will, on the question of the age of the earth. They differ from each other by tens of thousands of years. But if they agreed in placing the age of the earth at any vastly distant period of the past, there would be no conflict with the Mosaic story. For interpreters there have been, even from the second century, who have stoutly insisted that the opening verses of Genesis describe an indefinite past age in which God created the matter out of which he subsequently shaped the earth, as recorded in the succeeding verses of the sacred story. And not only are geologists divided among themselves, but they are in conflict with leading naturalists like Agassiz, and especially with leading astronomers like Thompson, who deny the immense age of the earth which is claimed by the theories of leading geologists. The "latest phase of science," is a difficult thing to be ascertained; for these phases chase one another like cloud-shadows across a mountainside, so that it requires a nimble eye to keep even some general knowledge of them as they come and go.[1] It

[1] Lamark held to "spontaneous generation" and the "variation of species." The view was so modified by Darwin as to be made antagonistic in fact to Lamark's speculation. But Romanes' "physiological succession," if given any large place, is equally antagonistic to Darwin's "natural selection," while Le Conte contends for intermittent advance. Wallace insists that Darwin's great doctrine of natural selection is not proven; and if proven would be entirely inadequate to account for the origin of man. Owen con-

may be that the Darwinian theory of the "survival of the fittest," finds its real application when applied to the multitudinous theories of scientists. And yet all truth that is really gained, from whatever source, is gladly welcomed by intelligent believers in the Scriptures. For they hold that the facts of the world of God and of the word of God will stand. Science is the name we give to the interpretation of the one; theology is the name we give to the interpretation of the other. Neither science nor theology can add a fact or change a fact. There are the facts in the world and in the word. We simply classify, and, as best we can, explain them. They often are mutually explanatory; for they show in many things that they have a common origin in the mind and heart of God. When after the clash of theories, the truth has obtained the victory, when that has survived which was not always the most confident and most noisy in its claims, it has always been found hitherto that science and religion, the interpreters of God's world, and God's word were not aliens but friends.

We can afford to wait when adverse theories rise with eminent men as their defenders. For the history of science, while it has its living achievements, is also a strand sown thick with opinions once earnestly defended and honestly believed, but now regarded not only as

tends for the physical unity of the race, and Agassiz, while granting the *moral* unity of the race, contends for different pairs in different geographical centres.

untrue but absurd. The truth about a created nature and the truth about an inspired Bible will survive ; and all the record of the past warrants the belief that these truths will be found evermore in essential agreement.[1]

Another objection to the inspiration of the Scriptures is drawn from the *history* of our usually received sacred books. It has been alleged, that the selection of these books was arbitrary ; that uninspired ones may have been included and inspired ones rejected; that what is called the "Canon of Scripture," was made by men, their taste and judgment deciding what to accept and what to reject from a multitude of writings all professing to be inspired.

The reference is to the fact that some few hundred years after the death of Christ, a Council or Convention of churches made public declaration to the world as to what books had been believed from the first to be genuine Scriptures. For there were forgeries in that age. Heretics, unable to introduce new verses into the well known documents, devised new Gospels ; and here and there a man had been for a time deceived. But these apocryphal Gospels have come down to us. And

---

[1] The grand old book of God still stands, and this old earth the more its leaves are turned over and pondered the more it will sustain and illustrate the sacred word.—*Dana.*

All human discoveries seem to be made only for the purpose of confirming the sacred Scriptures.—*Herschel.*

In my investigations of natural phenomena, when I can meet any thing in the Bible it affords me a firm platform on which to stand.—*Maury.*

any man who knows our four Gospels and then compares these apocryphal books with them, will not wonder an instant at the rejection of writings full of puerilities and absurdities—writings that carry, by their allusions to manners and customs absolutely unknown in the days of Christ, their own refutation; writings the whole tone of which is utterly unlike that of the New Testament. And this is so evident that if these rejected books are true, our Gospels are false, and if ours are true these are an imposture. The inventors of these apocryphal gospels never designed them as substitutes, but only as additional gospels. But they go not together; "the new agreeth not with the old."

It is customary for some church creeds to make declaration as to the books they hold to be inspired. Churches did the same in the second century. This is done to-day where Romanism prevails, to show that Protestants do not regard the Jewish books called the "Apocrypha," as having divine inspiration. A church of Christians at Salt Lake City would be very likely to make a statement of their belief in this matter, so that none should suspect them of believing in the pretended revelations of Joseph Smith. But he who should assert that such a declaration, made to-day, was an arbitrary or accidental settlement of a question that was not settled as much before, would hardly be more wide of the truth than those who insist that a similar declaration in the second century was accidental and arbitrary; and that it was then, for the first time, claimed that these books were inspired. God's people are intrusted with his Word, and it is their duty to make statements to the world of their belief. So did the early churches ; so do those of to-day.

The alleged *discrepancies* of the Scriptures have been urged as an objection to its inspiration. It is admitted, nay claimed, that there have been and still are things in the Scriptures "hard to be understood." But their number is rapidly diminishing. Under discoveries in sacred geography, under explorations in ruins where long buried inscriptions give the missing facts that have explained hundreds of apparent discrepancies and have thrown light on verses of the Bible that seemed almost contradictory, under researches in natural science and ancient history, the things once thought to be stones of stumbling are many of them among the strongest confirmations of the truth of Holy Writ. And when larger investigations have been had, other difficulties without doubt, will vanish, and in their place shall stand new evidences.

And when it is remembered that these books of the Bible were written by men who lived in lands widely distant from each other, in different ages, in different languages and dialects, in centuries in which there were different ways of computing time and also different eras from which to date the years, in which periods of time of the same name were of different lengths, and even days were differently arranged as to their hours, the only wonder is that we do not find more difficulties of this kind—difficulties that do not seriously impair the confidence of any candid man in the integrity of religious teaching of the Bible. These writers in giving lists of families, quoted from public official documents, and any error in official tables that did not affect their immediate purpose it was not theirs to examine and expose; they used here Jewish and there Roman methods of computation; and probably, sometimes, Assyrian and even Grecian methods. The inspired Ezra reëdited Moses, and gave, exactly as is done in modern works, a word or two as to the author's death. Different writers, living years apart, give in different words, and from different points of dating, the facts of Jewish history. They copy public documents in one case or rely upon personal memory in another, with exactly such small disagreements as might be expected. The differences touch nothing vital; and all of them may be yet explained by our fuller knowledge, as has been the case with other difficulties in the past.

Our ignorance must not be set down as against the Bible itself. In nothing perhaps is our ignorance so great as in this matter of chronology.[1] And we have

---

[1] "Chronology is peculiarly difficult when we have to do with oriental modes of computation which are essentially different from ours."—*J. R. Thompson.* Hebrew and Arabic permit one to write first the units and then the tens and then the hundreds, or to *reverse the order*, and write the highest first. Hence con

exactly the same trouble in making out the figures of Josephus and other ancient authors as in the case of the Bible. The ease with which mistakes may be made when, as in all the older records of the race, letters are used for numerals, is acknowledged by every scholar. That such errors in matters not vital may have crept in, would not be denied by many fast friends of revelation. And yet others after the most careful study of years, find no need of admitting that there are such errors. In either case they never affect the reality of Christian fact or the substance of Christian doctrine. For the truth, which, as its friends claim, is here given, is not the truth of inspired science as of Geology or Astronomy or Chemistry. It is *moral* truth as supported by the great historical facts of the dispensations which culminated in the advent of Jesus Christ. Nor do the friends of the Bible claim any miracle in its preservation but only such providential care that the books shall not become worthless for the purposes for which they were given. For we may be certain that the God who guides the fall of the sparrow would not allow an inspired book which was of any use to the world to-day, to be lost. For this age needs, as does each age, a directory reliable and sure ;

fusion and the liability to terrible over-statements in translation. The case in Samuel is an illustration, where " fifty thousand three score and ten men," are mentioned. Literally it is " seventy " and " fifties" and " a thousand,"—which *may* mean either as in our version, or it may mean one thousand one hundred and seventy a volume without admixture of error in its statements of moral fact and human duty.

In short, all the objections ever urged have one defect. They forget that the book is professedly *human.* They forget that the presence of the human element, so far from being an objection, is the very thing for which the friends of the Bible contend. No matter if Paul uses bad grammar, if Jesus speaks the impure Aramaic of his time, if Matthew writes with Hebrew idioms; no matter if Luke uses round numbers rather than exact figures. These men are men; and it is *men* for whom we claim inspiration. But they are men used of God as the stronger uses the weaker; God's inspiration preserving them from error when they utter religious truth. Did you ever stand beside the pilot of a noble ship as she bounded over the billows a thing of life? Did you ever watch his eye as it glanced at the compass, then up at the sails, then over the side as he saw the coming wave? If every thing goes right he stands motionless. But if he sees that a flaw of the freshening wind is about to change his vessel's prow but a trifle from the true course, how quickly he turns his wheel to meet the new deflecting force. Or if a broad wave, gathering on her quarter, is about to strike his ship from the line of her progress, swiftly he reverses his wheel. And thus amid all the disturbing influences of wind and wave, the pilot, with hand on the helm, guides the ship surely and safely in her unchanged path. So God guides the men through whom he will make known his will. The helm governs the ship. God is the helmsman, and this is the bark. Amid all human imperfections, amid the veering of winds and the tossing of the waves, the helmsman never steers wildly, never loses his control, never is deflected from his course. Man's book, we most fully believe, has God's inspiration.

There is proof that this volume is the inspired word of God.

1. It is *reasonable* to believe that God will give somewhere an inspired volume. No one has any too much light about religion. The wisest man, the loftiest soul among the Greeks declared that "the great want of the race is a book inspired of God." See the failure of men without it. They are like the dove sent from the ark, unable to find rest for the weary feet. Some tell us that reason is enough without revelation. But the keenest and most philosophical mind of the ancient time, the Greek mind, was busy at the problem of religion for centuries. And the result of the study of the finest, clearest, most penetrative thought of the race is seen every where else. In literature, in the plastic arts, in oratory, that mind leads still the world. But how about its religion? What is the result here? Just this; that the traveller seated on one of the prostrate columns of the temple of Jupiter Olympus at Athens, is compelled to remember that "Jupiter, king of the Gods," has not a worshiper on earth to-day!

Is reason then of no avail ? Very far from that. We only say it is no substitute for revelation. It teaches just this ; the need, and so the probable supply of the great want of our race, viz., a revelation of God in human literature. It is reasonable to believe that God has revealed his will and our duty somewhere in the course of human thought. He has revealed himself in other ways. Why not here, in the line of human literature ; and as a man discloses his thought in a book, why not God use the same simple and obvious and expected method in revealing *his* thought unto the race ? Indeed such a book is a necessity for us as much as light for the eye, and air for the lungs. God made the want in us, and God has made the supply. Otherwise we are left to men's conflicting guesses, and inevitable weaknesses, and perpetual mistakes in matters most vital to our souls' interests. There are things we need to know, and which we never can know unless God tells us ; for only God can know them of himself.

And if God must reveal himself in literature we may expect it in inspired documents concerning his Son Jesus Christ. And if this Bible is not that revelation, then somewhere in connection with the record of these facts it must be found. There is no competitor. It is this or none. There is not even the resemblance of a claim anywhere else. Even Mahomet claimed no revelation directly from God. It was through the *angel* Gabriel that his pretended inspiration came. Outside this Bible I do not know a book on earth claiming *divine* inspiration.

The *intuitions* of our hearts teach us this need and also prepare us to expect that somewhere there is a revelation from God about religious truth. Some have said a man's own intuition or spiritual insight is enough. But how is this? Theodore Parker's insight affirms "man is immortal." But Mr. Newman, over the sea, declares that his consciousness says nothing about it. Mr. Herbert Spencer "thinks we cannot know anything by our consciousness, insight, or in any other way about God, whether there is or is not such a being;" while Mr. Parker thinks that "we are all directly conscious of God."

The truth is that, left alone to their own consciousness or insight, men can never come to an agreement as to the beliefs at the basis of religion. Their divergences on first truths show the need of a revelation from God to take us up just where our feeble intuitions fail, and to carry us on and out of the twilight into the perfect day.

God is. But who save he himself can tell us what he is? For who but he knows? Man is immortal. But where, and in doing what is that immortality to be passed? Who can tell save God? For none but he, with omniscient eye, can see the interminable future. Is there a heaven and a hell? and are they eternal? God must tell us. What will men do in eternity? God only can see and know as of himself. We know only as he tells us. We are sinners. It is the consciousness of the race. Can sin be forgiven? God only knows on what terms he will forgive? We know from him, and if he has told us; not otherwise. The soul of man can never rest except in some authoritative expression of God. Our great soul-want is for something more certain than guesses about religion, or the differing conclusions of reason, or the partial intuitions of our hearts. We need something reliable, and sure; we need "the truth without any admixture of error." All the vast systems of ancient belief proclaim this want; all the struggling of men's souls to find a resting place declares it. It is one of the most unmistakable wants of the race. We claim that God has undertaken to supply this want. And will he be likely to do it by an imperfect book? Will he give us a revelation with error in it when the only purpose of giving it at all is to save us from error? We can err and guess without a Bible. What we need is not the mere afflatus of the poet or the dream of the enthusiast; but a book of certainty with the divine stamp upon it.

It is worthy of note that every man has a final authority in this matter of religion; if not the Bible, it is something else. The Romanist declares that the Bible alone is not enough; it must be interpreted by authority of the church—a company of men. The modern sceptic seeks his authority in his own reason.

He says "This or that thing in the Bible is unreasonable to me; I cannot believe it. This fact, plainly, is impossible; that doctrine goes against my convictions." And so he sets his own private authority higher than God's word. But mark it; Sceptic and Romanist agree in trusting human authority; one trusts man, the individual; the other trusts men, the church. But both have something they call authority, though it is only human authority. For there must be some final ground for rest. We take God. They take men.

We claim that there is an absolute need of *divine* authority, if men are to *know* about religion. We want a revelation from God;—inspired too, in every part, by God's Spirit. For a book sometimes true, sometimes false is worse than none; just as a guide sometimes trustworthy and sometimes treacherous is more dangerous than no guide at all.

Again the *early Christians* received these books as inspired. We have the writings of persons who conversed with Matthew, Mark, Luke and John. And these uninspired but honest men, always quote our sacred books with marks of respect; putting a wide difference between these and all other books. These early Christian writers, call them the "Divine Scriptures," "Scriptures of the Lord," "Divinely inspired Scriptures," "Sacred Books," "The Ancient and New Oracles," "Gospels," "Divine Oracles," "Holy Scriptures." Surely these names are significant. Moreover they quote not from general tradition but from these books when they wish to state the facts and the doctrines of religion; quoting them as final authority. So frequently did they quote the New Testament that scholars have said that the whole volume could be collected from the citations in the writers of the few earlier centuries.

Again; the Book *claims inspiration.* A former chapter has been devoted to the question of the general truthfulness of the Bible. In the book itself we find that God promises divine guidance. He said to Moses "I will be with thy mouth." The prophets were to speak, "in the name of the Lord." And these prophets themselves claimed this inspiration. "Hear the word of the Lord." "The Lord hath spoken." "Thus saith the Lord," is their usual formula. Moreover our Lord and his apostles indorsed the Old Testament. "Search the Scriptures," said Jesus. And he was continually saying "as it is written," and "that it might be fulfilled." It is said, "All Scripture is given by inspiration of God." "Holy men of God spake as they were moved by the Holy Spirit." If it is possible by any words to enter the claim of inspiration from heaven it is done in these declarations. Nor is this all. Jesus promised to inspire his disciples. He promised the Holy Spirit, who should "bring all things to their remembrance whatsoever he had said, and should also guide them into all truth." Can any thing be more decisive than such a promise? If then we have not an inspired volume, containing "all truth," Jesus spoke not truthfully, or his biographers have misrepresented him. His disciples, after his death, claimed this promised guidance. Says one of them, "ye received the word of God which ye heard of us, not as the word of man, but as it is in truth the word of God." How sharp the distinction made by the Apostolic pen between words which possess only human authority, and those which have also that of God! And this is only a single instance out of the multitude of similar claims.

Something must be done with such claims. They are too frequent, and too broad to be ignored. They occur continually in the Bible. They are either quietly assumed or expressly declared in the whole volume. Open the Epistles any where you please. Hear the writers announce the most momentous truths. Do they reason as with human logic? Do they offer to prove them as do ordinary writers? On the contrary, they generally announce them in a way which shows insufferable arrogance if they are not inspired; but which is just what we should expect if their authority was the divine guidance they claim. And thus it comes to be true that these immense claims are either very arrogant and wicked, and I had almost said, blasphemous; or else they are rightful and just, and demand reverence as coming from heaven. Very bad men, and very wretched enthusiasts were these writers on the one hand; or else on the other they were good, honest, and righteous men ;—men who were imperfect in themselves, but, as they claim, infallible when, under God's inspiration, they were teaching religious truth. In this claim of inspiration they were outrageous liars, whose pretensions should move our ridicule if not our indignation, or else they were true men, "chosen of God," to speak "as moved by the Holy Ghost." Scepticism in our day compliments the Bible as an excellent book with many valuable things in it; but hesitates to allow it to be inspired of God and an infallible guide. We rejoice that this ground has been taken. It is a slippery ground. No man can stand long upon it. For the Bible claims to be inspired. That claim is true or false. If false, can we trust any thing in the book? If false, this is a most prodigious falsehood. A little error in a man's words may not vitiate the main sentiment even when it awakes a degree of suspicion. But if the error be of large import, and lie at the very basis of the whole statement it is far otherwise. Now here is a claim continually made in the Bible, and a most important claim, nay, the most important of all its claims. If false, the whole book is radically false ; if true it is "the word of God." There is no middle ground. It insists not that it is simply a very good book, with excellent sentiments, not that it is, like any production of good men, of merely human authority. It disclaims this in claiming to be very much more.

We believe the volume is true. We accept it as

written by man, but written under divine guidance. They who have received it "not as the word of man but as it is in truth the word of God," have felt the more sure of its inspiration as they have studied it, and have yielded their hearts and lives to the control of the facts and doctrines. It has done them good to take it as an inspired book. They make it their final authority. "Thus saith the Lord," is the basis of their confidence in any religious belief.

And there is one thing about this book, by which, over and above all our reasonings, we may settle the whole matter of its truth or falsehood. We may use the Baconian method with it—the method of experiment and trial, and then of inference as the result of our experimental method. "If any man will do his will," said Jesus, "he shall know of the doctrine." This is perfectly fair. We are not asked to do things evil that good may come; but only to do what is obviously right; to begin with the nearest duty; to practice at once on precepts that commend themselves. The book asks you to *try it*. "Come and see," its grand message. Here is a personal test that a man may make for himself. As far as it commends itself, obey it. It bids you pray for wisdom. Do it as you would be a fair minded man and prove yourself desirous of knowing the truth. Enough has been shown in the argument thus far on the genuineness, authenticity and inspiration of the Scriptures to convince every thoughtful reader, that this book is worthy of a very careful examination. Can you give it so much as this, without prayer for guidance and the solemn determination, just here, to *do right in regard to your Bible and your God.* For as you would not call him an honest man who used carefully his ears and would not use his eyes in investigating the common things of life, so in these higher things, it is needed that a man use not only brain but heart, not only the method of ordinary search but the peculiar method that befits this kind of investigation—the method of prayer.

Yes; God has spoken to man. And there are thousands of the race who have listened with the reverent ear of the soul. And the utterances of God in his Word have made them men of a higher purpose and a better aim. The lowly have come and made God's truth their comfort and hope, and it has lifted them to a higher manhood. And think of how many of the most lordly souls the world has seen have brought their treasures of learning and of science to the feet of him to whom the Magi bowed. For the world's scholarship and science, and art, and culture are on the side of the Bible.[1] Little eddies of opposition there are in every

[1] "Who founded Prague and Vienna and Heidleberg and Leipsic and Tubingen and Jena and Halle and Berlin, and Bonn? Who founded Salamanca and Valladolid and Oxford and Cambridge and Aberdeen? They were Bible men. When the rest of mankind were caring for the mere necessities of the physical life, Bible men were holding the torch of science; and these men were the predecessors of the Bacons and Newtons. Who founded American colleges? With very few exceptions, they were Bible

age; "the opposition of science falsely so called." But the little eddy near the bank could not exist if there were not further out, even in the broad and deep channel, a vast volume of water floating steadily down towards the sea. And these great souls, the real leaders of the world's thought, have weighed all the difficulties that any sceptic has ever raised; for the modern objections have little of newness. And these men have gone through all this sea of difficulties; and did not stay weak and floundering in that Slough of Despond as feebler souls have done. They have landed on the further shore of a careful belief. They know why they believe the Bible. But, over and above every other reason, they can say with Coleridge—and men in every grade of intellectual and moral development can join in the utterance,—" I know the Bible is inspired because it finds me at greater depths of my being than any other book."

men. Newton was only one of hundreds, who, given to science, loved his Bible. From his day to this the succession has been complete. And the science that in our day boasts such Bible men as its Faraday, its Forbes, its Carpenter, its Hitchcock, its Dana and its Torrey, cannot be considered as occupying a position hostile to the Bible."—*Howard Crosby*, D. D., L L. D., Lecture before New York Association for Science and Art.

"Now if Christianity is the foe of science has she not taken a singular method of demonstrating her enmity? Christianity was the first as she still remains the fast and fostering friend of science. The devotion of the Christian church in this century to education is one of the notable facts, and it points with pride and satisfaction to its educational institutions."—*J. G. Holland.*

CHAPTER IV.

DIFFICULTIES AS TO MIRACLES AND TEACHINGS.

IN BUNYAN'S "Pilgrim's Progress," midway between the city of Destruction which Christian must leave and the wicket gate opening into the narrow way where he would enter, there was a certain bad piece of ground called the "Slough of Despond." Into it every pilgrim must go. Some retreated after a few steps, coming out on the same side on which they had entered. Some remained hopelessly fastened in the terrible quagmire and perished there. Some also, went on, went through, and came out safely, nor did the mud cleave to their garments when they stood once more on the firm ground. In like manner, there is a period, more or less definite and continued, in every young man's life, which may be termed the *period of natural scepticism*. It is the time when doubts come up like thick banks of cloud in the eastern horizon from a wintry sea; the time when a young man sees and feels the force of the objections to religion; when he finds grave and serious difficulties in his Bible.

A young man has been tenderly and carefully trained. He has religious parents. He has every advantage of

Sabbath-school and sanctuary. He hears indeed of objections to religion. But they are mainly answered in the books he reads, and in the family conversation to which he listens. He believes his Bible. The men about him who live it and strive to practice it, though imperfect men, are widely different from the noisy profane crowd that he occasionally encounters. He is a believer in religion. He holds fast to his Bible. But there comes a change. He feels the strength, the vigor, the impatience of authority, the natural independence, which is inevitable as the young man takes his place in life. He feels competent to undertake almost any thing. He hears new objections to particular portions of the Bible. It occurs to him that a good deal of his faith in the Scriptures is the result of education. He has taken many things for granted. He is beginning to think that, had he been trained up a Turk, he might have been a Mohammedan; or educated a Hindu, he might have reverenced the Shasta. This is all true enough; and it amounts simply to saying that if a man had been badly trained the results would be likely to be bad. As an argument against a correct religious belief, it is as poor as would be the argument against sound learning that bad text books would tend to make poor scholars. Right views of science are none the less correct because a man was trained up to know them. But our young man is independent, self-reliant, able now to investigate for himself. And he is tempted to think it only fair to do what sceptics assert is the mark of independence; that is, to let all *education in religion count for nothing.* And afraid that he may be unduly balanced in favor of the Bible by his education, he leans the other way. Now, he harbors every difficulty. Early training must not solve it. He will meet these things himself. He falls in with some one who suggests that religion, especially as a father and mother believed in it, has had its day; that it is old, puritanic; that the march of mind has left it far in the rear; that it is independent and manly and strong-minded to doubt. Objections to this miracle, to that doctrine, and the other duty get a good deal of force in this state of mind. And the way is prepared for listening to one of those oily-tongued men who affect to pity persons who still hold to the Bible, and still believe in Christianity. "They wish they could," so runs their conversation, "believe in the Bible with the simple faith they had in childhood; but they regret to say they cannot! They have very grave doubts; would like to have them solved; but have no hope that they ever will be." They tell the young man, "Ah! when you know more of philosophy, and of the progress of free thought, you will feel differently about your Bible; and a young man of sense and spirit and originality like yourself, will never be content to believe a thing is true because your mother told you so."

Now in this state of things the appeals of religion are not felt. The young man's faith is more thoroughly undermined than he himself suspects. He does not exactly disbelieve. But he does not feel sure. He asks himself whether there may not be some mistake; whether there may not be error in the Bible after all; whether it may not be true that religious men over-state Christian doctrine. At least one must not be in haste to commit one's self for or against religion. And this is the point at which the scepticism of our day is all directed. It does not ask that a man be a disbeliever, but only an unbeliever; not that a man deny but only that he should doubt. For if there be such objections to religion, such difficulties in the Bible that its truths are neutralized, it is all that scepticism can expect to gain in an age like this.

I want to put out a helping hand to any young man who has entered in any degree into this Slough of Despond, and who feels embarrassed by the difficulties he finds in his Bible.

There are two ways of meeting these difficulties. One way would be to state each of them at full length and then answer it. But this would require volumes. There is another way. It is Peter's way when he said, "Lord to whom shall we go; thou hast the words of eternal life." Some were leaving Christ because of their difficulties. Peter stops a moment and bethinks himself. I seem to hear him as he reasons with himself, "Suppose I leave Christ and his doctrine, what shall I gain? To whom shall I go? Shall I find no difficulties in rejecting the miracles and teachings of Jesus? What account can I give of all these evidences of his religion; for these will be prodigious difficulties to me as an unbeliever." And then, turning again to Christ, I seem to hear him say, " Lord, to whom can we go, Thou hast the words of eternal life." To every young man troubled with difficulties in his Bible I say stop, and think a moment as to what would you gain by rejecting the Bible? Are there not prodigious difficulties in taking that position? There are difficulties *with* the Bible; but there are ten-fold more without it. There are difficulties in believing; but there are infinitely more difficulties in the position of the sceptic and even of the doubter. Let a man magnify these difficulties a thousand fold and it would be still true that the difficulties of unbelief are far more formidable.

We shall see this, first, if we name certain Scripture *facts* in which men have found great difficulties.

I name *miracles* as one of them. The Bible certainly contains a narrative of miracles. They are interwoven with the whole texture. It is impossible to believe the Bible and interpret it fairly without believing that miracles have been wrought by God in former ages of the world. Some join issue just here, declaring that miracles are incredible in themselves, and some asserting that a miracle is impossible.

But when a man asserts that a miracle is impossible, he should stop and ask himself if he is aware of what he assumes ; of the prodigious difficulties he takes upon himself. "Miracles are impossible," he says. *How does he know?* Is he omniscient ? Is he omnipresent ? Does he know all the things that have transpired or that are now transpiring in this universe ? If not, then the thing he does not know may be a miracle. There is a prodigious difficulty in the way of a finite man who would acquire infinite knowledge. And one would think there would be some difficulty in finding a man whose modesty had been so far forgotten as to allow him to make the assumption implied in the statement "a miracle is impossible,"—the assumption of omniscience ; the assumption that one is himself God !

Is it said again, " that if not impossible miracles are very *improbable;* that the laws of nature are uniform ; that God would not be likely to institute an order of nature and then arbitrarily break through the laws he has established." To all this the reply is instant ; viz., That no one alleges miracles to be common ; that, common, they would cease to be miracles. It is admitted at once, that they are not probable as every day occurrences. Nor is their commonness claimed. But only this ; that at certain periods of time, when they were needed, God thrust in miracles for man's good. In all those great crises of human destiny, in all those eras when a new dispensation was to be inaugurated, when Moses was to be God's instrument in introducing the legal dispensation, when the prophets were to appear

AS TO MIRACLES AND TEACHINGS. 101

with divine credential, when Jesus was to come from heaven to give testimony of a new way of salvation—at each and all of these points of intense interest, we urge that it is not only probable that God will thrust in his hand of miracle, but without such miracle the world would have been more astonished than with it. For God made man to expect miracle, to demand miracle, and, when the miracle comes in the very hour of greatest need, to believe in it and to magnify the name of the Lord for what he has done. Has God put this expectation of miracle in man, as a deep and vital thing, on purpose to disappoint it ? The absence of miracle under such circumstances is far more improbable than its presence.

And here, a word about the laws of nature, to which as has been alleged, "God has bound himself." But where has he bound himself thereto ? Surely no man can show the pledge that God will never override physical law when he shall choose so to do. What is a law of nature ? It is God's usual way of doing things. What is a miracle ? God's unusual way of doing a thing. Is it any more difficult for God to do his will in the one way than in the other ? Surely no law binds him to do it in a particular way. For in that case God would be imprisoned in his natural laws. And these laws would be the grave of his omnipotence. Even the silk-worm that spins its own winding sheet, at length bursts through its prison. Is the infinite one entombed in his own world? Besides what are these " laws of nature,' considered as a restraint upon a being endowed with will?

It is a law of nature that my arm shall hang down at my side. It weighs just so much avoirdupois weight; and is attracted by just so much force to the centre of the earth. When I lift my arm I overwork the law of gravity. My will, practically, and within a limited range, suspends the results of law. The law exists. It acts. But I counteract it. A new force, supernaturally, is thrust in. My will is above nature; is stronger than nature; is *supernatural.* Now if I can work right over nature, right above her laws, cannot God more also? If I am not a prisoner of law, is he bound thereby? If there is a human supernatural, according to which I act above nature, thrusting in a new force, is there any difficulty in believing that there is a divine supernatural which can work *miracles?* It would be strange that a man having the power of will should never use it by lifting an arm or leg; and it would be even more strange if God, with the power to work through law or over law, by law or in spite of law, should not, when miracle is called for, work the needed miracle. The real wonder is that miracles are so few; that God so holds himself to law, *i. e.*, does things so much in similar ways. The entire absence of miracle under these circumstances is the most improbable of things. If God had not, at the fitting time, thrust in his hand and wrought marvellous works for signs, wonders, tokens

AS TO MIRACLES AND TEACHINGS. 103

unto man, and if the Bible had not contained this record of miracles, the omission would be a greater hindrance to our faith in God and in the Bible, than any other that I know.

That God should perform miracles is, then, not only possible but probable. And he who says that God cannot, or that he will not do it, involves himself in a host of difficulties any one of which is overwhelming.[1] That the Bible should record miracles is only what it professes to do. For, just as ordinary histories record for the most part ordinary facts, so God's word records those extraordinary instances in which divine love and power have spoken in the language of miracle to arouse attention, confirm truth and overthrow the powers of evil. Nor let any man when in his Bible he meets the record of a miracle say, "O, that is a miracle,"—as if a miracle were somehow less credible, and less certain. Who objects to a book on mathematics that it contains figures, or to a book on botany that it describes plants? It was intended to do so. And God's word describes among other things those deeds which men recognize as miraculous. It was intended to do so. Ponder these wondrous works, these mighty miracles. They are not freaks of power. They do not stand up apart. They are a portion of a mighty structure. They have

---

[1] "I will not believe a miracle."—*Voltaire*.
"I will not believe that water becomes solid in winter, and men walk on it."—*Japanese Prince*.

an appointed and an estimated moral value. As one studies them in their place, they exactly meet the needs of the hour when they were wrought. They exactly fit into the edifice that God is rearing. They are divinely given object-lessons for the instruction of the human race. The moral ends of miracle are the greatest things. For moral ends are final ends.

Again; there are objections to these facts of the Bible because of their *remoteness*. " They occurred so long ago; there is so much opportunity for mistake; they do not come home to us like the things done in these last critical centuries;" so runs the objection. It is replied, that it is impossible to thrust all events into one century. This nineteenth century cannot spread over more than one hundred years. A man's difficulty on this score with his Bible is a mere impression, and is unworthy of him. And as to the antiquity of the events, of course they are ancient; that is what the record asserts. And as to the authenticity of the more ancient of them, we have to go back only to Christ's day; to the time which all allow to be far within the period of authentic and reliable history. *He authenticated* Moses, and David, and Solomon, and Isaiah. He indorsed the Old Testament miracles, reasserting their truthfulness, confirming the most difficult things in Moses' account; so that now we believe them, not only on Moses' testimony, but on the comparatively modern, and also superhuman testimony of Jesus Christ himself. There are difficulties, it is said, in the narrative of these ancient events. Well. Be it so. But the difficulties are absolutely insuperable in the way of believing that our Lord Jesus Christ sent men to the Old Testament, saying, "search the Scriptures," when he knew the first pages of Genesis to be false, and the prominent events of creation and early human history to be misstated. It is said, "that even eighteen hundred years is a long while ago, and that since that time there have been opportunities for falsification of facts." The reply is that all the world believes in events recorded hundreds of years before Christ's day by ordinary historians. Those were for the most part ordinary events. But here in the New Testament are extraordinary events, recorded in solemn and authentic documents. Within a few years after the events are said to have occurred, the writers gave names, dates and places; they said that in a certain town just over the hill from Jerusalem, Jesus raised a dead man; and his very name, Lazarus, is mentioned; his sisters' names given; their house specified; the very sepulchre described. They said that yonder, he fed five thousand men in the wilderness: they gave these facts in all this minuteness of detail. Any body could examine the facts. These things were not done in a corner. They were noised abroad. They created intense interest. If there had been any mistake, the able and acute foes of the new religion would have proclaimed it. The Jews said the miracles were done by Satan. The heathen said they were done by magic. But both admitted that the things were done. And both appealed to our Matthew, Luke, Mark and John, as the historians of the facts. Here are the records in the Bible,—a book existing to-day. The sceptic is just as much bound to account for the book as it now exists, as is the Christian. But the sceptic has the most prodigious difficulties in his way. And if any young man attempts to stand between the two, to stand as a doubter, neither believing nor rejecting, then he is swept by the batteries of both sides. For, whoever is right, the man who is undecided is certainly wrong.

With reference to many a *speculative question* often associated with the discussions of Christianity, nothing is gained but much lost by leaving Christ's teachings. There are the inquiries about the introduction of sin, the transmission of diseased moral natures, of the prevalence and cause of sorrow and death, of how so much suffering can exist either here or hereafter and yet God be good, of the sovereignty of holiness and yet the allowance of sin, of God's all comprehending plan and yet how evil can come in as an ordained part while infinite holiness is unstained, of God's supremacy and man's freedom and so accountability—these are examples of the questions to which I refer.

I am free to confess that on these and kindred subjects there are great difficulties. But will there be less difficulty if we reject the Bible? Did the Bible originate these questions and will the rejection of the Bible solve them? These questions have been discussed by all thinking men, whether heathens or Jews, whether Mohammedans or Christians, whether Infidels or Believers. Outside of religion they have been debated as earnestly by sceptics, as ever among devout and prayerful men.

He who rejects the Bible is as much bound to account for the origin of evil, as really bound to show how man's free agency and the divine sovereignty can coexist as is any other man. For, if he is a Deist he holds to a belief in a Sovereign God; and, on inspection of his own powers, he finds himself free. If he is not a Deist, he has other and more formidable difficulties; he leaves doubt for darkness, difficulty for impossibility; he plunges into depths which, fairly considered, would turn the brain of a sane man.

All these inquiries belong really to another domain; they are questions of philosophy. They would rear themselves with the same frowning aspect if the Bible had never been given. Sir William Hamilton has said, "There is no difficulty in religion that has not first emerged in philosophy." Only as we have all been reared among Christian influences, we have heard these questions discussed in their religious bearing, until we associate them with religion itself, and so unconsciously we transfer the difficulties in the one to the charge of the other. This is unfair. Hume spent his life over these very questions, looking upon them as a philosopher. Let no man present as his reason for the rejection of Christianity those speculative difficulties which undeniably exist, which are as formidable without the Bible as with it, and which, if not completely solved by revelation, are, in not a few respects, relieved and mitigated.

If we reject the explanations of Christ so far as he gave them, what then? To whom shall we go?

As with speculative questions so with *practical facts*. There are perplexities about them. But one gains nothing by rejecting Christ's religion on this account. Certain things the Bible finds in the world. It did not make them. It is not responsible for their continuance. It simply records the things it finds to be the actual facts. Who thinks of charging a historian with the crimes he narrates, a writer on jurisprudence with the violations of law which he discusses, or a writer on medicine with the diseases he describes? Common history as well as sacred history records the fact of human guilt. Could a man write a pretended history of a nation who were not sinners, and get our belief that he was describing actual *men!* What, men—a nation of men, and not sinners! No! The world over, men distrust their race. Bars and bolts and heavy safes and careful locks guard property.

Sin is a fact. The denial of Christianity is not the disproval of human sinfulness. Nay, if the doctrine of Scripture depravity seem at first view to be harsh and repulsive, think a moment that the sad fact is more frightful and awful if surveyed outside the limitations and alleviations of the Biblical presentation. The mass of the world's sin has been actually lessened by the conversion of millions through the Gospel. Christianity has been an elevating power over against this depravity I can think better of the world with than without the Bible, see less depravity if the Scripture is true than if it is false. For if religion is a delusion or a cheat, then not only do we behold the depravity of wicked men, but the added depravity of good men, who in that case, are miserable pretenders or else are most sadly deceived; in other words, are either mentally or morally depraved beyond all the rest of mankind. And in addition to all other cheats and shams and lies under which men have groaned, we shall have, if we reject the Bible and take the infidel view, the most stupendous cheat and lie and delusion of Christ's religion. We must have some doctrine of depravity. It must be either the Christian or infidel doctrine, and the infidel doctrine is far more harsh and awful than that of the Bible.

And the sorrow of this world and the other world which men charge against religion is not due to it, but is true in spite of it and in opposition to it. It is often urged that much suffering of conscience is endured by persons who believe in religion but do not actually obey the commands of Christ. This is true. But religion does not ask a man to disobey and so to suffer under an accusing conscience. Religion asks this man to go on unto "peace in believing." And it is unfair to charge the reproaches of conscience and the agonies of fear and the dread of losing the soul, which some endure in their theoretical belief but their practical rejection of Christianity, to that religion which offers to the penitent calmness of conscience instead of agitation, and love and hope instead of fear and dread. If a man disobeys, and so is made sorrowful, let him complain not of religion but of himself.

But men have felt anguish of soul who were far enough from being influenced, even in opinion, by religion. Men have felt remorse who never heard of Christ or saw a Bible. In mid Africa or on the shores of further India men have had deep soul-sorrow as the conviction has forced itself upon them that they were sinful and depraved; and these men have made efforts almost superhuman to quiet, through worship and penance and sacrifice, the voice of inward reproach. Sceptics have died in sorrow, cursing the hour of their birth; or, where great despair has been absent, there has been sometimes a puerile levity or an insensibility which seemed befitting only to a beast; and the want of all that is comforting and elevating has been more sad than any despair, to the thoughtful beholder.

Did any man ever hear of one who died cursing the religion of Christ because it had led him into sin, because it had defiled and ruined him?—But thousands have died with bitterest maledictions on the infidelity which destroys both soul and body. And in regard to the dire calamity of death, surely the gain is in the Christian view. Some insist upon associating the ideas of death with those of religion. As they turn instinctively from the thought of the grave's loneliness and corruption, so, since the thoughts are connected to them, they turn also away from religion. Death is indeed a stern *fact*. All must meet it. It comes to the swearing as well as to the praying man. O, in this matter, we are all brethren ; and all of us must go down into the dust of death. If there is or is not truth in Christ's religion, this is true, we must all die. But, rejecting Christianity, we refuse the light from beyond which gilds the gates of the grave. And as to the sorrow beyond the grave, religion names it that we may avoid it ; discloses the gulf that it may show us how to escape the unending grief and gain the unending joy. Even if it were a thousand fold greater, no man need endure it. Even if it were unjust, he who does right has nothing to fear. The more terrible the future sorrow, the more reason for not being among the wrong-doers against whom it is threatened.

If we leave Christ and his doctrine we shall give the lie to all the best impulses and deepest intuitions of our nature. There are instincts, there are voices from reason and conscience. True our voluntary nature does not always obey them heartily, but the voices are there.

The words may be somewhat indistinct. For the voices of our voluntary nature are louder, and we obey the wrong heart, rather than the right conscience, and therein stands our sin. But the other voices speak; and sometimes the man must listen. "We are immortal," says a voice within us. Guilt may wish it were not so. But the reluctance to admit this inward testimony of men has not availed, and men for the most part believe in a life after death.

This belief the Bible assumes. It does not so much prove it, as take it for an accepted fact. But the doctrine standing in outline only, or perverted by false teaching, is comparatively uninfluential. Christianity takes it, develops it grandly, clears it of all error, lifts it up from a dead belief to a living motive and a thrilling hope. It teaches every man how to make his immortality the grandest of blessings.

Now suppose we leave Christ, what then? We fall back upon our general intuitions; definiteness is gone; all influential motive has departed. Is it said that intuition gives us more than the bald and bare fact of immortality? I must deny it. Men rejecting the Bible have widely various beliefs about the kind and character of this immortality. It will not do to trust self; for other people's reasons teach them, as they say, differently; and they may be as keen as we. It will not do to trust others; for how collect the world's opinions and balance them in search of truth? It is

Christ's teaching or none. It is to him we must go that the intuition may become an influential faith.

Another of these great ground principles of human thought and action is this; that what we do now bears upon all our future. The belief is instinctive. We act and reason upon it daily. Few persons deny it; and they, only in the matter of religion. All men see how results follow character and deeds. To-day you and I are experiencing partially the result of all former days. It will be so down to the last day of life. It will be so the day after death, the year, the eternity after death, if man continues to be man.

The Bible owns this principle, and carries it out more fully, bids us act daily upon it, and tells us definitely what the result will be of certain courses of action. "He that soweth to his flesh shall of the flesh reap corruption; but he that soweth to the spirit shall of the spirit reap life everlasting."

And now if any man objects to such a result; if, wishing the doctrine not to be true, he shall throw aside his Bible, what will he gain? He will not have annihilated this belief in the principle, which all men naturally entertain, whether believers in any religion or in no religion, and which all men act upon in daily life. The Bible indeed extends the application of the principle further than we, unassisted by revelation, can do; just as the telescope extends our vision deeper into the heavens. The Bible tells us of two future eternal

H

states. Of the holy joys in one, of the sinful sorrows of the other. And before any man denies these utterances of the Bible let him ask what he will gain by the denial? Thrown back upon the general principle, he must own that; and Christianity simply sheds new light along the old line of man's natural and instinctive conviction of immortality.

If we leave Christ we shall do the greatest violence to our reasons by rejecting the immense amount of testimony which has *convinced thousands of the best minds* of the truthfulness of Christ's religion. Look at the fact that the mass of men who have given deepest and most earnest thought and study to religion for eighteen hundred years have received the religion of Jesus. The men of most knowledge on this subject accept the Bible as God's revealed will. They are intelligent enough to know all common and some uncommon objections, and yet they see where is the overwhelming weight of evidence. That great mass of educated mind which, as presiding over colleges, teaching in seminaries, has made Christianity a specialty, a single undivided object of investigation, is more than satisfied with the evidence for these books of the Bible. Intelligent men have indeed rejected the Bible. But general intelligence is one thing, and the special study of a life-time by thousands of the best educated men of each Christian century is quite another thing. The overwhelming mass of ability and learning has had but one voice.

Here is a stupendous difficulty for the sceptic; a fact absolutely unaccountable by those who would have men leave Christianity.

It is the same with the *interpretation* which the holy men of all centuries have put upon the doctrines of religion. They are really one in this thing. They differ in explanations. The errors of their times influence their modes of statement. But the deeply religious, the really holy men of all the centuries are one in essential belief.

They all agree as to man's sin and ruin and exposure to God's displeasure; in redemption by Christ's death; in salvation only by faith in him; in the inward change of the Holy Spirit; in the hope of eternal life through Jesus Christ for those who believe; in the resurrection, the judgment and eternal awards. This is the Christian faith. The mass of devout men since the reformation three centuries ago, hold this as the truth. The mass of *holy* men in the Romish church have held to these verities of our religion. Time was when the Roman church was a simple Gospel church on the banks of the Tiber. In subsequent centuries she was corrupted, not essentially in her creed, but in her rites, in her forms, which overlaid and well nigh, for many, extinguished her creed. And the reformers protested not against her creed, but against the mummeries which to many usurped its place. Her creed to-day is essentially right. Thousands in her communion think only of the mummeries and forget the creed. But many we believe have thought of the creed and have forgotten the mummeries. She has nurtured holy men. It is the same with that vast body, the *Greek Church*. Some have caught at the deeper truth and held it in spite of the tradition which stands to so many in place of the Gospel. And in those old Syriac churches, older than the churches in Rome or Constantinople, it is the same. The holy, the truly Christian men, those who give noblest evidence of piety, have clung to these few central doctrines of faith; they are one in this interpretation of Christianity. And here is a fact which those would do well to ponder who are tempted to give up our Christian doctrines. These holiest men are in essential agreement. They hold one language about sin's ruin, and Christ's atonement, and the change of grace and the way to heaven. These are truths which they have tested by experience. These are the ground-work of their religion. And these are the pious men, if there have ever been pious men. Leaving Christ, in this matter, where shall we find genuine piety ? These holy men, the Edwardses, Paysons, Judsons of America, the Luthers and Calvins of the Protestant churches, the Thomas à Kempis, the Quesnels of the Romish church, the Chrysostoms of the Ancient Greek church, the Jeromes and Gregories of those old Syrian churches, the men who prayed and thought and preached on the hills and in the valleys that had seen Christ and his apostles, all these holiest men, out of the depth of *one* experience have had *one* faith, and were *one* in their proclamation of the essential facts and doctrines of Christianity. We will not leave these men. To do it would be to leave the united conviction of Christendom.

And, further, to cast off Christ's religion would be to leave all the dearest hopes both of our personal advancement and of the world's moral progress. Intertwined with the facts of Christianity are our dearest affections. So that we must say with Paul, if the facts are not as presented in the life, death and resurrection of Jesus Christ, "we are of all men most miserable." We hear men sometimes with flippant tone announcing their belief that Christianity is false. But if that be so, say it sadly, and with tears, as you would tell a loving child of the death of the mother that bore it and nourished it and loved it. Say it as the most sorrowfu¹ thing that human lips can utter, that the credentials of Christ—his mighty deeds and more mighty words—are not enough, and so never can God give a proven revelation to man. Say it with mourning, that the perfect purity and elevation and stainlessness of Christ's character in the New Testament is all a mistake ; that he did not live, or that if he did, his disciples devised his words and imagined his deeds, and that such deception has led the world's enlightenment, and so that we are all a duped race led by dupes, a race of maniacs led by fools and knaves ; and yet that these fools and knaves have wondrously helped men to be better, and made men holier, and broadened their views, and informed their intellects and enriched their moral natures, and made them to live nobler and more self-denying lives and to die sweeter, holier, happier deaths, looking onward to a still holier state ; and yet that all this is delusion, deception, mistake, imposture ! In striking at Christianity with iconoclastic hand one strikes at humanity as well as its dearest hopes, its sweetest consolations, its best ideals, its strongest impulses, its most praiseworthy charities and moralities. If it must be said at all, say it with bated breath, that Christianity is untrue ; for if untrue, it is the most awful of untruths and we ought at once to weed it out of human literature, out of common language and common life ; we ought to begin with childhood and stop it in its repetition of the Lord's Prayer, to forbid infant lips from ever again uttering the words "Suffer little children to come unto me for of such is the kingdom of heaven ;" we ought to stop the rites of burial and cast out of them the words "I am the resurrection and the life," to tell the mourner, though it will make him twice a mourner, that he has not only lost his friend but his Saviour ; we ought to assure age, though it will tremble all the more to know it, that there is some mistake as to the Bible which has been the staff on which it leaned, and that the Heavenly Father did not say, "I will never leave nor forsake thee," nor Christ promise, "He that believeth in me shall never die."

And as with personal hope, so with the inspirations of genius and the progress of art and of learning ; for, the support of Christianity gone, there is for them a mournful future. Before the advent of Christianity, how much of art was too abominable for description. But the single conception of the Virgin and her Child cut in a thousand marbles, painted a thousand times on canvas, in every variety of detail, has revolutionized and elevated art. Nothing blotted out the old ideals until Christianity flooded the realms of painting and statuary with a new and tender beauty. So always through the centuries this religion of Christ is purifying every thing it touches, and is doing it exactly as far and as fast as men take into mind and heart the great facts and doctrines which are its distinction and its glory.

Nor art and literature, but the common impulses of common life, would be ruinously affected if the religion of Christ were left as untrue. All the higher motives that lift men from a merely physical condition would droop.[1] With it would go all higher views of God, of duty, of the nobility of man, of just and humane law ; and society must inevitably decline, since the great

[1] That this is not a mere speculation the following quotation from the elder Pliny will show: "The vanity of man, and his insatiable longing after existence have led him to dream of a life after death. A being full of contradictions, he is the most wretched of creatures, since the other creatures have no wants transcending the bounds of their natures. Among these two great evils the best thing God has bestowed on man is *the power to take his own life.*"

teachings of morals which have extorted the world's admiration have been connected with a system called Christianity, which the world now leaves because false; —and if the one part false how the other true?

It has been thought by some that we might drop all the miracles and the doctrines that are distinctive, and still have all the impulses and moralities of Christianity. Yes, if moralities are mere outward things, mere wax flowers from milliners' shops, instead of genuine flowers growing on stems and out of seed and soil as God made them to grow. There is a natural belief in immortality. But it is inoperative aside from the light of revelation. And as it has never been efficient apart from the Biblical disclosures, so it never will be for any length of time after the Biblical doctrine of it has been left. For a single generation, possibly for two, if Christianity were discarded, there would remain a little of the Christian sap in Deism; but it would soon depart. It is doubtful if mere natural religion would live long enough to draw another breath after the going out from it of all that is distinctly Christian in thought and feeling and belief. Says one of the best thinkers and best known educators of our day: "The course of things if Deism should be the ultimate religion, can be easily foretold. As long as the recollections and influences of Christianity survived its fall, earnest souls would hope on; they would stay their souls' hunger on the milk drawn from the breasts of their dead mother. But a new age would toss about in despair. If a sense of sin remain, the life of all noble souls will be an anxious gloomy tragedy. Or if that burden be cast off, then the standard of character will fall and the sense of sin grow faint so that pardon will not be needed, and the utmost frivolity be reached in life and manners."[1]

Nothing, absolutely nothing is given us in return if we surrender either our theoretic belief in Christianity, or our practical obedience to it. What else can do any thing for the deepest yearnings and largest wants of the soul? Giving up Christianity is giving up the thing that ought to be true, just as there ought to be light if there are eyes, and sounds if there are ears, and air if there are lungs. And as the bodily organs are furnished with that on which they can best thrive, so the faculties of mind and heart can best be developed by the religion of Him who came "that men might have life and might have it more abundantly." For the deepest and most important intuitions man possesses are seized upon by religion and are made clear and influential. The germ of these truths is developed by the Scriptural doctrine, and they are made potent for man's good. All the difficulties are at least as great without as with the Bible; as great in the germ-truth, as in its form of growth and bud and blossom. And then there is the added difficulty of accounting for this fact; how it is that if

[1] Pres. Woolsey, in "Religion of the Present and the Future."

Christianity is false, it can so singularly, powerfully, beautifully take up and develop these germ-truths in the mind and these most blessed hopes in the heart, and thus purify, elevate and ennoble the man who believes and practices it.

CHAPTER V.

DIFFICULTIES FROM GEOLOGY.

It has come to be believed by many persons that there is a direct conflict between Genesis and Geology ; that the Scriptural account of the creation of the world and of man is entirely at variance with the results of the best modern scientific study. And there has been not a little doubt awakened in the minds of many young men as to the accuracy of the Scriptures on this particular subject. It is believed that these difficulties, stated so often in newspaper and magazine, in popular lecture and scientific volume, are the result of the ignorance of some scientists as to the actual teachings of revelation ; and also of the equal ignorance of some Biblical scholars as to the actual teachings of science. There is undue haste on the part of some men of large but exclusive acquaintance with science, to denounce the Scripture story; and equal haste on the part of some friends of the Bible to denounce science as atheistic. Crude theories in the interpretation of the book of nature or of the book of revelation are often at blame for the apparent antagonism of things in which, rightly understood, there must be unity.

Our best Biblical scholars who have a fair knowledge of scientific facts gladly welcome any light that science gives to religion, acknowledge gratefully their indebtedness for the past, and express their fervent hope and belief that more light is to come from every department of human knowledge in aid of the study of that book which they hold more and more firmly to be the attested Word of God. "All knowledge," said Cicero, "is of use to the orator." And every student of the Scriptures will say the same about the interpretation of that volume. And, on the other hand, the geologists are indebted, as some of them gladly and reverently own, to the Biblical story for the wonderful help it furnishes toward the explanation of the facts which they cull from the natural world. Truths never disagree when you get at them and bring them together. The outer court of nature and the inner court of revelation were built by one hand; and the architect and builder is divine.

I propose that we read together the *first chapter of Genesis* in the light of modern science. To do this, it will be necessary to ask, first, what the author of that chapter really teaches us about the origin of nature and of man; to inquire next as to the settled facts of science as substantially agreed upon by the best modern authorities in the scientific world; and then to note the points of agreement between the two.

1. Of the Mosaic record. At the outset it should

be very carefully remembered that the *methods* of science and of revelation are entirely different. One goes backward, the other forward. One starts with facts and asks the cause. The other starts with a great First Cause and then speaks of the facts as they proceed from his creative hand. In the arithmetics we used to study, there were examples in which now one factor and now another was wanting. If one was gone, it was sought by multiplication; if the other, the answer was sought by division. In like manner the methods of science and revelation are exactly opposite. Compare them at any point, until the problem is solved, and they may not agree. But in the end, when the grand result is reached—as it is not yet—the two methods, the reverse of each other, like multiplication and division, are mutual proofs of the correctness alike of science and of religion ; of the book of Nature and the book of God.

Then, too, the *language* of the Bible is popular, while the language of science claims to be exact. The popular language is just as true for its own purposes as that of science. It states facts as they appear to be. When I say "the sun rises and sets," I speak optical, but not scientific truth ; and the man must want to quarrel with me who would convict me of falsehood because I speak of sunrise and sunset. I could not be understood in a popular lecture if I used any other phrase, though other terms might be more scientific. Moses does the same. Indeed, no other way was possible. If he had used the scientific terms of Egypt—and they were the only scientific terms with which he was familiar—they would be false terms to-day. If God had inspired him to use *our* scientific terms, Moses himself and all those who have lived during thirty centuries could not have understood him. If he had spoken in the language of the science of twenty centuries to come, his words would have been riddles to us, as well as to all former generations. It is not the object of the Bible to teach science but religion. Its references to the facts which are now called scientific are few, and given only in popular language. And the facts are named only in their religious bearing.

In studying this first chapter of Genesis, we must not forget that it does not fix *any time* for the creation of the matter out of which the earth was formed. We have two verses in which the origin of the *substance* of the earth is named. Moses is careful not to say whether the heavens and the earth were created six thousand or six million years ago. He says, "In the beginning." The time is expressly indefinite. If the geologist can show proof that the creation occurred a thousand millions of years ago, Moses in the first two verses of Genesis does not contradict him. No age or date is given. It had a beginning. It was not eternal. It had a Creator. God created it.[1] That is all these two

---

[1] Moses uses a word signifying *created* in the first verse of Genesis. Afterwards as in the fourteenth, he uses another

opening verses say about it. What millions of centuries were passed in chaos before the world was finally fitted up for this race of ours in the last six days' work, no man can ever know; for God has no where told us. Nor is this interpretation of the two opening verses of Genesis any thing new. Justin Martyr, and Basil, and Origen, who were among the fathers of the Christian church, over fourteen hundred years ago, gave this interpretation. All the best modern commentators say the same thing. Lange, Stewart, Murphy, Conant and others, all agree that the opening verses of Genesis describe the creation of the original matter out of which the earth was subsequently through vast convulsions fitted up, shaped and formed anew, for the abode of the pre-adamite creations, and at length, for man.

And as the period of chaos is indefinite, so is the length of each of these six "day-periods," of Moses. It cannot be proved that they were days of twenty-four hours each. It is certain that the sun had not shone upon the world to make the first of them such days. The writer Moses is a prophet. He elsewhere uses the term "day," just as we do, to describe any period which had a beginning and an end. Any limited time in which a thing was commenced and finished is "a day." The whole six days work in the first chapter is described in the second chapter as the work of "one day;" the

word signifying *fashioned* or *shaped*, as out of materials already created.

writer thus using the word as we do both in the definite and the indefinite sense. A Christian pastor said to his congregation these words "I bring you as a text for to-day the words, 'Behold now is the accepted time: Behold now is the *day* of salvation.'" In one part of the sentence the pastor used the word "day," to denote a particular Sabbath, a day of twenty-four hours; in the other part of the sentence he used the same word to signify a day-period covering now eighteen hundred years, and to cover, it may be, centuries more—a day, or a period in which God will receive returning sinners to salvation. So Moses uses the word "day." When he talks of the "tenth day of the month Nisan," we know that he means a day of twenty-four hours. When he talks of a day of creation we can see that he is not so limited. It may cover thousands of years. It is of *periods* in which God began and finished certain parts of the creation, that he speaks.

Nor must we forget that Moses describes creation *optically, i. e.*, as it would have appeared to an eye witness on the earth.[1] God made these things to pass be-

[1] Is not this also the fair and honest way of interpreting the passage about the sun and moon as standing still, which is incorporated, evidently from a poetic composition or ode, into the Book of Joshua? It is optical language. Says the great astronomer Kepler, "The only thing that Joshua prayed for was that the mountains might not intercept the sun from him. Besides it had been *unreasonable to think* of astronomy or of the errors of sight; for if any one had told him that the sun could not really move in the valley of Ajalon but *only in*

fore him. Some have supposed that he was permitted to behold an inspired vision of these creative scenes. He describes them as a man would have done had he been there. Such a man would have seen the actual things exactly as Moses was permitted to see the vision of them. In the Midian desert it may be, on six successive week days followed by a Sabbath,—each of these week-days beginning and closing with "the evening and morning," which made the one literal day of twenty-four hours—on these literal days, God may have allowed the vision of those vast day-periods, in the great characteristics of each, to pass before the mind of Moses. No human eye saw the actual creation. But Moses is to see the vision of it, as if he had been the eye-witness of the earth's wondrous changes under the creative hand of God.

And thus the account of creation, declaring as it does God's glory, was to be transmitted, through the leader of the chosen people, to the entire world. He

relation to sense, would not Joshua have answered that his one wish was to have the *day prolonged by any means whatsoever.*" That the Jews understood the language not scientifically, but phenomenally, is also plain from the words of Josephus," That the *length of the day* did then increase is told in the books laid up in the temple." The Samaritan copy of Joshua says, "the day was prolonged at his prayer." Similarly Dr. Chalmers says, " I accept it in the popular sense, having no doubt that to all intents and purposes of that day's history, the sun and moon did stand still ; the one over Gibeon and the other over Ajalon." To those in the conflict it so seemed, and a Hebrew poet put it into verse, and a Hebrew historian quotes a stanza of the poem.

sees at first the elements, created indeed, but still in wildest chaos. There was dim light. It was not sunlight but nebulous light. It endured for a time and then came darkness. The first day of Moses' vision, corresponding it may be to the first *great day-period* of God's creative work, was ended. Next, the mists are partially lifted. The beholder would have seen vast masses of cloud, or portions of the firmament above the earth. It was the second day. Then comes the dry land, followed by herbage vast and gigantic ; growing, not by sunlight, but in the steaming heats of the earth now cooled down so far as to allow of plants and trees, which were afterwards to be turned into coal for man's use. It was the third day. Next, Moses sees for the first time the light of the sun shining clearly on the earth. That sun might have existed for untold millions of years. But through the mists and the murky atmosphere of the world, its rays had never before pierced. Now it appears in the heavens, the appointed ruler of the day. Then come into view the huge monsters of the deep, and the fowls of the air, the vast dynasties of the fish, and the beast and the bird. Last of all, at the close of the sixth great day-period, comes *man*, created in the image of God. Such is the order in the first chapter of Genesis. It is the spectacle of creation as vouchsafed to Moses. It was not intended to be scientific. It was the general order, described by the *characteristic of each great period*. Nor is it needed that we understand each day-period of creation as exactly matching the prophetic period of the inspired vision. The general object is to describe the creation, as it would have appeared to an observer had there been one present to watch the earth as God was preparing it for the abode of man.[1]

Turn now from the book of Revelation to the book of Nature, and let us ask, next, what does science, and especially the science of geology—the science of the rocks—say about this same creation.

Here, too, a few preliminary words are needed. One is, that the science of geology is yet in its infancy. It is not a hundred years old. Instead of making the boldest assertions of any of the sciences, and so drawing down upon itself their condemnation, it should be modest. It is also to be remembered that geology has changed its fundamental theories again and again. A book that was an authority twenty years ago, is no authority to-day in geology. The next twenty years may witness greater changes. New facts are discovered. But new theories are made even faster than new facts

[1] "The seven days are not literal days of twenty-four hours, nor yet seven *definite* historical periods. But as the seven seals, vials, trumpets of John's Revelation represented human history by a typical representation of each of its grand divisions without any one of them being chronologically defined, so these seven days of Moses represent in a dramatic or typical form the changes at creation, each grand feature being boldly sketched out in one scenic representation *characteristic* of that period"
—*Primeval Man Unveiled.*

are obtained. Nearly every leading geologist has abandoned his own most startling theories, and some have gone through a dozen of them. Lyell has discarded his former views about the age of the world, and the time of man's appearance on it. Huxley, who had claimed millions of years for the earth, under the telling blows of Lord Kelvin, easily the first mathematician of Europe, has just been compelled to own that the claims of geologists about the tremendous age of the earth are not proved. It is the same with the age of man on the earth. Huxley thinks that as star dust is the material out of which the earth was formed, so there is a *physical basis* for all plant, animal and human life. Agassiz denounces Darwin's theory of "natural selection." And then in turn is denounced by the whole scientific world for insisting upon the *moral* unity of the race and yet holding that man sprang not from one centre but from several centres—not from one human pair but from more than half a dozen human pairs.[1]

The scientists are not agreed in their theories.

---

[1] Spencer insists that his "theory of force" suffices to account for the world and for man. Lamark exalts "variation of species." Darwin depends on "natural selection" and "survival of the fittest." Weisman has dealt telling blows at both Lamarkism and Darwinism by showing that "all the evidence is against perpetuation by heredity of characters acquired by the individual." Cope declares for the "origin of the fittest." There are monistic, agnostic, infidel, and Christian naturalists. Certainly, Miller, Dana, Le Conte and Dawson are names equal to any, and they maintain the theory of one human pair.

They agree only on some general facts. What are these facts?

Modern science now almost universally adopts the doctrine that the earth was first of all in a fluid, gaseous or nebulous state. This gaseous mass was intensely heated. Somehow motion was communicated to the mass. This brought out heat; and this heat was attended with a feeble light—scientific men call it cosmical light, to distinguish it from sun-light.[1] Thus, without intending so to do, the scientists exactly describe the first of the Mosaic days of creation.

Next came, according to modern scientists, the huge rocks called Primary,[2] the granites and the different

---

[1] "How could there be light before the sun?" So cried Voltaire, and a thousand voices have echoed the question. And this objection has probably done more to unsettle the minds of young men in past generations than any other difficulty of the Bible. Those who believed in revelation had no other reply than to ask men to wait. The waiting has been richly rewarded. For now no respectably informed man ventures the question. Humboldt's words about cosmical light are well known. He claims the existence of light " which is a similitude of the dazzling light of the sun. The existence of this illuminating power we discover also among the other orbs." And Proctor, in writing of a late solar eclipse says, "We recognize the existence of envelope after envelope around the sun until our earth is reached and overpast."

[2] Nomenclature has been cast and recast so many times and on so many different systems that no one of them may be followed exclusively. Twenty years ago, naming them according to their supposed order of strata, the division of the rocks was into Primary, Secondary and Tertiary; next, with regard to the appearance of life, it was into Azoic, Palæozoic and Mesozoic, etc. Subsequently the nomenclature made popular in America by Lyell was employed. But he has himself

ingredients of granite. As the boiling mass cooled down these became the basis of all the rest. It was once almost unanimously maintained that no animal or vegetable remains had been found in them. It has, however, been recently claimed that there are indications of the skeleton of one animal. If so, it is the oldest thing that had life. But it is singularly complex in structure, as it ought not to be on the principle of spontaneous life.

This Primary age was followed by the Secondary or Palæozoic period. "In this appeared," says Sir J. W. Dawson, "at once a vast accession of living things as if by a sudden production. New forms appear which it is impossible to connect genetically with any predecessors." New vegetable forms arise in steaming air and without sunlight; then follows the carboniferous period, when these vegetable forests were turned to coal through some tremendous change by fire and water. "There was," says Dawson, "the introduction from time to time of new groups, as if to replace others." Some of these plants, though appearing so early, are more complex, and more perfectly formed, and of higher grade, as we study their remains in the rocks, than are their successors in our modern world.

But that age passed. The period of the animal

reconstructed his vocabulary, at least as to the Pliocene and Post-pliocene ages.

world arrived. Gigantic creatures roamed the earth and seas; in many respects the superiors of their degraded successors as seen in our own age.

It was a time singularly fruitful of life and equally destructive of life. A few years since geologists insisted, their eyes on the proof of these immense changes, that there had been "successive periods of the *entire* destruction and restoration of all life." Then, in the swing of the pendulum, it was insisted that the progress was uniform and steady from lower to more complex organizations in plant and animal life. But now the tendency is toward recognizing what Mivart, Le Conte, and Dawson call "critical periods," and "intermittent creations," and "prolific periods." And yet, on the whole, there was progress; the great plan of God taking in, as it did, the destructions and reproductions which appear to have been sometimes gradual and sometimes sudden. And thus the progress was not linear, in straight lines, but by a series of circles overlapping each other, like the links of a chain.

Then came another convulsion.[1] The temperature

[1] "In the distant past, not a trace of man's presence has been found. He is 'of yesterday.' While the stone volume has preserved for us the slight impressions of the Annelid and the foot-trail of perished Molluscs in the soft mud over which they crawled; while it delineated, on carboniferous columns, fern-leaves exquisitely delicate in structure as the finest species of modern times; and while the rain-drops of long

fell. All the continents were buried beneath the sea. Some claim that this was done by sudden and volcanic agency; some, that it occurred by the gradual subsidence of the land. At this time vast fields, and even mountains of ice, were formed over all the face of the desolate world. This was followed by the drift period, so called, when, this whole North American continent submerged, the great icebergs floated from the north-west, dropping from their bases those vast mountains of gravel and those vast boulders which are found all over the continent to-day. Says Humboldt, "the Alps were beneath the ocean." Says Lyell, "All land has been under water." "The highest mountains," says Tenny, "have been the ocean bottom." And then came the last great act before man. The continents were lifted out of the sea, and the waters gathered into the rivers and oceans. And at length on the last of these great day-periods man was created.

Such is substantially the course of creation as our scientists now hold it. A few of these points are still disputed. But these conclusions are all but universally held, and are as certain as any scientific facts can ever be.

bygone ages have left imprints which reveal to us the course which even the wind followed; not a trace of man is visible. Only at the close does he appear; science finds him where the Scriptures placed him, and sees in him the crown which continuous type had long foreshadowed."—*Fraser.*

A few words, thirdly, as to the general agreement of the record in the Bible and the record in the rocks.

First, all science says that there was originally a *Creator*. Even Darwin, often called an atheist, says, "life was originally breathed by the *Creator* into a few forms or into one." Owen says that "law is only secondary cause," but he holds that law is guided by the intelligence of the Creator. Herbert Spencer leaves a place for God as the author of force. While Agassiz, Hitchcock, Dana and Guyot all insist that science no less than revelation declares those grandest of words, "*In the beginning, God!*"

Secondly, all science declares that originally the earth was chaotic, sunless; its vast boiling, surging masses of melted rocks, surrounded by clouds of steam and mist, were lit at first not by sunlight but by cosmical light. Exactly so says Moses. A hundred years ago men said, "Moses is surely wrong in not making the sun to shine upon the earth until the fourth day." But no carefully-read man now makes that objection. The huge forests, which now are turned to coal, grew then in the steaming atmosphere as they could not have grown in the sun's light. Astronomers, geologists and chemists all agree that there was light before the direct rays of the sun touched the earth. How strikingly is Moses vindicated, or rather God, who spake through Moses, in the sacred narrative.

"Let there be *light*," was said on the first day. "Let the *sun* rule the day," was said on the fourth day.

Thirdly, science declares that the life-periods became observable only after the formation of the earlier rocks. The granites are conspicuous before the vegetable forms in the order of creation.

Fourthly, science is now insisting that there have been successive eras of manifestation or creation. Vast forests existed—they were swept away. Vast sea monsters existed—they have disappeared. Others have been introduced and destroyed. No less than twenty-seven of these distinct creations and destructions are insisted upon by some of our best geologists.[1] Professor Owen claims that some species survived these convulsions. But Agassiz, and with him the mass of more careful scientists, insists upon it that these eras have come and gone. He says: "There was a succession of beings on the earth's surface. But the *fishes of one age are not the descendants of those in the former geological age.* There is no parental descent among them. God has

[1] Geologists long debated the question of steady progress or of sudden convulsion as the mode in which these changes came about. The older theory made much of immense convulsions; the newer theory made much of the uniformity of advancement. It is coming to be seen that both had their place and their play, each more manifest than the other at some periods and at some eras. Concerning any *special form* of a development hypothesis, the wiser and more cautious men, so often inclined themselves in former years to stake all on a theory, have learned wisdom; that there is yet "a boundless region to be explored."

created all the types of animals that have passed away, to introduce man upon our globe." How wondrously is this in accordance with the chapter in which God is said to have made the fishes and made the birds and made the beasts and then made man.[1]

Fifthly, the general *order* of creation is another remarkable fact. The order of the scientists is in outline—we could not expect agreement in detail, for science is not yet perfect—is in outline, that of revelation. There is steady progress from chaos up through primary rocks, then on and up through secondary rocks with traces of vegetable life; thence upward still by new creations unto the mammal age and then into the highest created forms of the mammal age,[2] when man himself appears.

Sixthly, science also teaches of the classification of plants according to their "seed" and "kind," or structure. The Linnæan system had obtained for years a place in the scientific world. But it was felt after all

[1] " There is not an existing stratum in the body of the earth, there is not an existing species of plants or animals which cannot be traced back to a time when it had no place in the world. The forms of organic life had *a beginning in time*."—*Lyell.*

" Species appear suddenly and disappear suddenly."—*Agassiz.*

[2] The waters were repeopled with beings which were not repetitions of the forms just exterminated, but original conceptions; and yet not *fundamentally* different, but united to the old by such identity of the fundamental plan as to convince us that the intelligence which brought death to all terrestrial existence continued to prosecute his own unchanged purpose through all succeeding epochs.— *Winchell.*

that a classification by flowers was incorrect. And today the botanists of the world have gone on to their new classification, which is only the old classification in the first chapter of Genesis. "Let the earth bring forth the herb yielding seed, and the fruit tree after his kind whose seed is in itself." "This new trophy of science," is only an old laurel from the wreath woven so many years ago by Moses.

Seventhly, science puts vegetation before animal life. Scripture likewise, in describing the day-periods, places the plant kingdom before the animal; and here again the two records agree.

Eighthly, science puts man as the last of the beings that has appeared on the globe. He did not appear until the close of these tremendous convulsions by which the earth was shaped. Revelation makes man appear at the close of the sixth great period.

But when was that? When did he appear on our earth? No man can tell us. The Scripture on this point is silent. We have no definite chronology in Genesis, but *only historic periods in their general order.* Attempts have been made to ascertain the age of man from a purely historic basis; but this method is clearly unreliable when taken alone. For the Hebrew method and the Samaritan method and the Septuagint method are widely divergent. In one, the period from Adam to the flood is sixteen hundred years, in another thirteen hundred years, in another it is more than two thou sand years. In the period between Adam and Christ they differ by fifteen hundred years. What wonder that we have different systems of chronology by men like Ussher, Hales and Poole and Bunsen, none of them agreeing in the age of the human race. The system which, until within a single generation, has obtained most widely, is that of Ussher, which places the creation six thousand years ago. But the Scriptures say nothing about six thousand years. And if the time of Ussher should even be doubled, there is nothing to prevent it in the Mosaic record. The tables of genealogy in the Bible were constructed to show the descent of Christ from Adam. And the word "generations," is plainly used in the older Scriptures with the same indefiniteness as the word "day"—a usage found also in the New Testament, and common also in our own century and language. "The extreme uncertainty," says Dr. Hodge, "attending all attempts to determine the chronology of the Bible, is sufficiently evidenced by the fact that one hundred and eighty different calculations have been made by Jewish and Christian authors of the length of the period between Adam and Christ. The longest make it six thousand nine hundred and eighty-four years, the shortest three thousand four hundred and eighty-three years. If the facts of science or of history should ultimately make it necessary to admit that eight or ten thousand years have elapsed since the creation of man, there is nothing in the Bible in the way of such concession. *The Scriptures do not teach us how long men have existed on the earth.*"

It is well known that on the subject of man's age on earth the geologists have taken the lead of all other scientists in demanding that we extend into an almost immeasurable past the time of man's appearance. Wallace talks of "ten thousand centuries," and supposes "a time when man possessed no powers of speech nor those moral feelings which now distinguish the race." Others think two hundred thousand years enough. There was also much talk about pottery found at the mouth of the Nile, which, reckoning in a certain way as to the deposits annually made by the river mud, was thought to be twelve thousand years old. But since that day, at a greater depth, in the same deposit, Sir R. Stephenson found a brick bearing on it the stamp of a modern ruler of Egypt. And more recently it has been proved that the said piece of pottery is of *Roman* origin. Of the so-called fossils at Natchez on the Mississippi, said at first to prove man's existence one hundred thousand years ago, Sir Charles Lyell, an advocate for the longest times, declares, "it is allowable to suspend our judgment as to its high antiquity." So, too, it is of bones in European caves, and of Swiss dwellings submerged in lakes, and of arrow heads and flint hatchets which have been found mixed with bones of extinct species of animals, and with human bones. Lyell says, they "were probably not coeval." And some of the most eminent geologists declare, in the words of one of them, "It cannot be proved that these remains may not have been washed up, drifted and reassorted from earlier deposits dating back at the utmost but a few thousand years."

It is the same with the immense age claimed for the Egyptian Pyramids and other monuments—viz., seventeen thousand years before Christ. Recent discoveries have effectually banished the old illusions. Champollion declares "no Egyptian monument is really older than two thousand two hundred years before Christ." Wilkinson decides that "Egypt has nothing older than a century or so before Abraham's day."

But if geologists have demanded immense periods for the past history of the race, and have been followed by a few orientalists, their claims have been disputed strenuously by another class of scientists. Astronomers, with Sir W. Thompson at their head, while desiring to extend the period further than Ussher and the mere historians, have dealt severe blows at the geologists; for they have proved that, not many thousand years ago, such was the temperature of the earth, that man could not have lived upon it. It is then a settled thing that the sciences cannot determine accurately the period of the advent of man on earth.

The historians generally favor the shorter, the geologists the longer, and the astronomers the middle ground. The general drift, however, of scientific and philosophic thought inclines to the extension of the period of man's existence by a few thousand years. If the development theory should at length be shown to have a scientific basis, if even that particular form of it which is called the Darwinian theory should be accepted—a theory less brilliant and less popular than that of the "vestiges," which it supplanted, only in turn, as we believe, like it to sink out of sight—it would not be necessary to reconstruct a single verse of Genesis. If more than one *physical* origin for man is ever proved, nothing in the Bible can be alleged against it. *Moral unity for our race* is all that is really required. The doctrine of "diverse origins for man," was defended by a theologian on theological grounds and as a necessity of interpretation more than two hundred years ago. If it should ever be proved that, before Adam, there were creatures having man's physical form, and that at length it pleased God, in Eden, to take this being, whose body centuries before had been "formed out of the dust of the earth," and, then and there, to breathe into him a higher kind of life in which he became endowed with new capacities for moral character, with a new sense of right and wrong, with an immortal and responsible soul—all this would not be in any necessary conflict with the Scripture story. For nothing is said as to how long a time elapsed between the formation of man as a creature of mere body with an animal life in it, and the subsequent inbreathing of a responsible and immortal spirit by which the race became what we see it to-day. It would, in that case, be just as true that "God hath made of one blood all nations of men for to dwell on the face of the earth;" just as true "that by one man sin entered into the world and death by sin." In that case, the moral unity of the race, taught as a historical fact by Moses, and by Christ, and also incorporated doctrinally with the teaching of Paul, could be held and defended just as firmly, though on other grounds, as Christians hold and defend this fact and this doctrine to-day.

Indeed, in so recent and authoritative a work as Lange on Genesis, we have a note of the translator which reads thus : "this does not exclude the idea that the *human physical* was connected with the previous nature or natures, and was *brought out of them;* that is, that *it* was 'made of the earth,' in the widest signification of the term ; he having an earthly as well as a heavenly origin." Without adopting any one of these theories, nay more, holding that the time is not ripe nor the evidence all in for a careful verdict about any one of them, a Christian may rejoice that no truth will ever displace that of the Scripture record; that, positive as to some statements, the Bible is purposely left elastic and uncommitted about many a minor question. The agreement is clear of the two records as to a Creator, and as to one race. Equally clear is the statement that only a few thousand years since man did not exist, and as to that other fact, that the time will come when this earth will be no longer his abode. Says Sir W. Thompson. "Within a finite period the earth must have been, and within a finite period to come the earth must again be, unfit for the habitation of man. There is a process of events toward a state infinitely different from the present." Who can fail to recall, in listening to such testimony from scientific lips, those words of the Scriptures, "The elements shall melt, and the earth also and the works that are therein shall be burned up." "Heaven and earth shall pass away."

Science, again, declares that men are *a race*. This is regarded as proven by bodily structure, by human language, and by mental and moral likeness. Says Owen : "Men form one species, and differences are but indicative of varieties." Max Müller declares "language has one common source." And above all other proofs is that of mental and moral science ; showing as it does the capacity of man, and man alone, for faith ; the ability for moral ideas ; the powers for knowing God and duty ; for loving the pure and seeking the heavenly. For, no matter what theory of man's origin be adopted, this at least all grant, that man's soul to-day is not an ape soul, or a swine soul, but a human soul—a soul capable of faith in the unseen, capable of love to God as "our Father in heaven." And here Scripture comes in, declaring that "through faith"—faith in testimony being a human characteristic—"we understand that the worlds were made," and that "God hath made of one blood all nations of men for to dwell on the face of the earth."

And thus young men are taught to hold fast to their confidence in the Bible. Scientific theories for a time may oppose the statements of it. A fact here and there may as yet appear strange. Wait a little. Let the men who run their theories against Biblical facts have time enough, and they will be compelled to alter their theories. The *settled facts* are so many illustrations of Scripture truth. Let no man be afraid of Scripture; no more let him be afraid of science. God's handwriting is never contradicting when truly read.

And we can also see that we have each our duty as members of the race of men out of which Christ came. Adam has sinned. The taint comes on us. We inherit it, as we do diseased bodies; as we do the liability to physical death. But after all we are voluntary in yielding to any sin; for *any* sin is a sin "after the similitude of Adam's transgression." And so we are responsible for being sinners before God. But as we receive taint from Adam through the race bond, so we receive gracious offers through Christ, the second Adam. Here, too, it is our voluntary act to believe, and to accept the Holy Spirit, whereby we are recreated in the image of God. Paradise can be regained. The race-bond in Jesus Christ is the hope of the world.

We are prepared, by the thoughts already presented, to welcome the Scriptural idea of the "new heavens, and new earth wherein dwelleth righteousness." Vast have been the convulsions of the old earth both through flood and fire. But the floods shall come no more. The next great convulsion is to be, according to God's word, by fire. The earth and the things in it are to be burned up. Then every mark of man's sin shall be obliterated. Every trace of evil shall be destroyed. And the purified earth is to be visited by a higher form of life than ever before. Steadily has the earth gone on. Fit only for coarser and lower forms of life in the old geologic six day-periods, it has been now for a few years the home of sinful man. Beyond the great day of God, it shall be reformed and remodeled, and become the spot that holy souls from heaven shall love to visit. Thank God that the old world—now the type of hollowness and deceit, so that worldliness is another name for sinfulness—is to be so changed as to become an outlying borderland of God's holy heaven!

CHAPTER VI.

Difficulties from Astronomy.

A YOUNG MAN states to the writer his belief as follows. "I believe in a God who has a general superintendence over the affairs of the world. I believe in the immortality of the human soul. I believe that what a man does here affects generally his condition after death. Any thing farther than this I doubt."

Urged to tell why he doubted, the reply was that, substantially, of thousands. "God seems too great to concern himself minutely about our human affairs. It is too much to believe that he who has the care of the whole universe will condescend to notice all the thoughts of a being so insignificant to him as a single and separate man: too much to believe that he will hear him pray and do any thing because he prays that he would not have done just as soon if the man had kept silent: too much to believe that this infinite God had such a care for this world—a mere dot among the starry worlds, a mere grain of sand in a corner of his universe—as to give his Son to die for those dwelling upon it, whole nations of whom are but as the invisible dust in the balance."

And when this argument is pressed at night and out under the vast canopy of the winter heavens, with unnumbered worlds in view, and when it is remembered that new telescopes and larger glasses are multiplying these worlds, each as worthy, so far as we can see, to be visited by a Saviour, each as worthy of the divine care and providence as our world, the impression, to some minds, grows stronger, that we must not be too definite in our belief about the minute care and providence of God. "Is not a man's creed best when it is briefest; when he ventures only on a mere outline belief as to God, the soul and the future life?" So say some. Others feel it. And they hold to Christianity but loosely, because of the starry worlds, and the planetary spaces and the vastness of the universe.

It is believed that these doubts are without foundation; that the vastness of the universe confirms faith rather than suggests doubts, when carefully considered; that, since God is no where general in ordering the stars but every where special in the realms of astronomy, the inference is in favor not of a general and outline creed, but of a special and distinct and Christian belief. David's song, "When I consider thy heavens, the work of thy fingers, the moon and the stars, which thou hast ordained; What is man, that thou art mindful of him? and the son of man, that thou visitest him?" was not the minor strain of doubt, but the song of holy wonder and thankful praise. Others might doubt; but he must believe and adore and pray.

Look at the *minuteness of the arrangements* in the starry sky. The first impression is vastness. World upon world, sun upon sun, system upon system, crowd each other to the very verge of space. But where is the verge of space? Through the best telescopes, counting a little patch of worlds in the distant star dust where they are sown with only average thickness on the sky, and then multiplying the whole horizon by that star patch, astronomers count billions of stars. And when larger tubes shall be pointed against the sky, it is believed that the number now known will be but a mere fraction of those then to be seen. Figures get to be meaningless as we try to number the stars. The universe is immensity. Think, too, of the spaces through which these worlds are distributed. Our world spins its annual round of two hundred million miles, and never gets within thirty million miles of a neighbor star. Our sun has for its nearest neighbor sun a star forty-six million miles away. And if this is nearness in the skies, what is distance? Looking only on this vastness we are abashed and confounded; and we are almost ready to say that God's care can be nothing beyond general over the worlds, and especially over man the minute insect here in a mere outpost of the universe. But then, this temporary feeling yields in a single moment to our firmer and calmer reason.

For surely all this immensity tells of an infinite God. It is exactly what might be expected of him. It scatters atheism, driving it beyond the stars. There must be a God of immensity, when the universe, the work of his hands, is so immense.

Now mark the fact that this God of immensity is *great in the minuteness of his arrangements.* These planets are racing through the sky at the rate of thousands of miles each moment. But see how carefully God keeps time on this race course. Jupiter never gets in at his goal at any given point, a moment too late or a moment too soon. One mistake of a second here, would wrench the system past all computation. The most unwieldy of the stars comes exactly to time. Turning from the evening sky the astronomer said, "God is a mathematician." And as the *motions* are exact, and timed to the millionth of a second, so the *masses* are arranged and guarded with the minutest care. God stands with scales more exact than those of the goldsmith, and weighs out to each planet its grains of sand, never one too many to Jupiter or one too few to Uranus. A handful of dust in the wrong place would upset the machinery of the heavens. God is minute as well as vast in his universe. If his lines and angles stretch across the universe, the measurement is exact. Nothing is simply and only general. Every thing is carefully poised and specially considered. God has its vastness, because he has the minuteness of the universe in his hand. What, then, is the religious inference from these heavens ? Is it that God is simply a general God, who has made only the cast-iron frame of the machinery, and has left the exact fitting of each cog of every wheel pretty much to itself; that he is to be believed in as having only a *general* care for mankind, who in turn are to have only a general faith in his existence, a general idea of religious duties, which duties are only the general doing of things that are about right ? Nay! Nay! Is not the inference in favor of the special belief in a God ever near, who hears prayer, who has cared for man, and who reveals the moral glory of his grace in Jesus Christ even as the glory of wisdom and power are displayed in these radiant worlds above us. The stars do not say Christ. But they tell of a minuteness of God's care for worlds, that is exactly matched in God's care for the souls of men.

The young man whose doubt I am discussing argued in a very similar style from the revelations of the *microscope*. And since the reasoning—that from the immensity of minute things, as in astronomy from the immensity of great things—is very similar, the answer to it is found in the same line of thought.

The microscope is simply the inverted telescope. That looked among the mighty orbs, this looks down on the minutest things which God has made. It discovers insects so small that twenty-seven millions of them would make but a single inch. It finds vast families of various kinds of them in the cavities of a common grain of sand. In each drop of stagnant water is a world of animate beings who have as much room in proportion to their size as have the whales in the Pacific ocean. In a single leaf it finds swarms of insect life grazing as cattle on a hill-side. It finds a down on the butterfly's wing every fringe of which is so exact, that human art in its nicest and evenest productions is only clumsy and bungling. God has finished off and elaborated the wing of an insect that lives only a single day. Surely no man can doubt God's minuteness in his care for man, after seeing through the microscope, what he does for beings lower than man. If the telescope humbles us, when we invert it in the microscope it exalts us. Little in one view, we are large in the other. Shall God care for the polish on the beetle's wing and have no care for an immortal soul? Doing nothing slightly, but all things well in nature, has he no concern for the greater as well as for the lesser things of man's life? I can better understand Christ's splendid example of a special providence in the numbering of a hair and the falling of a sparrow, when I see what God does down among the living insect world as the microscope reveals his handy work.

Then, too, when we think of the myriad races lower than ourselves, is man quite so contemptible a being? Compared with God, man is feeble. But compared with the insect, he is almost a God. His world is small among the starry worlds, but it is vast as compared with the world of the insects that live in a sand grain. If God has guided the instinct of those minute beings so that each does his appropriate work, will he refuse to hear a man's earnest prayer for guidance in doing a work that involves the eternal interest of a priceless soul? If he has cared so much for their bodies that they may be saved to fulfil their destiny, will he have no plan of salvation for man's soul, that the highest and noblest being that walks the earth may not through sin be utterly ruined?

Then, too, these manifestations of God in nature, so far from awaking doubt, prepare us to believe in his manifestation in *humanity*. In the midnight sky he reveals his skill and his power. He does not launch worlds into space as boys throw their snow balls into the air from the mere feeling of sport, and the exuberance of power. He has the motive of *revealing* before intelligent beings his wisdom and his might. But why stop there? Why skill and might displayed, and all else hidden? Ah; but mere things will not show the deeper perfections of God. Yet being God, he must desire to display these movings and motions of his heart. He can only do this to man *through man*. Yet a *mere* man cannot show it. He himself must then be incarnate in man, God manifest in flesh. Grant me this only, that the worlds of the midnight sky were not made in sport; that their maker God, desired to reveal himself in these, that only a part of his nature could shine in them, while he himself could be enshrined in man, his image—and the inference is clear that he may, that he probably will come among us as Immanuel, *"God with us."* The stars do not hinder me, as I study them, they help me to believe that, manifesting his glory and power in them, he will also manifest himself in a human form. They prepare me to accept the great fact that Jesus is the God-man—who came to show us the beating of his heart even as these stars show us the working of his hands.

Again; turning from the works themselves to the attributes of God as indicated by them, doubt is lessened rather than increased. "He is so great that he has greater things to do than to notice each man," says the objector. But is that the true inference from the fact? Why not state it thus: He is so great, that, doing all things else, he can also notice each man. He is great at condescension. He is great in providing for the things that men would call trifles. In this universe the smallest things are the hinges on which turn the gravest events. Any trivial thing not carefully worked, the least accident in a trifle, may unhinge every broadest plan. An insect of an hour may inflict a fatal sting upon an emperor; and his death may destroy a nation and change the map of a continent. A God every where or a God nowhere is the alternative. He must have **every event in his control**, or he will loose the reins, and cannot govern his world. He must, then, care for man. And if he have any care, it must extend even to man's *thoughts;* for these are the sources of his acts. And so because he is God and therefore cannot be ignorant even if he would about any minutest thing, and because if ignorant of the lesser, he could not govern the greater, we feel sure of the Christian doctrine which teaches that God is near man, watches every deed, marks every purpose, and will bring every thought into judgment whether it be good or whether it be evil. Surely there is no general care for man that is not first special, no general providence that is not particular; no superintendence for the whole earth, that does not take in every particle of its dust; no watchfulness over any man's soul which does not include the minutest things that touch his mortal and his immortal life.

And as we reason from God's works in the starry skies to his nature, and to the manifestations of himself he will be likely to exhibit on other fields, so we reason from *man* and from his capacities for understanding something of the divine ways and works. The stars are mere masses of matter. They do not know themselves. They do not know God. They do not know man. But man knows them; and looking on them can thank God for them. They have no likeness to God. God is their Creator, not their Father. God is Father only to souls. Shall he have such interest in those stars that know not any thing, and only a general outline care for a human soul, which alone can know of his works? Is there no evidence that God loves to be appreciated in his world? Did he not make man his highest work to understand and interpret the other works of his hands? One soul is worth more than all the stars of the skies. Those stars are burning out. Year by year astronomers discover a star on fire. It burns on its months and then vanishes—a token of what God says is to be done with our earth at the final day.

But souls do not cease to be. They have an immortality. God has done so much in endowing them already, that we should be surprised if he did not do more. We have seen why he who reveals his power and glory in the stars, should also reveal himself in humanity; why God should manifest himself in Jesus Christ. But this spiritual nature of man carries us further. The great thing about a man is not his avoirdupois. The mind makes the man; the soul stamps him as of worth. Shall God reveal his thought in the stars, and shall he refrain from revealing it likewise in man's realm of thought *i. e.* the *literature of the world?* Shall men reveal their thought in books; and shall God have no Book? Shall his thought shine in every department except that where man's thoughts shine brightest? Is it not of all things most reasonable; nay so reasonable as to be absolutely certain, that God will reveal himself in a book, a Bible, a revelation in human thought and language about himself. There must be a Bible, a book of God, given through men, and having a *divine* inspiration, as all the great works of human genius have a human inspiration in them.

A few years ago astronomers said that there were strange perturbations in the motions of certain planets What was the trouble? Some one suggested that if a planet existed between two of those already known it would account for the disturbance. The disturbance was carefully calculated and the position of the supposed planet ascertained, and when they pointed the iron tube at the spot, there stood the waiting star. There was need for it; and so the star itself was there.

I reason in the spiritual astronomy of religion in the same way. I find a deep want. Here is a God whose notice of me is exact and minute. He will require of me a strict account at the last day. But I cannot do the duties of this life without some knowledge of the life to come. If that life takes on any complexion from this, I must in some way know about that coming life. No one but the eternal God can tell me certainly about that future world, what it is; how to escape its terrors, if it has terrors; how to gain its joys, if it has joys. I must have, not the inspiration of human genius, but the divine inspiration of God's thought in my human language; in other words I must have an inspired Bible to teach me of the future and so of the present. If I do not know about that life, I cannot in this world get ready for the future. I do not go upon the journey of a week without preparing for it. Can I go the eternal journey without making any special preparation in this life? How can I know in what way to prepare for a journey so solemn, and on which I may start so suddenly? If there be a God with any care for me, he will tell me. He will not leave me to be tossed on the ocean of human guesses. He will give me my directions and instructions. And so I reason with heart and head that there must be a Bible; just as, to those astronomers there must be a star. The need of it is the proof of it.

We may go further. Man has deeper needs than those requiring direction. He needs *redemption* from the guilt and bondage of sin. The stars are guided in their courses by one whose skill provides for every inch of their course and every second of their time. Their every want is supplied. A thousand influences would draw each of them from its orbit. But God provides for them that they dash not off their track to ruin. Unlike them, we can and do turn away from our appointed duty. But shall we think that the God who would rescue a star from its ruin, could look on and see men lost in sin, and make no effort at their salvation? I see him give Jesus Christ. I see Jesus Christ dying, the just for the unjust, that we may be saved. And I feel that he who cares so closely for the stars in their orbits, and who holds them to their course, is doing all this work of redemption for man, his child, the being with an immortal soul—doing it because it is like him to do it; like him *here* to show his heart, as *there* in the sky to show the wonders of his hand.

In short, I am compelled to feel that he who has so garnished the evening sky, so carefully settled the paths of the stars, so timed each planet, and weighed to a grain of sand each orb, who is never general but always special in his care for every thing great and for every thing small, is a God who has not left me any poor general outline creed in the infinite matter of religion. He is—thanks be to his name, as becomes him, and as becomes man, his child—especially careful and exact, especially full and explicit in telling me what to believe and what to do in religion, and how to gain a holy heaven. The stars do not make me doubt. They help my faith. They intimate, they more than intimate a Bible which teaches me all I need to know.

Thank God that we are not left to any man's guesses in religion. I ask you, young men, to come to no uncertain science in this matter of religion. God is our authority here. The clear doctrines of his Word shine out in the moral as do these stars in the natural firmament. Nay, these stars are only for the eye. But God's truth is for the soul. We can prove it to the intellect. That is well. But, young men, the God of those heavens and of this Bible, asks your hearts. He has worlds enough. But he wants appreciative and loving

L

souls. He stamped its radiant glory upon these overhanging heavens. The vast spaces of the ether blue were the groundwork on which he wrought out the pattern, so brilliant, so gorgeous, for the gaze of the worlds. He has another firmament, higher, grander than this of the evening sky. Souls are the stars studding that firmament. They have a peculiar lustre. Coming into existence at first, as the world was created, in chaos, the Spirit of God, which changed that old earth-chaos into the orderly and beautiful world where we dwell, has called these souls "out of nature's darkness into his marvellous light." They are destined for the higher firmament of heaven. They are to be at length stars, not for man's gaze, as are these evening orbs; but they are for God's delight, for the garniture of his own heaven.

God wants hearts. He can take the weakest and most guilty, if it be freely given to him, and out of it he can make an orb the radiance of which shall shine when these "heavens are rolled together as a scroll and the elements shall melt with the fervent heat."

CHAPTER VII.

DIFFICULTIES ABOUT HISTORIC FACTS.

VISITORS at the White Mountains are taken to see that great natural curiosity which is known as the "Old Man of the Mountain," or " The Profile." On the front of a lofty cliff, hundreds of feet above him, the traveller is shown a great stone face with its gigantic features sharply cut against the morning or the evening sky. But the perfection of the resemblance is discerned only when the spectator takes his stand on a specified spot. Seen half a mile in either direction nothing is visible on the mountain side save a rugged mass of uninteresting rock. Everything depends upon the right approach and the correct position of the man himself as he comes to the study of this great natural wonder. What if it be the same with other things; with wonders in the *moral* as well as in the physical world ? What if it be a very especial need when a young man comes to his Bible, that he should approach it in a peculiar way and occupy a certain definite position.

We have seen that the book which we call the Bible is a peculiar book; that its claims are unlike any other volume in existence; that it is a great moral wonder.

Is it then out of analogy that it should demand a peculiar mood of mind, a certain suitable state of intellect and heart, in those who approach it? The poetic mood is needed for the poem. The philosophic mood is needed for the study of the volume on philosophy. The scientist claims that a peculiarly calm and patient mood is needed by him who would come aright to the great problems of science; that, not the poetic spirit, nor the philosophic spirit, nor yet the theologic spirit, can be any substitute for this mood. And he is right. By all means, the scientific spirit for the scientific problem. So, too, the philosopher, devoted to the broadest inquiries, insists that there can be no substitute for the philosophic spirit, if one would study the volumes of Leibnitz or Descartes, of Hamilton or Hickock. And he is right. Are we then out of analogy when we insist that here, in the study of the great moral problems of the Bible, there is needed a definite mood, a certain reverent and devout tone of mind; and that neither the scientific or the philosophic spirit can be substituted for this obvious and necessary requirement. Everything depends upon the position of the beholder in looking up to this great moral wonder of a Divine Revelation. For the Bible is not made for the scientist as such, nor for the philosopher or poet as such, but for them all as men with moral wants, and for all other men, young and old, as *moral beings*. For it is not our scientific or philosophical capacities, but our moral capacities that are to be awake and receptive as we come to the Book the grand object of which is moral teaching.

And yet, I can understand how it is that exceedingly shrewd men, overlooking this very necessary condition, should make such sad work when they come to the more wonderful facts of the Scriptures. They are puzzled, confounded and led on to infidelity by their wrong ways of approaching these things. They would come to "the feeding of the five thousand," or to any other miracle of the Bible, just as they would come to any alleged fact on the purely natural plane of common things. But that miracle does not profess to be a common fact, nor to have been wrought down in the plane of nature. It refuses to be questioned by the agriculturist, by the chemist, or by any man either of vulgar or of learned curiosity. It was not wrought for wonder-seekers. It declines to let the philosopher talk to it of "laws of nature," and of fixed principles. It is its own principle. It is a physical fact with a moral meaning, and coming in under moral laws, in a system higher than nature. It is a moral doctrine incarnate in a physical fact. No man has any right to consider it out of *moral connections*. It is to be studied only in its relations to the Christ who performed it, to the time when it occurred, to the place it filled, to the truth it taught, to its bearing on the development of the Messiah's plan and aim, and above all, to the niche it was to fill in the great temple which God through Christ was building for the reverent worship of reverent men. To put these moral connections aside and out of sight in judging of "the feeding of the five thousand," is to ignore all the reasons that made the miracle a possibility, and all the conditions furnished by its author to us for our investigation of the meaning the character and the reality of the event itself. There are men who come as scientists with a profound reverence for "nature," and little for God, ready to refer any thing to *it*, but receiving the suggestion to refer any thing to *him* with the shrug of impatient and irreverent unbelief. And these men, in this mood, would apply their methods to the miracles of the Bible! Nothing can be more absurd, unless it be the proposition of those who with a confusion of terms which would be amusing if the theme were not so serious, propose to ascertain "the scientific value of prayer;" as if anybody ever thought it had a scientific value; as if any Christian thinker had ever dreamed of measuring moral values by physical standards; as if one could ask of his grocer a bushel of right or a peck of wrong, of his tailor a yard of truth or of error, or leave with his apothecary an order for the chemical analysis of a man's love for his child and the likelihood of a father to grant his child's petition! Christianity requires tests. Men are "to prove all things." But it suggests there is a proper way to do it. It says, put your crucible and scalpel where they belong in nature. Study your laws whether of the physical world or of the mental world, in the obvious and appropriate ways that are open to you. And when you come to religious facts come also in appropriate ways, and seek moral truth by moral methods. We object to the claim of any set of men, that we are to take their methods, excellent elsewhere, in the study of the miracles. For the miracles are not mere phenomena, mere freaks of power for vulgar curiosity or for scientific and philosophic inquiry. They are parts of a mighty moral system. And they are not to be approached except from this point of advance. They are to be studied with reference to moral ends; and this neither the scientist nor the philosopher, as such, proposes to do. The miracles are for man as a moral being.

And the same is true of many an incident of the Old and New Testament which is not miraculous, but which nevertheless is very strange, and it may be almost absurd when seen alone. But when studied in its place and seen as an object-lesson of God for the moral teaching of men, it becomes not only credible but instructive; not only probable but morally certain, as an event needed for its moral impression at the very point of time, at the very place, and in the very circumstances described. So that if there had not been some such event occurring in the process of the divine tuition of the race, we should have wondered more than we wonder now; the absence of such events being more remarkable than their presence in human history. Considered simply as a method of healing human bodies how absurd the "raising of the serpent in the wilderness." But seen in the setting of the story, seen as God meant it to be seen, as a teaching and a prophecy of Christ's uplifting on the cross; seen as a renewing of the primal promise given after the primal sin; as the palpable objective demonstration of the great moral fact of an atoner and an atonement; seen as a lesson set to the whole world as to the place and the value of faith, the incident is not only redeemed from littleness, but it shines in such grandeur that its light is thrown across all the separating centuries. The entire language of the religious world has been colored thereby, and men everywhere have been led to associate the idea of the lifting up of Christ with the lifting up of the brazen serpent. Nay; the Great Teacher himself has interpreted for us the prophecy, has explained the object-lesson of God. He has said, "As Moses lifted up the serpent in the wilderness even so must the son of man be lifted up that whosoever believeth in him should not perish but have eternal life."

I would have every young man who approaches the Bible come to it with the true idea of *God's method of revelation* in his mind. For this is the key to the volume. That method is easily gathered from even a general perusal. God's method is to *reveal himself to mankind through a particular race, the Hebrews; and this revelation, he will have to culminate in a particular person, Jesus Christ.*

The Hebrew race were fitted to become the medium of this revelation by certain peculiarities.

One of these peculiarities was their *capacity for moral ideas.* True of all Oriental as compared with the Occidental nations, this capacity to receive and express such truths was pre-eminently a Hebrew trait. They were quick beyond any nation of the olden time, in what may be called religious receptivity. They were spiritual symbolists. They thought in figures and talked in metaphors. They went down naturally to the spiritual base of things. It was not poetry, but religious instinct and the moral insight which made them see in all things the broad shadow of God's thoughts. They saw him everywhere. And he was uttering to them spiritual truths where others saw nothing but bald bare physical facts. To the Hebrew mind material things were shadowy and fleeting; their main use being to remind man of the spiritual world so near, so potent, so helpful. This physical world was the world of the dying; the other world, overshadowing this, was the world of the living. The real world was the world of God and angels and souls, of love and of hate, of duty and of destiny; of heaven and of hell. Outward things were just the images seen in a mirror—not the realities, but only representations of the realities. And so every thing in Palestine was a shadow, a type, a semblance, a prophecy of some moral fact; a representation of some deep religious idea. Each object was bursting with moral meanings, and the whole world was alive with God's thoughts revealed unto man through temporal objects.

This religious idealism shows itself in all the Old Testament story. The Biblical history is unlike every other on this very account. Says Stanley: "Every incident and every word of a narrative is fraught with a double meaning, and earthly and spiritual things are put over against each other—hardly to be seen in the English version, but in the original clearly intended." Take the promise on the strength of which the Hebrews went out of Egypt and became a nation. It reads, literally rendered, that they should come to "a land of rest." To *us* there would be just this meaning; that after being vexed in slavery, they should come to a land where there was no task-master. But that was the very least of all the things which it meant to them. The physical was the mere alphabet for the spiritual idea. So to a child the mere letters of the word "men," take the attention. He says to himself that the first letter has three lines with curves and so it is "m;" that the letter curved at the top is "e;" and the last with two lines and curves in it is "n;" and that all together they spell the *word* "men." But a full grown man seeing that word on the page, does not stop upon the letters as letters; still less upon the word as a word. There is a *thought* in it for him. He grasps at once the idea of a broad race of mankind with unity in their diversity, with their social, their political, their moral relations.

The ancient Hebrew went through no lengthened process of logical deduction. No idea had he of reasoning by analogy. He did the thing instinctively. He did not set up the outward object and extract laboriously the metaphor, and then mechanically apply it to moral truths. To him the two were one. If either led it was the spiritual.[1] And when Moses gave the promise of "a land of rest," every Hebrew mind went backward to "God's rest," at the close of creation, and took up the idea of "Sabbath rest," that is of heaven itself, the serene abode of God. Nor backward only, but forward the word carried every one of them. "Rest," was not to them simply a state of bodily repose. The word was broad enough to denote God's smile, favor, blessing, in every form of political and spiritual enjoyment. It meant to them the best of earth and the best of heaven. They seized on the moral idea of the physical fact. And this was their great characteristic

[1] In this fact may be found the removal of a difficulty which some have felt as to "Solomon's Song." It has seemed to them too *sensuous*, as it sets forth the ecstasy of religious feeling under the allegory of a bride and a bridegroom. It may be too warm for our cooler occidental tastes. But the Bible is for the Eastern as well as the Western nations. A distinguished English orientalist has declared that, whereas once the book of "Solomon's Song," was to him a great trial on ground above named, his residence in the East, and his notice of the fact that the religious ideas of the people found constant expression through nuptial figures, had removed from his mind all his former feeling.

as a race, and the leading element of that national feeling which fitted them to be a peculiar people.

And here is the answer to the question pressed so often upon the young man who keeps his faith in the Bible, as to why such prominence is given to the Hebrew history. God selected the best instrument for his purpose. The plan of revealing himself through men once chosen, this was the race foremost in moral capacity; the nation who not only, by inheriting the traditions of the best ancestry, but by their natural constitution of mind, were best fitted to do his work in this thing.

And there was also to be a distinct moral lesson in the *development* of the Hebrew nation. Born in the wilderness, the nation had a unique training for their mission. Nothing like it before or since in human history. The escaped tribes go out of Egypt under circumstances without a parallel, and for a journey that was as singular as was their mission peculiar. Why that long journey of forty weary years? Some will hasten to say that it was for the sins of the people. But then the sins usually named as the reason for this journey were not committed until after the journey had begun, and there were indications at the outset that the journey was to be long, tedious and difficult. The course taken at the very commencement led them away from Palestine. The Land of Promise was but a little distance, had they gone in the direct way. There were fewer obstacles. They would have met no foes. Most of the brief journey would have been through a region of country desolate enough now, but then watered by "the river of Egypt," and connected by a grand system of canals with the Mediterranean. Had they taken this the natural and direct course, forty days, instead of forty years, would have sufficed for the journey. But they go away south-east towards the desert, rather than up north-east towards the fruitful plains of Southern Palestine.

There is a reason for this thing. May it not be found in the *teaching* God would give that people ? He would leave such a stamp upon that race by his communications to them in this wilderness, that all through human history they should be "a peculiar people." Such laws he would impose upon them that no contact with any other race should ever entirely obliterate the impression. Left in Egypt, this teaching could not have been given. No more could it, had they gone at once into Palestine. They must be separated from heathen nations for a time. They must be under direct tuition. On the one hand, they must be purged from the defilement of Egyptian ideas, on the other, special revelations must be given, and special discipline be received. The wilderness was their university, and God was their teacher. They were to cease to be tribes and become a nation. It was their period of childhood,—the period when what is learned abides ; when a single year tells on a life-time.

The most magnificent ritual the world ever saw was introduced, every rite of which was eloquent with the truths of the coming Gospel. New ideas as to God, his holiness, his justice and his mercy, were put before this people. Every minutest thing, even down to the fringe on a priest's garment, was significant, while the grand feasts and festivals, the appointed sacrifices, the more marked celebrations of the nation were intended to make them acquainted with ideas to which all other Oriental nations were utter strangers. Nor by laws alone, but by providences often miraculous, did God give them teaching. But the providences would have been of little worth for this end aside from the laws. Ordinary and extraordinary observances, days of atonement and of passover and years of Jubilee, all were to make them familiar with the root-ideas of the Gospel time. It was designed to indoctrinate a people in religion as never before. They were to be directly trained of God with no contamination from any surrounding nation. Taught of heaven, apart from all that could hinder the force of that teaching, and under the most favorable circumstances for that end that can be imagined, they spent those years in the wilderness.

And this teaching was not alone for the Hebrew nation. It was the human race that was in the eye of God. The tuition of the wilderness was to be written out. It was to be a story for the world's study. And so it has been. For Mahometan and Jew and Christian alike have pondered it. Thousands who know nothing of general history, know of the wilderness wandering. Thousands who could not give a connected story of the battles of their own land, can tell of the battle fields and camping stations of the Hebrew host on the way from Egypt to Canaan. And when any young man is pressed with the objection that "too much space is occupied in the Bible by the story of an old race which has now lost its importance in human history," let him be ready to reply that such an objection shows not only narrowness of view but an entire mistake as to God's plan of using that Hebrew race in their historical development as the medium of his revelation to mankind. Seen in its true relation, seen as an intentional lesson-paper for the world, the old story of that peculiar nationality is not a Hebrew idyl, nor a scrap of antiquity to be preserved by those curious and careful about the olden time. It is for us as well as for them ; a thing of to-day in meaning though of yesterday in fact. Its minuteness is not trivial, but intentionally careful. Its incidents are not accidents, but they are put into the record to be pondered, as they have actually been, by the most thoughtful and advanced souls of the race in their search after God's will.

Nor, again, can we overlook the *geographical* position of this Hebrew race. The land of Canaan stood out fronting other lands. It was a part of Asia, and yet was separated from it by a distinct geological formation that is without a parallel on the globe. In some convulsion of the crust of the earth, there has been formed a depression running north and south, so that the great Jordan valley lies a thousand feet, in some places, below the Mediterranean; thus cutting off Palestine from its own continent and thrusting it forth into the presence of the world. Along its eastern shore stretched the "great and wide sea," the Mediterranean, with its Joppa the oldest, and its Tyre the grandest sea-port of the ancient civilization. Waves that washed Europe on the one side and Africa on the other came dashing in upon the long sea-beaches of Palestine. It was central to the commerce of the world. It invited the ships of every clime to bring their treasures for exchange upon those fruitful shores. That grand old sea gives us the means of making accurate the division between ancient and modern history. For if modern history is the history of lands washed by the hoarse surges of the stormy Atlantic, then we may define ancient history as the history of the lands washed by the white surges of the blue and beautiful Mediterranean. But if Palestine stood fronting the sea and inviting its commerce, no less was the situation propitious on the landward view. If ships brought commerce over the sun-lit waves of the Mediterranean to her western coasts, the caravan, rich in treasures, on its way from Arabia and the lands of the more distant Orient, must pass through her eastern gates, and over the Jordan valley and up and into

Palestine, on its way to the wealthy cities of Smyrna and Ephesus, in Asia Minor.

So, too, on the south lay Egypt, the most fertile land on earth; and north lay Assyria and Babylonia, prodigal of gold and gems, boasting of mineral as Egypt of agricultural wealth. In the rivalries of trade or the fiercer rivalries of war, this land of Palestine was directly on the highway between the two. None could pass east of it, for there was the pathless desert. They must go directly through for trade. They must march their armies directly across the plains in time of war. In days of peace—and Solomon saw that " the empire was peace,"—the heaviest tolls might be exacted and were gladly paid. Hence the immense revenues of Solomon. Hence the riches that built the Jerusalem temple. In time of war—and this was nearly all the time—between the vast northern power and the vast southern kingdom, it was policy in the Jewish nation to take part with neither, but to furnish, at a regular commercial price, supplies to both. So that in a strict neutrality in war, and in a careful trade with the contestants, the advantages to them were nearly as great as those of peace. The great cities were back upon the spine of hills which runs up and down the land. And the Egyptian armies seeking their Assyrian foe, or the Assyrian hosts seeking their hereditary enemy of Egypt, always attempted to pass at the foot of these hills and between them and the sea. There were two plains along the sea-shore, varying from one to twenty-five miles in width and thrice that length from north to south. Both of them led into a vast valley-plain of twenty by thirty miles running directly across the country from east to west, the great plain of Esdraelon, the battle-field of the world. On this field armies of every ancient and of nearly every modern nation have met in deadly conflict. It has been trod by Babylonian armies under Nebuchadnezzar, by Assyrian armies under Sennacherib, by Jewish armies under Gideon and Saul, by Egyptian hosts under Necho, by Moslem hordes under Saladin, by crusaders from Spain and Portugal, from Germany and Italy, by English troops under Smith, and, less than a hundred years ago, by Frenchmen carrying the imperial eagles under the personal leadership of Napoleon I. of France. The world's history has been written in blood on this plain of Esdraelon, in Palestine. Those great conquerors whose disastrous fame has filled up with sickening fullness the records of human history, have all seen that Palestine was geographically the pivot of empire, and that the Esdraelon plain was the great field the winning or the losing of which carried with it all they hoped or all they feared. To this plain they have come either in person or by their armies. Here came the Persian Cyrus, the man whose rise to power is the most wonderful exploit in history; that Nebuchadnezzar who when he died left behind him "more buildings reared by his hands than any man who ever stood on this planet;"

that Macedonian conqueror who wept for other worlds to subdue ; that Roman Cæsar who by his vast hordes overrun Palestine, giving imperial names to her cities and to her beautiful inland sea ; that Richard of England whose fame is world-wide ; that Godfrey, at once the pride of Europe and the boast of his own France ; that great emperor Frederick Barbarossa, whose ashes are buried in the ruins of the old Christian temple at Tyre, near by this plain where he fought so nobly ;—these are some of the men who have seen in Palestine the very central spot of geographical position, the possession of which in their day was essential to their plans of empire.

And when any young man hears a sneer thrown at Palestine as if it were never of any importance, as if it had always been an out-of-the-way land, and had no right to such an eminence in the Bible, let him recall the fact that it has been coveted more than the gold of Ophir and the mines of Golconda by the great conquerors, statesmen, rulers of the world. And instead of heeding the sneer, let him pity the man whose knowledge of the history of the human race leads him to undervalue the importance of the land which geographically was the most important land of any on earth to the older nations. Let him recall also the fact that when the older nations faded out and their lands were occupied by newer peoples, there was still the same ambition to possess Palestine. Assyria and Egypt, broken and retired from the stage, there arose west of Palestine, two empires, one that of Greece, the other that of Rome. Both coveted the east, the far east. Between them and that far east stood Palestine. It was necessary to their project of universal empire to gain a foothold in Palestine and make it their base of operations. They came, a vast host, marching across Asia Minor, and whitening the Mediterranean with their vast fleets of transports. They effected a landing in Palestine. But when they attempted to advance inward, they were met by the hosts of the far east who swarmed in upon the plain of Esdraelon from over the Jordan and gave them battle. In a hundred fights the Greek and the Roman had a sort of success. They occupied, partially, and for a very brief time, the country, holding it in military duress. But in the end both were routed, and retired discomfited from the land. They had dashed against this rock and their dreams of universal empire were rudely broken. And then, too, when other centuries had come and gone, and the Holy Land was the possession of the Moslem of the east, there went forth a cry through the west of lamentation because the crescent instead of the cross held Jerusalem. The cry of lamentation became one of angry warfare, and the crusades were organized. It was the whole west warring against the whole east. It was a continent rising against a continent for the possession of a strip of land not larger than the State of New Hampshire, but which had been for long centuries not only the best known but also the most coveted land on earth. The last blow ever struck by the crusaders was vainly given on a little eminence of the Esdraelon plain, a few hundred feet only from the spot where Jesus uttered the "Sermon on the Mount." And from that hour the victory of the east has been secured, and the Moslem has held Palestine in his merciless grasp. And as with religious wars so with those prompted purely by ambition. Napoleon in the fullness of his lust for power craved the mastery of the east. He saw the worth of Palestine as the only possible base for further conquests. And he must try his hand at the task only to find his dream of eastern empire melt away on these shores where others before him had met a similar fate.

And thus God's choice of Palestine as a home for his people, as a place second to none in all the old world in its geographical importance, has been endorsed by the world's statesmen and warriors. It was no secluded spot. It fronted the continents. It took the eye of the world. All done there was done for the gaze of the race. And God's wisdom selected not only the people so keenly receptive of moral ideas, but the land for them to inhabit, that his purpose might be accomplished of giving to the race through them, as they dwelt in this central position, a revelation of his will.

The *historic* position of the Hebrew race in their home at Palestine is worthy of study as showing another feature of God's plan. There were centuries before them. There have been centuries after them. But had they appeared sooner or later in the calendar of historic time, they would have utterly failed in their mission. Back of them were the two great historic peoples of Babylonia and Egypt, but both were waning when the Hebrews appeared. After them the Romans were the world's masters. Parallel with them was the Assyrian empire in the days of its strength. A few centuries earlier the documents of Moses would have been impossible. A few centuries later the necessary tuition of the Hebrews in the arts of Egypt, could not have been had. Their geographical position was not more striking as they fronted the continents than was their historical position as they stood conspicuous in the world's thought. They took from the wisdom of Egypt all that was valuable, just as Plato took his philosophy from the old city of On near the banks of the Nile. But Plato and the Greeks developed what they took in one way, and Moses and the Hebrew hosts in another. From Egypt came ideas of agriculture and the arts of embroidery and of letters for writing; the knowledge of the astronomy by which the Hebrews fixed their numerous festivals, and the history by which Egypt became the second as Palestine the first of the Sacred Lands. And they left behind them in Egypt a moral impression, which was, in part at least, a revival of the more ancient Egyptian faith in the eternity of God and the immortality of man. From Pharaoh's reluctant lips they forced a confession of partial faith in Jehovah as God. When settled in Palestine their distinct belief was known to all the nations, and obtained respectful recognition. Hiram, king of Tyre, a hundred miles from Jerusalem, sent workmen to Solomon to assist in building the Temple on Moriah Cyrus gave a decree which shows that Hebrew ideas had penetrated the Persian mind, and that the enslaved race were masters in the realm of ideas of their captors. And so, in war and in peace, in victory and in captivity, now by voluntary and now again by involuntary teaching, the Hebrew ideas were slowly but surely working their way among the nations, and thus carrying forward the divine plan. And as God was ordering their historic position, so he was arranging the nations to receive the influence they were to exert. Parallel with them, during an important part of their history, was the Medo-Persian power under which flourished those sects nearest in religious belief to the Hebrews of any known to history. One of them, the world-famed "Magi," sent its deputation to Palestine at the birth of Christ. And when Jewish history culminated in the advent of Jesus, God had ready the one great empire of Rome, then the mistress of the world. Thus it was that the unity of peoples in one sovereignty made them, willing or unwilling, God's messengers to spread speedily the story of the cross over the inhabited earth.

And here, too, we find the reason for those peculiar *incidents* which appear in the Scriptures. These incidents are intended to be *object-lessons*. Mere words would be forgotten. But facts with a moral meaning in them would be remembered. We cannot imagine any better way, or, indeed, any other way, in which God could teach the primitive tribes and nations. A fact, a striking occurrence, a phenomenon singularly unlike any other, which these olden nations would at once connect with the finger of God, was surely the most impressive, most natural form of moral teaching and the one most to be expected. If Hebrew history were without its examples of striking incidents used as divine object-lessons, we should have wondered at it. Their absence would try our faith more than their presence. To a people apt in receiving this kind of teaching, God gave these object-lessons;—and the fact that they were accepted so readily, confirms our faith in the wisdom that selected the method.

Take the story of the first man's first sin. The whole series of circumstances, seem to be contrived for their moral impression. No need, so far as man's actual fall was concerned, of the events which took place in the garden, of the serpent's agency, of the sword at the gate. But the occurrences were to be for the world's teaching. The garden not only does symbolize, but was intended, as we know by Christ's use of the word Paradise, to symbolize the state of happy holiness, the fullness of which is heaven. And sin was to be made loathsome and foul; and temptation to be seen as stealthy and mean, a crouching serpent with slimy tongue and insinuating motion and beautiful form, to charm and then destroy men. And the historic fact of Satan's temptation through words that seemed not his own but the serpent's words, is not only named by our Lord long centuries afterward, but the moral teaching of it is enforced by him when he says, "Ye are of your father the Devil. He was a *liar* from the beginning." The whole series of facts was to be rehearsed in the earliest centuries by the patriarchs and thus handed down through the generations, until written language came to the rescue of an oral tradition, and Moses must put the story on the imperishable pages of Revelation.

And the flood is in the same line of object-teaching. It taught the world of the sin of attempting to do without God. And no less was the deliverance given to Noah a designed instance of palpable teaching. For it has so stamped our whole mode of thought that, in the religious language of the world, *the ark* is the symbol of salvation. So, too, we can understand the overthrow of Sodom only when we see it as God's teaching of retribution. In the pathway of the great caravans, on the world's broadest highway, situated where its destruction would be as conspicuous as its wickedness had been notorious, sure to be the theme of remark as an example of divine wrath in its singular overthrow, in its doom first by fire and next by burial in the sea the mists of which are a perpetual reminder of the "smoke of her torment," that old city, living in story though long dead in fact, has stood out on the sacred page as a solemn warning, the lurid light of which has caught the eye and alarmed the wickedness of all generations of men. And, in after ages the deserved destruction of the wicked Canaanites who were usurpers in Palestine, who had abundant opportunity to repent and to leave the land, but who made the approach of the Israelites a pretext for a war in direct defence of idolatry—this destruction, so often condemned, is to be seen in the same light. It is no isolated event to be judged by ordinary rules. The nations that then existed and that were to be born needed to understand that denying God and attempting to thwart his will was sure to bring ruin. And so, all through the prophets, we hear those iron tongued men ring out the threat that as God destroyed the nations in Canaan so he would destroy the Jews, if they walked not in his ways.[1]

But probably, the incident in the Bible which the young man will hear most earnestly denounced is that

[1] As to Psalms which contain prayers for the destruction of David's enemies, it must be remembered that he was not a private man wishing for private vengeance, but a king, and as such the rightful head of authority and the executive whose duty it was to punish evil doers. And, above all, he was, before the surrounding nations, the representative of the Jehovah worship. Hence the enmity of idolatrous princes was directed not only against his throne, but against his God and his religion. See the fifty-eighth Psalm, where we have in the eleventh verse an explanation of the malediction in the tenth verse.

concerning the proposed sacrifice of Isaac by Abraham. Though the act was not done, and was not intended to be done, yet there stands the command. The objector urges that such a command, though God intended at the last moment to stay the fatal knife, must have been an outrage on the moral sense of Abraham and of the whole world ; that it seems a blur upon the moral character of God himself for him to order the death of a child at a father's hands. It is true that the popular answer vindicates God from blame. It is true that we are to look at the "whole transaction, the command and the counter-command ; and that Abraham afterwards saw the scope and compass of it which cleared up every difficulty."[1] But is it enough that we simply clear God and his servant Abraham from blame ? This would leave the matter in its negative aspect. It would perhaps excuse, but would it justify the transaction ? Nor does it tell us the deep reason for this command, so unusual ; nor does it give us any hint as to why the story is so prominently recorded in God's Word. There must have been some great reason, lying back of all this, for allowing such a transaction as the attempted offering of a son in human sacrifice by the hand of a father who was the most righteous of all the men in his day.

Now what if we have here *God's object-lesson in redemption*—the "preaching of the Gospel." What if the full justification of the transaction, not only to the

[1] "Moral Difficulties of the Bible."—*Hessey*.

Patriarch's moral sense but to that of the whole world, is to be found in that which it was intended to teach men of God's love in its method of saving them, by the sacrifice of the only-begotten Son. Put it thus : There had come to Adam, in the garden, the primal promise, hard after the primal sin. It was no general declaration of a redemption, but the special promise of a Redeemer. This promised Redeemer was the one object of all the ancient faith. The belief in his coming was the one article in the creed of the "youthful world's grey fathers." Further on in history, the mass of the race had lost out the belief in the promise, and so were doing "only evil." God sent Noah, who, in the very form of deliverance granted his household, preached the Gospel in a figure—the ark being not only a type of salvation, but of its method by special Divine interference for those who believe and obey. Years go by. The faith in the promise is again almost lost. There is needed once more—this time for all the centuries—a *great palpable object-lesson* that shall stand up and out and take the eye of the world. But who should give this lesson if not this man Abraham, "the father of the faithful?" He was to set the world a lesson of human faith in obeying a divine command. Why not also a lesson as to the Divine Fatherhood, as it was to show itself in making sacrifice for human redemption ? Can any other way be imagined so awful, so tender, so impressive as that of a father giving up his only son !

Now, what if God, the atoning idea ever present in his thought and ever craving expression, took this man Abraham as it were at his word. What if he appoints to him such a lofty proclamation of this fact as was allotted to no other "preacher of righteousness." Abraham shall, in a sense, represent God. He shall show what God's love is like. He shall help prepare the world for the Calvary scene. Through this father's devotion of his son to death and through his receiving of Isaac "from the dead, from whence he received him in a figure," there was set forth, as nearly as could be done by any human transaction, the great fact of God's gift of the Divine Son to die and to rise from the grave for human redemption. And so this whole scene is to be judged not at all by our ordinary rules of moral judgment as to right and wrong. And if we fail to see how as a merely human transaction we can quite justify it, we are happily delivered from all difficulty when we see in it a divinely-ordained setting forth of the great redemptive fact. That it has been looked upon generally through the Christian centuries as our greatest illustration of that fact, is no small evidence that it was *intended* so to be regarded by God. And thus it was a prophetic scene ; a great objective *representation* to those who lived before the Messiah's day. Only thus can we understand this transaction, or justify it, or admire it. The Messianic idea is the key to many an event in the Old Testament. And nowhere do we more need it, and nowhere, when seen, is it more instructive than in this great object-lesson of redemption which is here furnished to the world.

And a young man's difficulties are removed and his faith is established by noticing what may be called the *timing* of the miracles and "wonderful works" of the Scriptures. This thing grows on one who studies the volume. The miracles are no longer a confused jumble of strange events. Each takes its place; its *own* place; and it is seen that it could not have come in at any other time. No two of these miracles can change places. The flood does its work at its own epoch. Abraham's attempted sacrifice is the event for that hour, and for no other. No Old Testament miracle could have occurred in New Testament times. Those that appear somewhat alike are so only in appearance. The New Testament miracles are exactly ordered as to the point where they occurred. They are progressive. The "raising of Lazarus," could not change places with the "turning of the water into wine," except by an entire destruction not only of the Gospel story but also of the harmony of Christ's own character. He could not, being the Christ he is, have inverted this order, if he would be understood by men. Embosomed in a family known only in the social circles of a Galilean province, it was exactly fit that his first miracle should be the *consecration of domestic life*. But the grand resurrection miracle was best done near Jerusalem, just when all teaching and all miracle were culminating at the close of his ministry.

And this element of time is to be noticed in an event mid-way between the two just named—the transfiguration. It grew out of a want that did not exist either at the outset or at the close of Christ's earthly life. It was needed alike by the state of mind in which the immediate disciples found themselves, and of the scheme of his own life as shown by what preceded and followed the event. He had just told them of his coming death. It surprised them more than all his miracles. Eight long weary days they pondered the strange fact so unlikely if he were really "the Christ." He told them that they might also have to lay down their own lives. They think of him as failing, of his mission as ending in defeat and of their own utter loss as those embarked in a ruined cause. Never was their faith so low. In this condition they fail utterly to do the mighty works they had performed so easily a month before. He takes a part of them up Tabor; or, it may be, a spur of Hermon. They are weak in faith in him as "the one sent of God." But in the Tabor manifestation they see at once *who Christ is!* The heavenly glory is about him. They can doubt no more. The conversation of the denizens of the other world is about that death which these disciples thought so shameful, but which now is so glorious. Their faith needed a palpable object-lesson. Tabor gives it. They accept his death, perhaps also their own, as an event connected with the eternal glory. And how much the transfiguration meant to the world at large as the completion of its idea of Christ! He had shown his power over nature, in stilling the tempest, in feeding the hungry thousands; over man's body by healing his diseases, by giving sight to the blind and tongues to the dumb; over man's soul by forgiving sins; over the lower world of evil spirits by casting out demons from those who had been allowed to receive that peculiar visitation. But there remained one other department in which there was need that he should show his sovereignty. Had he power over the world of holy souls? Was heaven also allegiant to him? Would it acknowledge him? Would those who do God's will in the highest places of the universe, the most select spirits, come at *his* bidding as demons had gone at his command? See! The heavens open. Moses the greatest of lawgivers, and Elias the greatest of prophets, who for centuries had been serving in heaven, *came at his word!* When works are done that show power over nature the world thinks, though incorrectly, of physical might. When works are done that show power over the world of evil souls, men can say that Satan has them in allegiance. But none save God himself can command the allegiance of the holy, and have them obey. More striking was the Bethany miracle. More impressive to the general sense of the world was the resurrection of our Lord himself. But no event of all his eventful life so exhibits his power, his majesty, his glory, as does this obedience of the souls so long disembodied, so long serving in the interior service of heaven; the souls standing nearest the Great White Throne.

And it will help a young man's faith if he will see the *setting* of these miracles and these wonders in their moral teaching. In the miracles of Jesus this is very evident. The feeding of the five thousand grew out of three things which occurred together at that very point. There was, first, the multitude physically hungry. Ordinarily they could have gone to the city and bought bread. So too, they were hungry for truth. One of those movements, inexplicable except by the theory that God's spirit sometimes moves peculiarly on men's souls, was in progress. Truth had impressed, but not yet done its whole work in conversion. Should the process be stopped in the soul for want of a few loaves? So, too, there was a lingering doubt about him in their minds. He meets at once the physical, the intellectual and the moral want of these men.

And, more, he is shown to the world, when the event goes upon the Gospel page, as the master of nature, able to perfect in an instant its processes; and at the same time, while so great, he is also shown as caring for man's "daily bread." And yet the fitness of miracle to teaching, and of them both to the idea of Christ which the world was to receive is not more striking in this than in the case of every miracle of the Bible.

And the miracles, especially of Jesus, are not merely accompanied with teaching, but they have *a meaning in themselves.* They are not separate wonders but orderly facts in the development of Christ's doctrine. Hence their prominence. They stand right out. They strike the eye. They are not only signs and evidences of Christ's authority, but divine object-lessons, to which our Lord appeals. He told men that, if they were doubtful about his words, there were his works. If they did not understand the one they could the other. He did not look upon his miracles as merely physical facts. They had moral relations. And so too the Apostles regarded them. The resurrection of their Master was the great miracle—so great that, if true, there could be no objection to the other and lesser miracles which they proclaimed every where. It is to them no pretty fable, no beautiful myth. In their way of telling it, it was *a fact with a moral meaning.* It carried with itself the whole moral system of Christian facts and doctrines. And when the lesson of each miracle is seen it is no excrescence to the growth of the fair tree of revelation. Its teaching is the most miraculous thing about any miracle. No miracle was simply a "sign" in the physical world. It was chiefly a "wonder" in the moral realm. The miracles carried with them an eloquence most convincing. Their light went out through all the earth and their words to the end of the world. There is no speech nor language where their voice is not heard. They are stars in the moral heavens that declare the glory of God and show his handy-work.

The miracles have not only moral ends, but they are themselves teachings. There is the marrow of some Gospel doctrine in every miracle of Jesus. A miracle is a doctrine incarnate. And the old-time miracles, in the destruction of Sodom, in the crossing of the Red Sea, in the healing by a look at the lifted serpent, in the descending manna, in the divided Jordan, in the thrown-down walls of Jericho,—what are these but God's great object-teachings, even if no word be uttered in explanation?

And only as one sees the grand setting of these miracles, their place, time, order, purpose, in God's great unfolding of his redemptive plan, do these things that, all alone, to the merely philosophic or scientific eye, appear like blemishes, become beauties; these hindrances helps; these difficulties of faith its best arguments and supports. The key-stone of the arch standing alone would be an impossibility. But then it does not stand alone. It is to be seen in its place with other stones. And in the temple of God's revealed will these miracles are no hindrance to the use, and no excrescence upon the beauty of the structure, when one shall rightly come to see and to hear and to worship with reverent heart. They have their place. There would be here a weakened arch and there an unfilled niche without them. Not one can be spared. There is no blemish as of a single useless thing. Nothing can be added, without harm, nothing taken away without loss. Each thing was in the plan of the structure as drawn by the architect. And the architect and the builder were one. So that each thing adds in its own way to the strength or to the beauty of the edifice which God has reared. It is a structure the foundation of which is his truth, and its top-stone his praise.

www.ingramcontent.com/pod-product-compliance
Lightning Source LLC
Chambersburg PA
CBHW020839160426
43192CB00007B/718

Léon Gautier

Regina Sæculorum, or Mary venerated in all ages

devotions to the Blessed Virigin, from ancient sources

Léon Gautier

Regina Sæculorum, or Mary venerated in all ages
devotions to the Blessed Virigin, from ancient sources

ISBN/EAN: 9783742860262

Manufactured in Europe, USA, Canada, Australia, Japa

Cover: Foto ©Lupo / pixelio.de

Manufactured and distributed by brebook publishing software (www.brebook.com)

Léon Gautier

Regina Sæculorum, or Mary venerated in all ages

REGINA SÆCULORUM

OR

MARY VENERATED IN ALL AGES.

Devotions to the Blessed Virgin,

FROM ANCIENT SOURCES.

Partly Translated from the French of
M. LÉON GAUTIER,

BY

E. A. M.

London:
R. WASHBOURNE, 18 PATERNOSTER ROW.
1875.

DEDICATION.

TO thee, O Glorious and Immaculate Virgin, do we offer this little nosegay culled from the wide garden of the Church; beseeching thee to grant that its fragrance may not only strengthen and refresh thine own children, but also that the sweetness of thy name, O Mother of our God and Saviour JESUS, Mother of our own Crucified and Glorified Redeemer, JESUS, may draw into the Fold of His Church, those yet without, for whose salvation thou didst bear JESUS, and JESUS died. To these, O thou who art as tender in thy loving compassion, as thou art spotless in thy perfect purity, and all-powerful in thy intercession,

Monstra te esse Matrem:
AND WIN THEM HOME.

AVE MARIA.

PREFACE.

ALTHOUGH various Books of Devotions to Our Blessed Lady have, within the last few years, appeared in England, yet none among them occupy the same ground as that taken by the present collection; for the greater part of which we are indebted to the valuable and interesting Book of M. Léon Gautier, entitled *Prières à la Vièrge, d'après les MSS. du Moyen Age*, &c. &c.,[1] its principal aim being to show from the most ancient, as well as from subsequent authoritative sources, how the devotion to Mary has ever been an integral part of the tradition of the Church. That it should not have been so, would be equally impossible to faith and to reason. The marvel is that it should ever have become necessary to argue in favour of

[1] Paris. Victor Palmé.

showing reverence to the Mother, with those who profess to honour the SON.

Our Lady's great panegyrist is the Archangel Gabriel,[1] who might be called the Prophet and Evangelist of the Incarnation. We read of him in the Book of Daniel, when he foretold it; in the Gospel of S. Luke, when he announced its precursor; and again as the favoured angel of the Annunciation. And who is he? He says of himself to the father of the Baptist, "*I am Gabriel, who stand before God;*" that is, in the immediate presence and glory of the very Source and Fountain of Grace. And when, fresh from the light of the uncreated Godhead, he speeds into the pure presence of Mary, the heavenly Ambassador salutes her with the words, "*Hail, FULL of Grace!*" using a word which, in the original Greek, we are told by Origen, occurs nowhere else in Scripture, and which implies that she was not only free from sin at that time,

---

[1] V. *Lectures on Catholic Faith and Practice*, by the Rev. J. N. Sweeney, p. 278, Lect. xv., *Mary, Mother of God.*

but that she had been formed in Grace, and "had not been infected by the breath of the venomous Serpent." Hers was no ordinary office, and no ordinary splendour surrounded her. At her coming into the world, Grace awaited her who was chosen to be the Mother of God.

The devotion to Our Lady naturally had its first development in the East. In the West, the early Christians traced her image in the gloom of the catacombs. The Cemetery of Priscilla might indeed be called the Catacomb of Mary, from the frequency and importance of the representations of her which it contains. In the Catacomb of SS. Peter and Marcellinus, Mary appears as the heavenly advocate, whose arms, outstretched in prayer, are upheld by two mysterious personages, as were those of Moses by Aaron and Hur on Mount Horeb. It is thus a great mistake to assert that no representations of Mary existed anterior to the Council of Ephesus. Even as early as the second century there was a particular type according to which the Virgin Mother was to be depicted, and which was generally adopted by the faithful.

In the ancient Liturgies, which, both in their substance and in the perfect similarity as to the order of their various portions, bear internal evidence of being all derived from the original ritual fixed upon by the Apostles themselves, our Lady is invariably honoured, and her intercession invoked. It may not be out of place to mention here also, that we find it to have been customary in the fourth century for the Bishop, in going to and from the Church, &c., to be preceded by a Deacon, who from time to time cried aloud to the people, "Be mindful of the Most Holy and Immaculate Mother of God."

Scarcely had the Church reached the period of tranquillity purchased by three centuries of persecution and by twelve or fifteen millions of martyrs, than, in the fourth century, arose the great constellation of Doctors whose teaching completed the evangelization of the Empire. To the voices of S. Ambrose, S. Augustin, and S. Jerome, were united those of S. Chrysostom,

S. Ephrem, and S. Epiphanius; and each of these great saints joined, as it were, in a hymn of praise to Mary, of which the prelude had already been sung by S. Clement, Tertullian, S. Cyprian, and many more. Already had the title of Theotokos been repeatedly applied to Mary by S. Denys of Alexandria, by Origen, and by S. Athanasius, before the Council of Ephesus, in the fifth century, to the enthusiastic joy of the whole multitude of the faithful, decreed it to be acknowledged as rightfully her own, in honour of her Divine Maternity; and before S. Cyril, at the first session of this Council, addressed the glowing words of love and veneration, which still remain, to her whom he declared to be "above all praises."

Mary's title to veneration being thus indisputably proved to have been acknowledged by the first five centuries of the Church's existence, it is needless to do more than touch upon the unceasing devotion to her through the successive ages which have followed; and we need only name S. Benedict, our own S. Anselm, S. Ildefonso of Toledo (the works of either of these great Archbishops furnishing whole litanies of titles of honour and praise of Our Lady), S. Bernard and the other doctors of the twelfth century, S. Dominic, and S. Thomas Aquinas; leaving many great and saintly names unmentioned.

In conclusion, we would observe, with regard to a doctrine of the Church which has lately come into prominence, that it was so early as during the fifth century that the Feast of the Conception came to be observed, and spread widely during the seventh and eighth centuries. Hymns written in honour of the Mystery had appeared in the fourth century. The celebration of the Festival began in England in the eleventh, under the auspices of S. Anselm. From Spain, where it was observed at an earlier date, it advanced into France, and so onward to the rest of the Churches. After this time the doctrine began to excite the warmest controversy within the Church. Great Doctors rose up to be its champions, but a whole Order (not, however, without many exceptions), deceived by a legitimate reverence for the supposed authority of its own Angelic Doctor, set itself against it. Scotus, the great Franciscan, rose in its defence, and with him were the Universities of Europe. It was opposed: it grew. Time went on, and soon it was received under the special protection of the Popes. All that opposed it crumbled away before its native vitality and Divine Power, and its former adversaries were to be now seen among its most strenuous defenders. At length there was a time of peace. No new heresy disturbed the silence of the Sanctuary; and the voice of Peter is heard once more in His own Basilica. The contest is over, the development is complete. Mary has triumphed, and the Immaculate Conception is an article of faith.

"TOTA PULCHRA ES, MARIA ;
ET MACULA ORIGINALIS NON EST IN TE."

TABLE OF CONTENTS.

PART I.

DAILY AND OCCASIONAL PRAYERS.

		PAGE
Prayers for Morning	... ...	2
,,	Mass	17
,,	before and after Confession	87
,,	before and after Communion ...	48
,,	during the Day	45
,,	Evening	47
Occasional Prayers		49

PART II.

PRAYERS ETC. TAKEN FROM THE PRIMITIVE LITURGIES.

The Apostolic Ages: and the Catacombs	75
The Liturgy of S. Peter	77
The Roman Liturgy	78

	PAGE
The Ambrosian Liturgy	83
Liturgy of Pope S. Xystus	84
The Græco-Sclavonian Liturgy	85
Greek Liturgy	88
Armenian	89
The Mozarabic Liturgy	91
Liturgy of S. James	94
,, of S. Basil of Alexandria	94
,, of Antioch	95
,, of Constantinople	96
,, of Ethiopia	97
Coptic Liturgy	98

The Early and Mediæval Fathers of the Church.

First Century—Letter of the Clergy of Achaia, etc. ... 99

Second Century—S. Justin Martyr; S. Irenæus; Tertullian ... 100

Third Century— S. Dionysius of Alexandria; S. Hippolytus; S. Gregory Thaumaturgus 103

Fourth Century—S. Ephrem Syrus; S. Basil of Seleucia; S. Epiphanius ... 106

Fifth Century — S. Cyril of Alexandria; S. Ambrose; S. Augustin ... 112

CONTENTS.

	PAGE
Sixth Century—S. Anastasius the Sinaïte	113
Seventh Century—S. Ildefonsus	114
Seventh and Eighth Centuries—S. Andrew of Crete	114

SAINTS OF THE MIDDLE AGES.

Eleventh Century—S. Peter Damian; S. Anselm Archbishop of Canterbury	116
Twelfth Century—S. Bernard; S. Bonaventure	118

EARLY ENGLISH HYMNS TO THE BLESSED VIRGIN.

I. The Five Joys of the Virgin	125
II. An Orison of Our Lady	127
III. A Song to the Virgin	129
IV. A Prayer to the Virgin	131

PART I.

DAILY AND OCCASIONAL PRAYERS.

NE SCRIBAM VANUM, DUC, PIA VIRGO, MANUM.
(Motto of certain Mediæval Scribes.)

소

PART I.

DAILY AND OCCASIONAL PRAYERS.

When the Day begins to appear.

LORD JESUS, Who art the true Sun of the world, Sun, ever rising and never setting; Thou, Who with Thy life-giving beams dost produce, nourish, and gladden all things in heaven and earth; O let Thy light arise upon me who now lift up my prayer to Thee, and grant that this brightness may drive far away from me the clouds of error and the night of sin. May I take this fair light for my inward guide, and accomplish all the journey of my life without offending Thee; may I walk therein unceasingly, as in the full light of day, pure and radiant, free from all the works of darkness. Amen.[1]

Hail! glorious Mother of God; hail, Queen of Heaven; hail, my Patroness. To thy tender and maternal love I commend myself through all this day which is now beginning, in order that all my actions may have for their end these three things, namely, the glory of thy Son, my own salvation, and my neighbour's good. In every tribulation, every sorrow, come to my aid, and to the aid of my friends. Come, O kindest Virgin Mary.[2]

At Daylight.

May Thy will, O God, be done IN US,

---

[1] *Thesaurus Precum*, Paris, 1578. The original appears to be: *Erasmi Preces*, Lugduni, apud Antonium, 1556. Ct. *Precationes*, Lipsiæ, 1575, etc.

[2] *Piarum precationum Thesaurus*. Parisiis, apud Petrum Rocollet, 1652.

THROUGH US, and BY US, this day and always here and everywhere. Amen.[1]

O God, Who by the light of Thy Word dost dispel the shades of ignorance, increase in our hearts the faith which Thou hast bestowed upon us; and grant that this fair flame, kindled by Thy grace in the depth of our souls, may never be extinguished. Amen.[2]

Let us all pray God to give us a place in His Paradise, where the dawn and the bright day have no end. "*Tug preguem Dieu que nos don von estal en Paradis on es clars jorns e l'alba.*"[3]

On Rising.

Blessed be the sweet Name of our Lord Jesus Christ: blessed also be the name of

[1] *Enchiridion, sui manuale quotidianorum exercitiorum spiritualium*, auctore R. P. Michæle Constantiensi, Lugduni. 1599.
[2] *Thesaurus Precum*, Paris, 1587.
[3] Bernard de Venzenac, troubadour of the 13th century.—Raynouard, *Choix des Poësies originales des Troubadours*, iv. 432.

the most sweet Virgin Mary, His Mother; blessed be He through eternity and beyond it![1]

In the Name of Christ my Lord I arise; I arise in the Name of Jesus crucified, Who has bought us all with His most precious Blood.

May He, even the God of Light, descend upon me, to guide, guard, bless, and keep me in all good works, this day and all the days of my life.

And after this miserable life may He bring me to the life eternal. Amen.[2]

Before Morning Prayers.

Virgin Mary, Mother of sweet Jesus Christ, into thy hands, and into the hands of thy dear and blessed Son, I recommend this day my body, soul, and senses. Guard me, Lord God, from all vices, from all sins, from the temptations of the devil, and the pains of hell.

[1] *Bibl. de l'Arsenal*, T. L. 624a, xv. century, &c.
[2] *Precationes*, Lipsiæ, 1575.

Enlighten my heart by Thy grace and Thy Holy Spirit. Make me ever obedient to Thy commandments, that I may live eternally in Thy presence, never to be separated from Thee. Amen.[1]

To Saint Anne.

Saint Anne, Mother of our Lady, and Grandmother of Jesus Christ, shew me the holy Paradise. "*Santo Anno, mero de Nouestro Damo, et mero grand de Jesus Christ, Enseignetz me tou sant Paradis.*"[2]

MORNING PRAYERS.

To God.

O most majestic Power of God the Father, Who hast created me in Thine own image and likeness. O sovereign Wisdom of God the Son, Who hast redeemed me by Thy precious Blood. O supreme Goodness of the Holy

[1] *Bibl. Nat.* 927, xv. century.
[2] *Chants Populaires de la Provence.* Published by Damase Arbaud, p. 13.

Ghost, who hast always impelled and inspired me for my salvation. I adore Thee with all my heart, with all my strength, and with all my mind; and I thank Thee for all the great favours that it is Thy pleasure to grant to me, and to all Thy creatures. My God, I desire for the love of Thee, to serve and praise Thee, to please Thee better and to love Thee more, and to this end I offer my soul to praise Thee, my heart to love Thee, my body to serve Thee, and my will to obey Thee. O my God, I humbly commend myself to Thee. I implore Thee, Thyself to direct me in the way of salvation. Hold Thou my hand in Thine through all my life, and especially in this coming day, guide me in all the actions I should perform, all the words I should speak, and all the thoughts which should fill my heart. Place the curb of Thy love and fear upon my tongue and all my senses, so that they may not do anything which is not to Thy greater glory, to my own salvation, the well-being of my kindred, and my neighbour's good. My

God, I protest that I would rather die than offend Thee by mortal sin. I protest also that I desire to live and die in Thy holy faith, and in the keeping of Thy commandments. Deign to give me grace so to do. I offer unto Thee, O Lord, all that I shall do and suffer this day in thought, word, and deed, in body or soul. O my God, behold my sole purpose and desire is this, that everything within me may be to Thy honour and love, and to the honour and love of Thy most holy Mother, the Blessed Virgin Mary, and of all the saints commemorated by the Church, to whom, even the whole court of heaven, I commend myself now and evermore. Amen.[1]

AVE MARIA.

All Hail, Rose without thorns, hail, Virgin, whose majesty the Divine Father hath placed

---

[1] Bibliothèque Sainte Geneviève, BB. 66. Commencement of the sixteenth century. *Instruction et manière de vivre pour une femme seculière.*

so high in the heavens, and whom He hath chosen to preserve immaculate.

Maria. Hail, "Star of the sea," who by thy Son hast been clothed with the very brightness of the Divinity, and whose glory is more resplendent than that of all the saints.

Gratia plena. The Holy Ghost has filled thee with all graces, having made thee the perfect vessel, chosen to receive the divine Goodness and Love.

Dominus tecum. By an admirable covenant, God is with thee; the Word of the Father took flesh within thy womb, and each person of the ever Blessed Trinity shared in this great work.

Benedicta tu in mulieribus. That thou art blessed among women, art thou declared to be by all the nations of the earth. Thou art established on the heights of Paradise, and the heavens cease not to proclaim thee "Blessed."

Et benedictus fructus ventris tui, Jesus.

Grant, therefore, that we may enjoy the presence of thy Son here on earth, within our hearts, as a foretaste of heaven; and after our death, in the eternal and beatific vision. Amen.[1]

A Prayer for One's own Necessities.

O Lord most merciful, grant me above all things to desire ardently, to seek prudently, to find surely, and finally to accomplish most perfectly, all that is pleasing in Thy sight. Rule my whole being in accordance with Thine own glory: and grant, O my God, that Thy servant may desire, know, and perform all that Thou dost demand of him. Grant that I may never yield to weakness, either in joy or in sorrow, that I may not be puffed up by prosperity, nor cast down by adversity. That in all my joys, thanksgiving may be ever on my lips, and that in all my tribulations, patience may be ever in my heart. Let that which draws me nearer to Thyself, O my God,

[1] *Enchiridion*, Lyons. 1599.

be the only subject of my joy: that which removes me further from Thee, the chief occasion of my tears. Let me seek to please none apart from Thee, and let me fear to displease none but Thyself alone. May I do all things, suffer all things through love; and may all those things seem to be naught, which belong not to the worship I owe to Thee. Grant that none of the actions of my life be performed from habit alone, but that with true and deep piety I may refer them all to Thee, my God. For thy sake, O Lord, I desire to despise those things which pass away, and to love ardently only the things of God, and Thee, O God, above all. All labour for Thy glory shall be to me welcome rest, all rest that is not in Thee shall be to me wearisome toil. Suffer me, my sweetest Lord, frequently to lift up my soul to Thee in the fervour of meditation; assist me frequently to weigh the gravity of my faults, and with tears to make the firm resolution to commit no more. Help me to be humble without hypocrisy, cheerful without excess, serious without dejection, and gay without levity. Bestow upon me the spirit of fear without despondency, and of hope without presumption. May I correct my brethren without anger, and edify them without pride. Give to me, most sweet Jesus, a heart which never slumbers, and which no idle curiosity may draw away from Thee; a heart firm and stedfast as a rock, which no evil passion shall have power to disturb or overcome, a heart invincible, which no tribulation can conquer or weary; a heart free from the tyranny of any form of self-indulgence. Bestow upon me, O Lord, the intelligence which has knowledge of Thee, the activity which seeks Thee, and the wisdom which finds Thee, a life which is pleasing to Thee, a faith which already beholds Thee, which possesses Thee already on this earth. Give to me, O Lord, penitence, grace, and glory. By penitence I shall be crucified with Thee, by grace I shall know how to use Thy benefits during the journey of this life;

and by glory, when I shall have reached the heavenly country, I shall possess Thy joy for ever. Amen, amen.[1]

Prayer for all Men.

O most sweet and gentle Jesus, our Lord and our God, we implore Thy mercy, that by the merits and intercession of the Blessed Mary, ever Virgin, and of all the Saints, Angels and Archangels, Patriarchs and Prophets, Apostles and Martyrs, Confessors and Virgins, it may please Thee ever to increase the faith within the bosom of Thy Church. Make Thyself the guardian of those whose mission it is to govern us on earth. Give health to the sick, serene weather to those who are at sea, a prosperous journey to travellers, and grant them safe arrival at the harbour of eternal salvation. Give cheerfulness to the sad, strength to the feeble, liberty to the oppressed, deliverance to the captive; to strangers a

[1] Bibl. Nat. Anc. Coll. St. Victor, 617, fourteenth century. Bibl. Mazarine, T. 814, MS. of Philippe de Mezières, fourteenth century. The text, attributed to S. Thomas Aquinas, is found in a great number of other Collections.

happy return to their own land, charity to those who love not, the true faith to all who have it not, and to the faithful departed eternal rest. Amen.[1]

Pater, Ave, Credo, Confiteor.

To the Immaculate Virgin.

O Holy Mary, Mother of God, and ever Virgin, O Daughter of the great King, O most merciful Queen; Consolation of the desolate, Mother of orphans, Way of the wanderer, the Helper of all who hope in thee;

Source of grace and salvation, source of comfort and kindness, source of love and joy:

In the name of that joy with which thou didst exult when the Archangel Gabriel announced to thee the incarnation of the Son of God, when the conception of the Word made man was accomplished;

In the name of this divine mystery which the Holy Spirit wrought in thee, and in the name of these inestimable graces of love,

[1] *Bibl. Nat.*, Ancient Latin Collection, 1153, ninth century.

mercy, and charity, which this entrance of the Lord God into thy revered bosom merited for thee, when He thus clad Himself in the vestment of our nature;

In the name of all the virtues which flowed to thee from that gentle look of thy Son, when from the height of His cross He recommended thee to St. John; and also when He raised thee above all the choirs of angels;

In the name of the Five Wounds of Jesus; in the name of all His Passion, and of all thy grief; in the name of the torrent of thy tears;

I come this day, O Blessed Virgin Mary, to entreat thee, and with thee all the Saints and the elect of my God, to be near to me and afford me counsel and support in all my prayers and petitions, in all my necessities and sorrows, in all that I am called to do, to say, or to think, every day, every hour, every moment of my life.

Obtain for me of thy Son all the virtues of which I stand in need, obtain for me heavenly blessings and consolations, the help and benediction of God, sanctification, peace, prosperity, joy, salvation, and sufficiency of all that is needful for body and soul.

Obtain for me the grace of the Holy Ghost, that He may dispose of me in all things according to His Will, that He may direct my body, elevate my soul, guide my life, rule my conduct, inspire my actions, realise my hopes and desires, maintain within me holy thoughts, pardon my sins of the past, correct those of the present, and preserve me from them in the future :

This grace, which shall secure for me a truly upright and honourable life, and to which I shall owe the victory over all worldly adversities, with true Peace of body and soul, with Faith, Hope, Charity, Humility, Chastity, and Patience;

This grace, which shall be the protectress and mistress of my five senses, which shall cause me unceasingly to perform the Seven Works of Mercy; which shall establish my belief in the twelve Articles of the Faith, and help me to fulfil the Ten Commandments of the Law; and which, finally, shall preserve me from the seven deadly sins to the last day of my life.

And for that last day, and that last moment, I entreat thee, O Blessed Virgin Mary, to warn me beforehand of their approach, and then be thou there, quite close to me, that in gazing upon thy countenance I may pass out of this world.

Grant this prayer of thy suppliant, and obtain for me eternal life.

O sweetest Virgin Mary, turn not away from me, Mother of God; Mother of Mercy! Amen.[1]

[1] Bibl. Nat., Latin Collection, 1177, thirteenth century; 1196 and 1367, fourteenth century; 13,307, fifteenth century, &c. Bibl. Maz. T. 812, and T. 815, fifteenth century. Bibl. St. Geneviève, BB. L. 56, 59, 66, 73, 76, fifteenth century. Bibl. de l'Arsenal, "Heures," said to be of Henri II., T. L., 331, &c. *Heures à l'usage de Rouen*, faites par Simon Vostre, pour Philippe Pigouchet, 1502. *Horæ Beatæ Mariæ Virginis ad usum Cisterciensium*, Paris, 1503, &c. This prayer, called *Obsessio*, is that one which was more widely used than perhaps any other throughout the Middle Ages, and which is in the greatest number of MSS. It is found, together with the *Intemerata*, at the beginning of almost all the books of "Hours."

MASS.

During the celebration of Mass in past times, it was usual on the great festivals, to sing what was called a *trope*—a little hymn or versicle — before the Introit. One of these tropes is given us by Father Ballerini (*Sylloge Monumentarum*, part i. p. 23), who ascribes its composition to St. Ambrose. Anyhow, the latest date which has been assigned to it is the latter part of the eighth century.[1]

Trope.

Candidissima uti lilia!	Hail, O whitest of lilies!
Salve æterni Patris filia;	Daughter of the eternal Father,
Salve, Mater Redemptoris,	Hail, Mother of the Redeemer,
Salve, Sponsa Spiritoris,	Hail, Spouse of the Spirit,
Sine macula concepta.	Conceived without stain.
Salve, Triadis electa;	Elect of the Trinity;
Salve, inferni Victrix aspidis;	Hail, Conqueror of the infernal serpent,
Illius expers sola cuspidis.	Alone free from his sting,
Salve, Triadis electa.	Hail, Chosen One of the Trinity,
Sine macula concepta!	Conceived without stain!

[1] *V.* Fr. Harper. "*Peace through the Truth.*"

PRAYERS FOR MASS.

On entering the Church, say to yourself:

Depart hence, evil thoughts, wrong desires, passions of the heart, and carnal impulses. And thou, my soul, enter into the joy of thy Lord and thy God, that thou mayst see what is His Will, and worthily present thyself within His holy temple. Amen.[1]

Before Mass.

Lord Jesus, Thou who didst deign to take upon Thyself within the womb of the immaculate and most glorious Virgin Mary true flesh for the salvation of mankind; Lord Jesus, who for us wretched sinners didst, by Thy own Will, endure so many humiliations, so many insults, blows, defilements with spittle, the cross, the nails, the lance, the crown of thorns, the gall and vinegar, and, finally, the ignominious death of crucifixion,

[1] *Aureum thuribulum.* Bambergæ, apud Aug. Crinesium, 1625.

deign favourably to listen to the prayer of Thy servants, preserve them under all the sorrows of this life, and save them eternally. This we implore Thee in the name of the unbloody sacrifice of the Mass, which, through all ages, unceasingly renews the bloody Sacrifice of Calvary! Amen.[1]

O Mary, Mother of God, and our own Mother; O St. Michael and ye holy Angels; O all ye Saints celebrated by the Church this day; O my especial patrons and all the Saints;

In order that in your honour we may worthily offer the Sacrifice of the Divine Body and Blood; in order that we may worthily receive them within us;

Give us of your purity, your love, your sanctity, your piety; and do thou, O Virgin-Mother, unite thyself with us, in praise and prayer to the Lord God. Amen.[2]

When the Priest is at the Foot of the Altar.

Let us consider devoutly the manner in

[1] *Bibl. Nation.* Lat. 13,287; Fifteenth Century.
[2] Enchiridion, Lyons. 1599.

which the priest has vested himself before going to the Altar.

The priest is our champion against the enemy, and for this reason makes use of the same armour which our Lord employed when He conquered hell.

The *Amice* signifies the bandage with which the eyes of Jesus Christ were bound on the night of His Passion. The two *Cords of the Amice* signify the cords with which Jesus was bound while He was beaten with blows. The *Alb* signifies the white robe which was put upon Him at the command of Herod, to prove that the Son of Man was mad. The *Girdle* signifies the whips with which Jesus was scourged at the pillar unto blood. The *Maniple* signifies the bonds which manacled the hands of this Pattern of Obedience. The *Stole* signifies the yoke which the sweet Jesus bore, by His own Will, unto death.

Consider the ox, in the days of September, toiling at the plough to produce the wheat of which the chaff alone will be his portion.

Thus our Lord, in His Passion, has only its anguish, and we its fruits.

The silken *Chasuble* represents the purple robe with which Pilate covered the shoulders of Jesus, on whose sacred Head had already been placed the mocking crown, when Pilate said to the Jews, " Behold your King!" The *Cross* on the Chasuble signifies the Passion of Jesus, and all the sufferings by which it was preceded, and which ought to be indelibly graven on our hearts. The *Chasuble* has also another significance; as it covers all the other garments, so all our other virtues should be enfolded in charity. It is because of this grand symbolism of the vestments of the priest, that we should regard them with great reverence. We ask of Thee, O God, to inspire us with this devotion. Amen.[1]

At the Confiteor and the Kyrie.

By the merits, by the intercession and prayers of the Virgin Mary, of all the holy

[1] *Bibl. Nation.* Lat. 13289; Fifteenth Century.

Angels and Archangels, Patriarchs and Prophets, Apostles and Martyrs, Confessors and Virgins, pour forth into my heart, O most merciful God, the grace of Thy Holy Spirit, excite compunction within me, strike the rock of my soul, and call forth an abundant flow of tears. Grant me the grace to know perfectly all my faults, and devoutly to make a complete avowal of them, followed by true repentance, that I may obtain for them pardon through the loving mercy of my God! Amen.[1]

At the Gloria.

"The glory of God has descended upon the earth, peace has come down to men, and goodwill." Behold, O my God, the *Gloria in Excelsis* in its fullest meaning. It is truly the song of the living in the heavens, and never can we join therein without exciting in ourselves the desire of being one day transported thither, where it is for ever sung. Blessed

---
[1] *Bibl. Nation.* The same MS.

angels and messengers of our Lord, harbingers of heaven, who come before our King to prepare the place to which He shall descend, I beseech you, in the name of your love for our God, teach me to love Him. Offer to Him at this moment, by your invisible hands, the same prayer that you presented to Him during that night in which Jesus was born of our Lady. *Gloria in Excelsis Deo!* — and deliver me from all that might hurt me, or that might be an obstacle to my prayer. Amen.[1]

At the Collect.

Glorious Virgin Mary, thou who art the true mediatrix between thy sweet Son and poor repentant sinners, pray for me. And do you, all ye Saints whom the Church commemorates this day, come to my aid. Unite yourselves with the Queen of Angels, to beseech of God that He may grant this day all that His Church asks for me. Amen.[2]

[1] *Bibl. Nation.* The same MS.   [2] Ibid.

At the Epistle and Gospel.

O ye blessed Apostles, Evangelists, and Disciples of Jesus Christ, it was for love of Him that you renounced the world, and that you so generously delivered yourselves to the torments of martyrdom. I beseech you with all my heart, as also my Lady, the Blessed Mary, to pray to the Lord God for me, that all the days of my life I may have part in the merits of His blessed Incarnation, and that I may be constant here below to that doctrine which shall lead me, by true faith and perfect love, one day to see Him in the glory of His Paradise! Amen.[1]

At the Credo.

Sweet Father, Jesus Christ, Thou who knowest all things, Thou knowest all my faults, and how simple and unlearned I am. But, O Lord, without reserve I believe and love the faith of the holy Church. And by the love of Thy precious death, I beseech Thee to

---

[1] *Bibl. Nation.* The same MS.

give me knowledge and understanding, that I may live and die in this faith, professed by the Apostles, Martyrs, Confessors, Virgins, and all the Saints, in union with the Virgin Mother. Amen.[1]

At the Offertory.

O God, Thou who by Thine own Will, and for the salvation of all sinners, didst fix to the tree of the cross Thy Feet, Thy Hands, and Thy whole Body; who didst permit, in outrage to that sacred Body, that a crown of thorns should be placed on Thy royal Head; who didst endure the cruel agony of the five wounds of the cross; and who, in Thy Mother's sight, didst redeem mankind by shedding all Thy Blood; bestow upon me, O Lord, the gift of penitence, chastity, and of patience, and grant unto me the light of understanding, and the knowledge of good. I implore this in the Name of Him who offered Himself for the salvation of the world! Amen.[2]

[1] *Bibl. Nation.* The same MS.   [2] Ibid.

At the Orate Fratres.

May the most blessed Mother of God, the Virgin Mary, all the Saints and all the Elect intercede for us, and may the virtue of the Most High cover us with His wings, that we may offer to the Father a mystery worthy of God and beneficial to man! Amen.[1]

At the Sanctus.

Come, holy and glorious Trinity, indivisible Deity, my hope and my salvation. Come Thou whom the angels in the heavens glorify, singing, "Holy, Holy, Holy is the Lord, Who was, and is, and evermore shall be." And I, unworthy sinner that I am, cast myself at the feet of the throne of God, and cry to Him, "Kindle within me, Lord, the light of Thy mercy, and the fire of Thy burning love. Satan and his ministers threaten me; be Thou my defender. Against all perils and all evils be Thou my shield."

[1] *Bibliothèque de l'Arsenal*, T. L., 624. Fifteenth Century, &c.

And again I say, uniting myself to the angels, "Thou art my true God, my blessed Shepherd, my sole Creator, my just Judge, my good Master, my loving Protector, my most victorious Leader, my powerful Physician, my living Bread, and finally my Light and my Salvation." Amen, amen.[1]

At the Consecration.

"To Thee, O my Lord Jesus, now I come, and in the name of Thy great charity I offer up my prayer this day; that charity which led Thee, the King of heaven, to suffer Thyself, *in the presence of Thy Mother*, to be suspended to the cross which the light of heaven made bright, Thy Soul filled equally with sadness and with sweetness, Thy Heart pierced, Thy Body covered with a thousand bleeding wounds. But lovingly didst Thou endure this fearful Passion, so consumed wert Thou by the thirst for our salvation. And it is in the name of this charity, with which Thy Heart of love, O most dear Saviour, was wounded for

[1] *Bibl. Nation.* Lat. 13,287; Fifteenth Century.

us, that I implore Thee to pardon all my sins, and according to Thy great mercy to grant to me a holy death and a joyful resurrection! Amen.[1]

At the Elevation of the Host.

Truly Thou art Jesus Christ, the holy One, true God, Son of God the Father; true Man, Son of the Virgin Mary. And Thou art entire in this sacred Host, within which, under the form of bread, Thy Body is contained. I believe in Thee, I adore Thee, I place in Thee all my hope, for Thou hast redeemed me by Thy blessed Passion. Have mercy on me. Amen.[2]

At the Elevation of the Chalice.

It is Thyself, again Thyself, sweet and blessed Jesus Christ, Who art also entire within this Chalice. Thy Blood is here under the form of wine, that Blood which Thou didst shed for us.

---

[1] *Bibl. Nation.* Same MS. A prayer very popular in the middle ages.
[2] *Bibl. Nation.* Fr. 24, 89; Fourteenth Century.

Again and again I adore Thee, and beseech Thee to be my Salvation.[1]

Memento of the Living and of the Dead.

And now, O my God, I desire to pray to Thee for all Thy holy Catholic Church, for all Thy reasonable creatures; for all Christians, religious and secular, for all those who believe in Thee, and especially for those who pass through this life labouring in answer to the call of Thy holy love; to these give perseverance, O my God.

O Lord Jesus, King Eternal, give chastity to virgins, sanctity to religious, mutual affection to those united in marriage. Pardon all sinners, be the support of the widow, the counsellor of the orphan, the friend and protector of the poor, the guide of the traveller, and the comforter of the sad. Grant that the wicked may amend their lives, and that the good may rise to higher excellence.

On examining myself, I find that I am guilty among all others, and sinful in all

[1] *Bibl. Nation.* Fr. 24, 39; Fourteenth Century.

things. O my good Father, O my most sweet and most tender Father, Thou who pitiest all mankind, suffer me not to live at so great a distance from Thy paternal love. Be Thou my Liberator, and pardon me all the evil thoughts and sinful deeds with which I have to reproach myself before Thee. Make of my soul, O my God, a soul which seeks Thee, fears Thee, loves Thee, and fulfils Thy Will. O God, blessed in all ages, and eternally glorious, pour forth Thy grace upon those who remember me, or who have remembered me in their prayers, and upon all those who are dear to me. Deign most mercifully to direct their steps, that they may never perish. Leave not without Thine aid those Christians who are still in this life, and to those who have passed away give eternal rest. Amen.[1]

Sweet and kind Virgin, full of dignity and bounty, Virgin sanctified in the womb, Virgin

[1] *Bibl. Nation.* Lat. 13,287; Fifteenth Century.

illuminated with grace, Virgin powerful as thou art pure, most glorious Mother of God, Mother most chaste and Lady most reverently honoured; I pray thee, of thy goodness, to preserve my body and my soul from all sin, and take them both into thy holy keeping. And may thy sweet Son Jesus give me, through thy loving prayers, patience in adversity, a humble heart in prosperity, the remission of my sins, and perseverance in well doing. Obtain for me all these gifts, O Mary, that I may never for one moment do aught that is displeasing to my God. May thy Son grant to my kindred and my friends the bliss of Paradise: may He convert the wicked and maintain the good in well-doing: may He put an end to wars, and grant us peace: may He pardon us all our offences, and bestow upon us an honourable life, a happy death, and eternal joy. May he not forget the souls in Purgatory, and award to them full pardon and a share in His glory. Amen.[1]

[1] *Bibl. Nation.* 24,685, formerly Cordeliers, 137; entitled, *Oraison bien belle à la Vièrge.*

At the Agnus Dei.

O God of Love, O tender and immaculate Lamb, Thou, O Lord, Who didst create heaven and earth, and Who dost hold the whole world within Thy divine Hand; Thou Who didst take upon Thyself our humanity, Who didst deign to submit to the Cross of ignominy, Who didst redeem the universe by the precious streams of Thy Blood, and Who didst promise Thy kingdom to all who follow in the footsteps of Thy Sacrifice, grant that we may love Thee with a pure heart, and persevere in Thy service. Pour forth upon us Thy love and eternal peace, so that, filled with Thy mercy, we may one day merit to be near to the Blessed Virgin, in the joy of the just. Amen.[1]

At the Communion.

In the presence of the true Body and the true Blood of our Lord Jesus Christ, O my God, I place myself most humbly and devoutly at

---

[1] *Bibl. Nation.* Lat. 13,287; Fifteenth Century.

the feet of Thy loving mercy. Make me to avoid sin in the present, pardon that which I have committed in the past, and guard me against it in the future. *Through the prayers of Mary and the Saints*, give me intelligence and faith, wisdom, sweetness, and the spirit of self-denial, even though I be surrounded by all the prosperity this earth affords, humility in good works, patience unshaken in all the trials and afflictions of this world, a true and active love for all my friends and benefactors; and I would especially address myself to Thy eternal glory and mercy in favour of my enemies, if any such there be. Finally, I beseech Thee, in behalf of all here present, for the amendment of our lives, space for repentance, the treasures of Thy grace, the consolations of the Holy Spirit, and perseverance in all good, so that we may, by Thee, be reunited to our Father in heaven, by Thee, O Lord Jesus, whose most sacred Body and Blood we adore at this moment on earth.[1]

[1] *Bibl. Nation.* Same MS.

O most delectable and life-giving Bread, Food most desirable and sweet; incessantly self-renewing, and abundantly satisfying all who love Thee; the Angels and Saints behold Thy unveiled glory in the light in which they live. Grant that amid the miseries of this world, where dwells my sinful soul, it may receive Thee with purity of intention, true faith, and to its own eternal benefit; and communicate unto it strength to attain unto Thee, in spite of the wiles of the Evil One. Amen.[1]

Hail Mary! To thee we owe it that we may partake of the most pure Body of Christ, and that we may venture to draw near to His dread Table. Ave Maria.

Hail Mary! To thee we owe it that we may eat of the true Bread, the Bread immortal. Ave Maria.[2]

---

[1] *Bibl. Nation.* Fr. 927; Fifteenth Century.
[2] St. John Damascene; seventh to eighth centuries, quoted in the *Scutum Fidei* of Conrad Boppert, end of the Eighteenth century, I. 180.

At the Last Prayers.

And now once more I commend myself unto Thee, O my God. I commend myself throughout the hours of this day to the keeping of Thy Angels, and I bring before Thee, for the same loving care, my kindred, my brothers and sisters, my friends, my benefactors, and all Christian people.

Be Thou my Guardian, O Lord; I implore this favour by the intercession of the most Blessed Virgin Mary Thy Mother, and of all the Saints. Deliver me from all impurity, from all sin, from all the snares of the devil, from sudden death, and from the pains of hell. Illuminate my heart with Thy clear light, and grant that nothing may ever separate me from Thee. Amen, Amen.[1]

AFTER MASS.

Lord Jesus, Thou who hast created and redeemed me, take into Thy keeping my body and my soul, which are the work of Thy

[1] *Bibl. Nation.* Lat. 13787. Fifteenth Century.

hands. Thou art my God, be Thou my strength and stay. Thou art my Redeemer, be Thou my Deliverer. Regard not my merits to exercise justice upon me, but hearken only to Thy mercy; and grant me the blessing of a happy death, so that when my soul, immaterial and invisible, escapes from the prison of my body, I may appear untroubled before Thee, and attain in peace to Thy heavenly kingdom, where I may rejoice in the vision of Thy glory, while from Thy most sweet voice I hear these blissful words, "Come ye blessed of my Father, enter the kingdom that has been prepared for you from the beginning of the world."[1]

O Most Blessed Virgin Mary, at the close of this Mass, I come once more to lay my prayer before thee with all the fervour of my soul. As thou wert present to sustain thy Son, so dearly loved, while He was suspended to the Cross, so deign to sustain all His priests, who, spread over the surface of the earth, offer

[1] *Bibl. Nation.* Latin, 13,287; Fifteenth Century.

up the Divine sacrifice this day, that, aided by thee, they may worthily present to the most Blessed Trinity, a victim well-pleasing in the sight of God, the Victim of Propitiation. Amen, Amen.[1]

PRAYERS BEFORE AND AFTER CONFESSION.

Virgin of incomparable merit, thou hadst no model nor exemplar; Virgin Mother, of whose virginity of body and soul our Lord made Himself the Guardian, that He might worthily take of thee that flesh which is the price of our redemption. I implore Thee, O most compassionate One, to whom, after God, we owe the salvation of the world, intercede for me, covered as I am with the defilement of sin, and wholly stained with iniquity, that God may grant to this most miserable soul the love of purity and a sincere delight in chastity. I, unhappy creature, have lost the grace of

[1] *Scutum fidei.* Conrad Boppert; end of the Eighteenth Century, IV. 261.

innocence and holiness, I have violated within myself the majesty of the temple of God. But what is this thing that I do? Behold I pour forth my sins, O my Mother, into thy pure ears! I abhor myself, O my Lady, my conscience accuses me. I feel, like Adam, my need of being clad, and own myself nigh unto death.

To whom then shall I expose the wounds of my soul, manifest my sorrow, tell my tears? And how can I be restored to health if it be no longer permitted to me to enter this resting-place of eternal mercy?

Lady have pity on me, have pity on this citizen of thy kingdom, self-banished from thy celestial home, who after long exile, many sighs, cruel deceptions, and countless sufferings, returns at last to his comforter, to his Mother. I call to mind that thou didst once deign to reveal thy name of loving memory to one of thy dying servants, that all sinners might be encouraged to turn to thy gracious patronage. When he was passing through the terrors of death, thou didst appear unto him, saying, "Knowest thou me?" He replied in trembling accents, "Lady, I know thee not." Then with what sweet and tender condescension didst thou say to him: "I am the Mother of Mercy."

No, there is no one to whom we can confide our miseries, our misfortunes, and our tears, no one like thee O Mary, who art the Mother of Mercy in very deed and truth. Holy Mother, Immaculate Mother, Mother of love, Mother of pardon, Mother of goodness, open thy loving heart and receive within it a miserable creature dead in sin, even him who is now before thee. Behold the Prodigal returning to his father's house; he is in rags, with bruised and bleeding feet, he has escaped from a place of horror, an atmosphere of gloom, laden with poison and infection. He sighs, he groans, and cries out to thee, his Mother, remembering that thou hast often clothed him when naked, warmed him when cold, and pleaded for him with his

Father. How good and tender is that Father! How sweet and gentle art thou, that Mother!

Regard us, then, as children whom thine only Son Jesus did not disdain to call His brethren. Thou didst feel the sword pierce thy heart at the sight of thy most innocent Son nailed to the Cross; how canst thou restrain thy tears at sight of thy adopted children, who, like me, are dead in sin? How can thy Mother's heart at that sight refrain from grief? We are led astray by the enemy, torn from our rightful home and cast into captivity. And there is no one to deliver us, no one to redeem us, no one who will one day stand forth and offer himself as surety for us.

Arise thou, O Virgin. Arise, O Merciful One. Enter thou into the heavenly sanctuary where God hearkens to all prayers, and there remain with those immaculate hands of thine, outstretched before that altar of God where will be effected the reconciliation between God and man. And easily wilt thou obtain for us that which we venture to ask through thee, and to thee shall we owe it, that the sins which fill us with fear will receive their pardon.

Could He suffer thee long to languish at His feet, praying for us? That Son, whom thou, sweet Mother, hast so often comforted, a little wailing child? And who could be worthy to appease the anger of this Judge, if not she who was not unworthy to be His Mother? Then delay not, O my Lady. The God to Whom thou art about to plead is my Salvation and my Glory. He is also of my flesh; He is the Head of us all. He knoweth us, for He knoweth well the work of His own hand.

I have but one boon to crave of thee for the sake of thy Son, and that is the ever present remembrance of thy own beloved name. Grant that it may be the sweetest food of my soul, and may it be present with me in all my perils, in all my trials, and let it be the first of all my joys. May I but obtain this gift from God and thee, I shall no more fear eternal death; for thy protection and thy grace will depart from me no more for ever. And though I should be plunged into the depth of misery, thou wilt go thither to seek me, thou wilt snatch me forth and restore me victoriously to thy Son, Who hath redeemed me and washed me with His Blood; to Jesus Christ our Lord, Who liveth and reigneth God Eternal with the Father and the Holy Ghost. Amen! [1]

II. AFTER CONFESSION.

Blooming Rose; Mother of God, all beautiful; Virgin most sweet; fruitful Vine; bright Dawn of Day, pray for us, that we may be worthy to find eternal happiness in eternal Light. The stars are thy crown; the sun is thy garment; the moon is beneath thy feet; the glory of Divinity is within thee, and in that magnificence of glory, thou dost

---

[1] Saint Anselm, eleventh to twelfth century. The ten first lines cannot be attributed to the great Doctor, for we have found them in a MS. of the tenth century, Bibl. Maz. T. 805. This was one of the most widely known and most popular prayers of the middle ages. Cf. the MS. 1195 of Bibliothèque Nat.; fourteenth century, &c.

rise above all the creatures of the world. O holy Virgin, thou who in heaven dost drink of the fountain of beatitude, pray for us. Grant that by thy intercessions our sins may be effaced, and do thou gain for us the joys of heaven. Amen.[1]

PRAYER BEFORE COMMUNION.

I.

O Mother of God, O blessed Virgin, behold I come, even I unworthy one, to receive the Body and Blood of thy dear Son Jesus Christ. Take me by the hand and present me before the most Holy Trinity; praying that through the worthiness of this Body and this Blood, God will bestow upon me a holy love, that He will deliver me from the snares of my enemies, visible and invisible, and that He will fill my heart with humility and all other virtues. Amen.[2]

[1] *Bibl. Nation.* 1201; fourteenth century.
[2] *Bibl. de l'Arsenal*, T. L. 320. *Livre d'Heures*, date, 1631.

II.

O Mary, after God my only hope, by thy intercession render me worthy in this life to participate without sin in the immaculate Body and Blood of thy divine Son, and in the next life also, to partake of the ineffable sweetness of the heavenly banquet, in that fair kingdom of God which is the habitation of all joyful souls. Amen.[1]

AFTER COMMUNION.

O my Almighty God,—JESUS:
O my most faithful Shepherd,—JESUS:
O my most royal Sovereign,—JESUS:
I, the least of Thy servants, poor and needy, with all my strength, with all my heart, with all my thoughts, and all my affections, I entreat Thee that Thy most precious Body and Blood which I have received, may remain

---

[1] St. Ephrem; Fourth Century, quoted in the *Scutum Fidei* of Conrad Boppert, towards the end of the Eighteenth Century, I. 200.

inseparably and for ever united to my heart. Amen. Amen.[1]

PRAYERS DURING THE DAY.

The Hours.

O our Lady, thou who wert present at the Passion of thy Son, grant that at every hour of this day I may recall those hours through which thou didst pass on the day of thy Son's death.

At Matins. During the night, at the hour of matins, it was announced to thee, O Mary, that thy Son remained a prisoner in the hands of the Jews, and that He had been led before Annas. Then did thy heart sink within thee as witnessing that ignominy suffered by thy Son. *Ave Maria.*

At Prime. At the first hour, O Mary, thou didst follow thy Son Jesus to the house of Pilate; with what grief thou didst hear the

[1] *Bibl. St. Geneviève*, B.B. I. 66. Commencement of the Sixteenth Century; *Instruction pour une femme seculière.*

false witness borne against Him. Thou didst see thy sweet Son defiled with spitting, thou didst see Him, alas with what anguish, most cruelly, most sacrilegiously scourged. *Ave Maria.*

At Tierce. At the third hour thou didst hear the tumult, and beheld thy Son led away to His place of torture; thou didst see Him clothed with purple and crowned with thorns. Thou didst hear him condemned to death, and watch Him bearing painfully on His shoulders the wood of His Cross. *Ave Maria.*

At Sext. At the sixth hour thou didst see the tender Flesh of Jesus Christ nailed to the cross, and suspended between heaven and earth. Thou didst witness that agony of thirst which He had nought to quench but gall, and thou too, even thou, wert stained by the blood of Thy Son. *Ave Maria.*

At None. At the ninth hour thou didst witness with thine own eyes the death of thy Son, and thine own ears did hear that supreme cry of anguish when He bowed His Head and gave up His Soul to His Father. Then did the sword foretold by Simeon transfix thy heart. *Ave Maria.*

At the hour of Vespers. In this hour, O Mother of Sorrows, thou didst breathe forth thine anguish before the Body of Jesus, which had been detached from the Cross, and restraining thy sobs, thou didst exclaim, " O staff of my declining years. O light of mine eyes." *Ave Maria.*

At Compline. At this hour thou didst come to the sepulchre, there to place amid sweet spices thy Jesus, bruised for our transgressions, the price of our salvation, and the Hope of our life to come. *Ave Maria.*[1]

At the Sound of the Angelus.

Hail Mary, Handmaid of the Trinity!
Hail Mary, Spouse of the Holy Spirit!

[1] *Bibl. de l'Arsenal,* T. L. 624, Fifteenth Century. After each hour a prayer is read: *Propter illius terroris commotionem; propter gemitus; propter cruciatus; propter Gravamen, &c.* These prayers were very celebrated in the Middle Ages. The first five lines have been added.

Hail Mary, Mother of our Lord Jesus Christ!

Hail Mary, Sister of the Angels!

Hail Mary, Promise of the Prophets!

Hail Mary, Queen of the Patriarchs!

Hail Mary, Mistress and Instructress of the Apostles!

Hail Mary, Strength of Martyrs!

Hail Mary, Refreshment and Reward of Confessors!

Hail Mary, Honour and Crown of Virgins!

Hail Mary, Consolation of all the living and the dead! Be thou with me in all my temptations, tribulations, necessities, sufferings, and weaknesses. Obtain for me the pardon of all my sins. And above all, be not far from me in the hour of my death, O most benignant Virgin Mary.[1]

At the Striking of the Clock.

✝ Almighty and most merciful God, Heavenly Father, I implore Thee, by the death of

[1] *Horæ Beatæ Mariæ Virginis, ad usum Cisterciensium,* Paris, Iolande Bonhomme, 1553.

Thy Divine Son, most beloved and most innocent, grant that the terrible hour when my soul shall be separated from my body, may be favourable for me. Have pity, O my God, on a miserable sinner.[1]

PRAYER OF ST. ANSELM.

To be frequently repeated in the course of the Day.

✝ Blessed Mary, intercede for me, so that after having lived holily, I may end my life happily, confessing my sins, in the true faith, calling upon the Name of Jesus, receiving the Body and Blood of my God. Pray for me, Holy Mother of God, that I may enter into that eternal kingdom, where thou, Queen of Angels, Queen of men, dost triumph in glory. Amen.[2]

---

[1] *Aureum thuribulum.* Bamberg apud Aug. Crinesium.
[2] *St. Anselm*, Eleventh and Twelfth Century, quoted by Conrad Boppert in the *Scutum fidei*, end of the Eighteenth Century.

VISIT TO THE CHAPEL OF THE BLESSED VIRGIN.

Most blessed Mary, and my Lady, I come to place myself, body and soul, under thy special care and protection, and in the embrace of thy mercy, not for this day only, but for all the days of my life, and particularly for the hour of my death. I also place in thy hands all my hopes, all my sorrows, all my cares; my life, and the end thereof.

Through thy merits and intercession, O blessed Virgin, I ask that all my actions may henceforth be conformed to thy will and to the Will of thy Son. Amen.[1]

IMPERATRIX REGINARUM.

Empress of Queens: *the Lord is with thee.*

Immortal Praise of holy souls: *the Lord is with thee.*

Flower of flowers: *the Lord is with thee.*

[1] *Bibliothèque de l'Arsenal*, T. L. 320, Fifteenth Century; *Precationum Thesaurus*, Paris, 1563, &c.

Lily of the valleys: *the Lord is with thee.*

Mediatrix between Jesus and man: *the Lord is with thee.*

Endless Joy: *the Lord is with thee.*

Thornless Rose: *the Lord is with thee.*

Virgin Incomparable: *the Lord is with thee.*

Virgin all fair and noble: *the Lord is with thee.*

Source of mercy: *the Lord is with thee.*

Shelter of the glory of God: *the Lord is with thee.*

Fruitful Paradise: *the Lord is with thee.*

House of Eternity: *the Lord is with thee.*

Living Shrine, containing the Old Testament and the New: *the Lord is with thee.*

Sanctuary of the Holy Spirit: *the Lord is with thee.*

Thou who, hearing the words of the Angel, didst conceive: *the Lord is with thee.*

Mother of Charity, of Mercy, and of Truth: *the Lord is with thee.*

Mother of the orphan: *the Lord is with thee.*

Consolation of the desolate: *the Lord is with thee.*

Salvation of all who hope in thee: *the Lord is with thee.*

Ark and temple of God: *the Lord is with thee.*

Star, making bright the heavens: *the Lord is with thee.*

Thou, who, true Virgin and true Mother, didst give birth to Jesus, true God and true Man, born for us: *the Lord is with thee.*

Mother of Him, Who for us was in the Temple received into the arms of the holy and aged Simeon: *the Lord is with thee.*

Mother of Him, Who for us was cruelly beaten, crowned with thorns, pierced with nails, and fastened to the cross: *the Lord is with thee.*

Mother of Him, Who for us, always for us, recommended His Virgin Apostle John to His Virgin Mother, saying to her, "Behold thy son," and to Saint John, "Behold thy Mother:" *the Lord is with thee.*

Mother of Him, who from the height of His cross, uttered that piercing cry : *Eloi, Eloi, lama sabacthani!* and bowing His Head, gave up the ghost : *the Lord is with thee.*

Mother of Him, Whose side was pierced with a lance after His death, (and from this Wound there poured forth Water and Blood for the remission of our sins, and the redemption of our souls) : *the Lord is with thee.*

Mother of Him, Who rose the third day and ascended into the heaven of heavens, in presence of His Apostles, to prepare an immortal abode for His most just and holy Mother : *the Lord is with thee.*

Mother of Him, Who will come to judge the living and the dead, and try the world by fire : *the Lord is with thee.*

Sweet Virgin Mary : *the Lord is with thee.*[1]

[1] *Horæ Beatæ Mariæ Virginis, ad usum Cisterciensium,* 1553. *Heures à l'usage de Rouen,* printed by Simon Vostre, 1588, &c. This prayer is found in a great number of Collections, and was very popular : a portion only is here given. The petition translated *Living Shrine* is in the original "*Living Library.*"

BEFORE AND AFTER MEALS.

Blessed be the Name of our Lord, and blessed be the name of the Virgin Mary, His Mother.

Blessed also be the names of all the Saints in Paradise. Amen.[1]

EVENING PRAYERS.

TWILIGHT.

Behold the shadows deepen around us: arise Thou in our hearts, fair dawn of Justice, so that, closing the day with thanksgiving, we may in the morning again be found by Thee, O God, employed in offering unto Thee our homage. Amen.[2]

WHEN IT GROWS DARK.

I.

Commendation to God.

The day is Thine, the night also is Thine, O Lord. Grant that the Sun of Justice may

---

[1] *Bibl. Nation.* 2139, Fifteenth Century. *Comment on doit rendre grâces apres manger.*

[2] *Thesaurus Precum*, Paris, 1601. Abel l'Angelier.

continue through this night to shine within our souls, keeping far from us the darkness of sin.[1]

II.

Salutation to the Blessed Virgin.

Hail, field of roses! Rose-garden of the Heavenly King; Queen of God's chosen ones, and fairest Lily of virginity.

Hail, Palace of the Word; Consolation of sinners; Abode of purity.

Hail, Sanctuary of the Spirit; Shelter of the Trinity; Garner of perfumes.

Hail, Cure of fallen man; Refuge, open to all souls; sweet Protection, beneath which none need tremble.

Hail, Strength of warriors; hail, Light of contemplatives; hail, Joy of all who pray.[2]

An Universal Prayer.

✝ Almighty and eternal God, Thou didst

---
[1] Same source as the preceding.
[2] *Bibl. de Stuttgard,* Man. Brev. 101; Fifteenth Century; *Ave Patris Rosarium,* Mone, *Hymni Latini medii ævi.* 11, 21.

send us Thine only Son, Who, without separating Himself from Thee in heaven, took upon Himself the garment of our flesh, and dwelt among us. By the teaching, by the admirable life and bloody death of this Thy Son, Thou hast raised us up unto Thyself.

We implore Thy mercy this day, humbly acknowledging our frailty. Grant, O heavenly Father, that henceforth we may follow our Saviour's footsteps, and may thus become pleasing in Thine eyes. Grant us, O Lord, the gift of tears, the sighs of penitence, the knowledge of our own heart, the love of prayer, the sweet savour of piety, and the eternal consolations of Thy love.

So that, our hearts being filled with the sweet nourishment of Thy words, and being illuminated by the splendours of Truth, we may obtain grace henceforth to be strong in adversity, humble in prosperity, joyful in tribulations, patient in trials, intrepid amid temptations, exact in our life, prudent in our plans, assiduous in spiritual reading, attentive in our prayers, and unwearied in our thanksgiving.

We ask of Thee, O Lord, a heart burning with charity, and an intelligence unceasingly consumed by desire for spiritual progress. Grant that our daily life may be fully enlightened and wholly spiritualised by the exercise of every virtue.

Pour into our souls, O God, the Spirit of Wisdom and Understanding, of Counsel and Strength, of Knowledge and true Piety, and, finally, the Spirit of Holy Fear. May the Holy Spirit accompany us in all our ways, may He direct and protect us, so that, with that Spirit by our side, we may pass safely through all the dangers of our earthly pilgrimage: and, when we reach the close of life's fearful combat, we may, O Lord, attain to Thy presence, full of confidence and security; that we may have joy in Thee, be enfolded by Thee, and be filled with Thee, praising Thee with all the joyous legions of Thine angels, and the choirs of all Thy Saints, in that fair heaven, where, by Thy grace, we may find eternal rest, endless praise, peace unalloyed, bliss ineffable, and the eternal vision of Thyself, O Lord. This we most humbly implore Thee to grant us, O most merciful Father. Amen.[1]

On going to Bed.

O Good Shepherd, who sleepest not, that we may be preserved from all dangers of the night; for the protection of our bodies and souls, O Lord our God, spread over us Thy heavenly wings, and during our sleep may Thy Majesty keep guard over all our senses. Amen.[2]

Before going to Sleep.

Jesus, Whom I adore,
Give me Thy love and nothing more.
Mary, most dear to me,
Thy love is all I ask of thee.

[1] *Saint Laurence Justinian*, Fifteenth Century. The Latin text is in the *Scutum fidei* of Conrad Boppert, I. 219, 220, end of the Eighteenth Century.
[2] *Thesaurus precum*, edition of 1587.

"Mon doux Jésus,
Votre amour et rien plus :
Douce Marie,
Votre amour, je vous prie." [1]

PRAYERS FOR TIMES OF PRIVATE AFFLICTIONS.

All you devout Catholics, true servants of the Blessed Virgin Mary, who in this present life are in perpetual fear and trouble; call frequently to mind, by pious contemplation, the great pains and sorrows which the Blessed Mother of God underwent for you, in order that you may with her reign in eternal joy. [2]

In Suffering.

In memory of the anguish which oppressed thy heart, O most loving Virgin, when thy sweet Son Jesus, in the hands of the Jews who cried, "Crucify Him, crucify Him," was judged worthy of death, and condemned to the

[1] *Bibl. St. Geneviève*, BB. L. 66, Commencement of the Sixteenth Century.
[2] *Bibl. Nat.*; 10,551; Fifteenth Century.

torture of the cross; in the name of this immeasurable grief, come to the aid of me a miserable sinner, this day, and during all the time that my suffering shall continue. Forget me not when I am tormented in body by sickness, and in soul by the evil one, and by fear of the terrible judgment; but grant that the sentence of eternal death may not be pronounced against me, and that I may not be delivered over a prey to everlasting flames. Amen.[1]

In Trial or Temptation.

Immaculate Virgin, Mother of God, receive my prayer. Help me in this trial and in all my necessities. Intercede for me, O Glorious One, with my Redeemer, even with Him, thy Divine Son, whom thou didst bear without spot of sin. Deliver me from every snare of the enemy, and from all carnal delights, that, by thy intercession, I may obtain the pardon of all my sins, a steadfast resistance to all my enemies, visible and invisible, and the amend-

[1] *Bibl. Maz.*, T. 897; Thirteenth Century.

ment of my life, protected henceforth by God. I ask this in the name of thy Son, whom thou didst bear according to the flesh, but Who lives and reigns one God with the Father and the Spirit, through endless ages. Amen.[1]

When the Trial becomes more heavy.

O ye holy Archangels, Michael, Gabriel, and Raphael; O all ye Choirs of the angelic hierarchy and of the blessed spirits; Cherubim, Seraphim, Thrones, Dominations, Principalities, Powers, and Virtues of Heaven, Angels and Archangels, with all the Elect of God, Patriarchs, Prophets, Apostles, Evangelists, Martyrs, Confessors, Virgins, Widows, and those who have in holiness fulfilled the marriage state, even all holy souls;—I entreat of you to salute on my behalf the Blessed Virgin Mary, and to pray to her for me, saying:

Ave. Hail, Queen of Heaven, and the Reconciler of sinners. *Gratia plena, Dominus*

[1] *Bibl. Maz.*, T. 895; Tenth Century.

tecum. O, Full of Grace, the Lord is with thee, God the Father Almighty, thy Creator, whose Daughter thou art. God the Son is with thee, thy only Son and the Only-Begotten of the Father, Who consecrated thee to His Virgin Mother. God the Holy Ghost is with thee, the Paraclete, who made thee fruitful, and of whom thou art the Spouse. God the Eternal Trinity is with thee: *Benedicta tu in mulieribus, et benedictus Fructus ventris tui Jesus.* Amen."

And behold, I also, a miserable sinner, who have so often dishonoured my soul and my actions by the deceitfulness of sin, I come, in my present tribulation, to find comfort in offering praise to thee: Hail, Festival of my heart; hail, Daughter, Spouse, and Mother of God, His Diadem, and the eternal theme of the praises of the Saints, who hast given unto us the Flower of Life.

Beauty to the Eyes, Music to the ear, pure and heavenly Fragrance;

Be my defence; mark me with thy seal,

and show me how sweet thou art; but above all aid me in the final combat of this life. Hail, Habitation of God; hail, our Refuge. *Ave Maria, Gratia plena.*[1]

When One has Enemies.

O most sweet Lady, Saint Bernard says that none ever have recourse to thee without being aided by thee; and therefore, O fair and gentle Virgin Mary, I repair to thee, and in this present great trouble of my soul, place myself under thy blessed guard: and I beseech thee, Mother of God, in the name of thy dear Son, and for the love thou bearest Him, to show favour unto me and defend me against all those who threaten me.

Guard thou my honour and estate, which I confide to thy kind protection, and be pleased to obtain for me peace for body and soul. Save all my benefactors and friends, and preserve them in thy love; have compassion on the departed, convert evil-doers, and make

[1] *Bibl. Nation.* 1201; Fourteenth Century.

them powerless to harm me; appease their hearts towards me, and maintain us all together in thy service, O sweetest Lady. Amen.[1]

In Sickness.

To thee O Mary, to thee it is that I commend the last day of my life and the last hour of my death.

In this last struggle my poor soul will be troubled: O merciful Lady, then look pityingly upon it.

With all the Saints, hasten to succour me. Preserve me from the eternal displeasure of God, and make me to be pleasing to Jesus thy Son.[2]

Against Sudden Death.

The Dwelling of Light, the chosen Vessel of the Holy Spirit, the glorious Mother of God, is she, who has destroyed the power of the Serpent. She is fairer than the sun, brighter than the moon, more resplendent

[1] *Bibl. Nat.* Fr. 927; Fifteenth Century.
[2] Ibid. 1291; Fourteenth Century.

than the stars. Let us, then, poor sinners, draw nigh to her, striking our breasts and saying: "O Virgin Mary, our tender Mother and benignant Lady, be pleased to obtain our deliverance from sudden death and from all evils, and make us to participate in the eternal glory of paradise. Amen." [1]

For a Sick Person.

O Only Pure! thou in whom is found the ocean of Peace, cease not for an instant thy prayer for thy suffering servant. Rescue him from sickness, that he may again and unceasingly praise thee.

Mother of the Creator of all things, cast from on high a pitying look upon our sick one, and soften the severity of his pain.

Mother of God, and ever Virgin, mighty Protectress; Gate, Wall, Ladder, and mystic Fortress; have pity upon our suffering one, who has recourse to thee.

O Thou whose purity merits so much praise,

[1] *Bibl. S. Geneviève*; BB. L. 66. Commencement of the Sixteenth Century.

Lady of surpassing goodness, mystic Olive, have compassion upon him who receives the anointing of the holy oils, and save thy servant.[1]

For One who is Dead.

O Radiant Gate through which our God has entered, ask of Him to open to thy servant the gates of heaven, that there he may sing thy praises in everlasting rest; O Mary, exalted Protectress of the human race. Amen.[2]

AFTER THE DEATH OF A CHILD.

Prayer of the Mother.

O thou who didst bring forth Him who is the Word and the Wisdom of the Father, behold the anguish of the wound which has stricken my soul; heal it, O my Mother, and assuage the woe by which my heart is torn.[3]

In Abraham's bosom, in the habitations of eternal repose, where joy and gladness have

---

[1] Ritual of the Greek Church.
[2] *Greek Liturgy: Officium Funereum in Sacerdotem vita functum.* Cf. the Euchology of Goar, p. 586.
[3] *Ritual of the Greek Church: Canon Funereus pro pueris vita functis.*

no end, in that fair country where the waters of life have their source, it is there, O my child, that we pray God to place thee, even God, who for thy sake became a little child.

Thou hast willed it, O King of heaven and earth; swiftly hast Thou borne away my happy child, as a little bird caught in Thy heavenly nets and placed by Thee in the nests of Paradise. Receive him, then, into Thy kingdom, that there may be another soul to praise Thee among the just.

The Child Answers:

Wherefore weep for my death? seeing that in truth I neither am nor can be in need of pity.

O God, my God, who has called me into heaven, be the Consolation of my home, which from hence I behold all filled with weeping.

I was their only child, and upon me alone were their eyes fixed.

Comfort my mother, O Thou who wert born

of the Virgin, and be the refreshment of my father's burning grief, Thou to Whom we sing Alleluia![1]

PRAYERS IN TIMES OF PUBLIC CALAMITY.

During an Epidemic.

O Immaculate One, thou art our most assured Refuge, and the hope of the despairing. Have pity, therefore, on thy children who are a prey to so terrible a calamity; visit them in their affliction, sweeten its bitterness, and lighten the pressure of their sickness; drive away from us this contagion, and save thy servants, O Mother of God.[2]

In Time of War.

O Virgin, Mother of Him who is the Mighty One, terrible in war; thy hand, O Mary, is likewise powerful and strong, deliver us therefore from the enemies who threaten our peace.

Thee, O Mary, do we invoke against our

---

[1] *Greek Liturgy: Canon Funereus pro pueris vita functis.* Cf. Goar, 594.

[2] *Ritual of the Greek Church: Canon in pestilentialis morbi periculo.*

enemies; thee, who art at the head of all the Christian host, its leader and chief.

Moses with outstretched hands put to flight the cruel Amalek; the hands of Moses were stretched out in the form of a cross. Do thou as Moses did, O Virgin Mary, and put to flight the enemies of thy people.

May all the kingdoms of the world acknowledge the might of thine arm, and proclaim thy unconquerable power; as for the nations which know thee not, they shall be confounded and perish.[1]

In Time of Civil War.

From civil war, from all destruction and revolt, from all tumult and secret conspiracy, from every perfidious attack, from every snare, and from all treason, deliver this city, O Immaculate Virgin!

Surround our city—this city which is thine—with the invisible legions of the heavenly chivalry, and with the cohorts of the angels.

[1] *Greek Liturgy: Canon supplex ad sanctissimam Deiparam in rumore belli.* Cf. Euchologion of Goar, p. 813.

Hasten, O Mary, to come down and aid us. Amen.[1]

For Peace.

Pray for peace, sweet Virgin Mary, Queen of heaven and Lady of the world, and by thy courtesy cause all the Saints also to pray for us. And do thou address thyself to thy Son, beseeching of His high Majesty to look favourably upon this people, whom He has purchased with His blood. War troubles all things, may Jesus drive away war! Weary not of praying, O Mary, and ask of God that peace which is the true treasure of joy.[2]

Biaux Sire Dieux en qui je croy,—
Par la pitié octroye—moy
Que mourir puisse en telle foy
Que sainte Eglise tient de Toy.[3]

[1] *Greek Liturgy.* Same source as preceding prayer.
[2] Charles of Orleans, Fifteenth Century. *Priex pour la paix, douce Viérge Marie.* Edition of Guichard, p. 139.
[3] *Bibl. Nat.* 10,528, at the end of Seven Prayers to Our Lady against the Seven Deadly Sins. It may be thus translated:—

"Blessed Lord God, in Whom I believe; for Thy mercy's sake grant to me, that I die in that same Faith which Holy Church holds of Thee."

To obtain True Joy.

O God, who didst give to the Blessed Virgin Mary, Thy Mother, the threefold joy of Thy Incarnation, Thy Resurrection, and Thy Ascension, have regard to her merits and to her perpetual prayers, and in spite of our unworthiness, grant that we may happily attain to the joys which have no end. Amen.

TO OBTAIN THE CONVERSION OF OUR BRETHREN.

For Preachers.

O sovereignly gracious and blessed above all women, Holy Virgin Mary, thou art in an especial manner the Espoused One, the companion, and, above all, the dearly-beloved Mother of our God; and therefore is it that thou art placed on high so near to our Emmanuel, above all the souls of the blessed.

Obtain for me, I pray thee, from thy Son, Who is the Word, living words, burning and efficacious. I ask not the false ornaments of

[1] *Bibl. Nat.* 1196; Fourteenth Century. This prayer accompanies the *Joys of the Virgin.*

human eloquence, but power to show forth the Holy Spirit and all Virtue, to set on fire the hearts of those who hear me, and happily to complete the work begun by our God; all for His glory, and for the eternal happiness and salvation of the whole Christian people. Amen.[1]

[1] Second Session of the Council of Trent, Feb. 4th, 1546, opening discourse by Father Catarino Polito, of Siena, of the Order of Friars' Preachers. Labbé : *Conciles*, xiv. 1007.

PART II.

PRAYERS TAKEN FROM THE ANCIENT LITURGIES
AND
EARLY FATHERS OF THE CHURCH.

PART II.

THE FATHERS; AND ANCIENT MONUMENTS.

The Apostolic Ages.

THE Virgin and Child is not a mere modern idea; on the contrary, it is represented again and again, as every visitor to Rome is aware, in the paintings of the Catacombs. Mary is there drawn with the Divine Infant in her lap; she with hands extended in prayer, He with His hand in the attitude of blessing. No representation can more forcibly convey the doctrine of the high dignity of the Mother, and, we will add, of her power over her Son. Why should the memory of His time of subjection be so dear to Christians and so carefully preserved? The only question to be determined is the precise date of these remarkable monuments of the first age of Christianity. That they belong to what certain Christians call "the undivided Church" is certain, but investigations have been lately pursued which place some of them at an earlier date than any one anticipated as possible. We have the *Imagini Scelte* of Rossi, published in 1863, and they are sufficient for our purpose. In this work he has given from the Catacombs, various representations of the Virgin and Child, the latest of which belong to the early part of the fourth century, but the earliest he believes to be referable to the very age of the Apostles. He comes to this conclusion from the style and the skill of the composition, and from the history, locality, and existing inscriptions of the catacomb in which it is found. However, although he does not insist upon so early a date, the utmost liberty he grants is to refer the paintings to the age of the first Antonines, that is, to a date within half a century of the death of S. John.

ANCIENT LITURGIES.

I.

Liturgy of Saint Peter.

Deign, O my God, to be mindful before all of the holy and illustrious Mary, Ever-Virgin, and with her, of all the Prophets and Apostles, all the Martyrs and Confessors, all the Priests and Just Persons who have found perfection in the true Faith, and in particular of Saint John, the Forerunner and Baptist; of Saint Stephen, first of the Deacons and first of Martyrs; and of all the Saints.

We offer to Thee their prayers, O God our king, in order that Thou mayest give freedom to all souls in bondage, and that Thou Thyself mayest govern those who have no ruler.

Make us to be worthy of the blessedness of all those who have served Thee in truth; of all those who have been pleasing to Thee, and of whom the memory shall never perish.

Grant that with them we may merit to praise Thee without ceasing, and to sing to Thee and to Thy Son a *gloria* everlasting. Amen. Amen.[1]

II.

The Roman Liturgy.

The Roman Church in her liturgy displays towards Mary a particular love and respect. This may justly be called the mother-liturgy, the universal and only one, which presents at the same time the three incontrovertible attributes of antiquity, authority, and unity.

The Roman Church does not hesitate to apply to the Virgin Mother all that the Scriptures say of the eternal wisdom, who was created before all other creatures by the breath of the Most High. "The depths were

---

[1] Liturgia Sancti Petri Principis Apostolorum, Renaudot, ii. 149.

not as yet, and already thou wert conceived, and through thee an immortal and inextinguishable light has arisen in the heavens. Thou hast sought thy repose in Jerusalem, and thy habitation in Sion. Blessed and glorious art thou, holy Virgin Mary. There is no praise of which thou art not a thousand times worthy, for the Sun of Justice, Christ the Lord God, is come forth from thy womb.

"Holy and immaculate Virgin, by what words can I glorify thee? I know not, for thou bearest Him whom the heavens cannot contain.

"Thou hast given back to us in thy glorious Son all that had been lost to us by the sin of Eve. It is thou who didst open the gates of heaven, in order that sorrowing man might enter into the land of light. O thou, whose name is as a sweet odour, thou who hast thyself alone destroyed all the heresies upon the earth, behold we come to thee!

"Succour the wretched, help the weak-hearted, strengthen the feeble, pray for the people, mediate for the clergy, intercede for the devout female sex. Let all who celebrate thy holy commemoration experience thy aid. We are captives, break our chains; we are blind, do thou give us light. Grant us all good gifts, and drive from us all evil. Show thyself a mother.

"That we may be delivered from present sin, and enjoy everlasting life, is what we ask of our Lord God through thy intercession O blessed Virgin Mary. Amen. Amen.[1]

"Hail Mary, full of grace, holier than all the Saints, higher than the heavens, more glorious than the Cherubim, more venerable than the Seraphim, and worthy of veneration above all other creatures!

"Hail, Dove which hast brought to us the olive branch, and after the deluge which has overwhelmed our souls, didst show us the gate of salvation! Dove, whose wings of silver shine with resplendent brightness,

---

[1] All the quoted texts are taken from the Missal and the Roman Breviary, *passim*.

flashing like the purest gold, the Holy Spirit illuminating them with His glorious light!

Hail, most sweet and spiritual Paradise of our God, planted in the east by His almighty and merciful Hand. Paradise fragrant with the odour of lilies. Paradise wherein is found the unfading rose, healing all who in the west have drunk of the bitter cup of death, the cup so fatal to their souls. Paradise, where flourishes that beautiful tree of life, whose fruits bestow the knowledge of truth and everlasting life on all who eat thereof.

Hail, Palace of the great king, palace of God, built with holiness, pure and immaculate, which the magnificence of God delighted in adorning. Palace where hospitality is freely offered to all, and where all find life in its delectable mysteries. In this palace was it that the Word — to recal lost and wandering souls, and to reconcile to the Father all mankind, whose sins had exiled them from heaven—made His espousals with our human nature.

Hail, shady and fertile Mountain, where has been nourished the spiritual Lamb that bore all our infirmities and iniquities; mountain from whence came that Stone, cut out without hands, and which has overthrown all idols and their altars, and become the Corner stone, wonderful in our eyes.

Hail, holy Throne of God, divine Sanctuary, glorious House, marvellous Adornment and chief Treasure of this sanctuary, Propitiatress for the entire universe, Heaven which declarest the glory of God.

Hail, Vessel of purest gold, Vessel which containest the most fragrant sweetness of our souls, even Christ our manna.

O Virgin most chaste, worthy of all praise and honour. Sanctuary consecrated to God, and first in the hierarchy of created beings; Virgin earth, flowering Vine, fruitful Source of waters, Virgin mother, and Mother virgin, hidden treasure of innocence, splendour of virginity. Thy prayers are favourably received on high, being endued with the force of maternal authority. Address them for us to Him whom in thy virginity thou didst conceive, even thy Son, who is true Lord and God, the author of all creatures. Amen.[1]

The Ambrosian Liturgy.

It is just and right to offer unceasingly our thanksgivings unto Thee, O Almighty God; and to celebrate, with the invocation of Thy Divine power, the festivals of the Blessed Virgin Mary. And to whom, in truth, do we owe the gift of the Bread of Angels, if it be not to the Fruit of her womb? Has not Mary restored to us all that the sin of Eve had wrenched from us? Is it not, on the one side, crime, and on the other, salvation? Between the Virgin and the Serpent, what distance! Between their works, what an abyss! To the one we owe the shedding abroad of the deadly venom; to the other, the mysteries of salvation. The one offers

[1] *Roman Liturgy*, Seventh, Eighth, and Ninth *Lessons of the New Office of the Immaculate Conception.* They are taken from a Homily of Saint Germanus.

us but a guilty temptation; to the other we are indebted for the admirable succour which has been afforded us by the majesty of the Redeemer. The Serpent brought in death upon the earth, and behold, the Son of Mary raises up again, and restores to liberty poor captive human nature.[1]

The Virgin Mary, the spotless Virgin, has shone upon the world like a brilliant star. Eve had closed upon us the gates of Paradise; Mary has opened them wide. We were in perfect darkness; Mary has brought back to us the joy of the ancient light. Virgin Mary, pray for us.[2]

Liturgy of Pope Saint Xystus.

(Martyred A.D. 120.)

Miserable and unworthy sinners although we be, O my God, we give thanks to Thee in all things, and because of all things.

[1] Ambrosian Liturgy, *Dominica Sexta in Adventu*, Præfatio.
[2] *Ambrosian Liturgy.* Preface to the Nativity and to the Presentation.

' Above all, and before all, we here make mention of the holy and blessed Mother of God, Mary ever Virgin. Be mindful of Thy Mother, O my God, and may her most pure and holy prayers obtain at last our pardon. Amen.[1]

Prayers from the Græco-Sclavonian Liturgies.

O Immaculate Virgin, God is made flesh by the hypostatic union with the body, which He took from thee, and yet remains, as ever, incorporeal in His Divine Essence.[2]

The voice of all creation salutes thee, saying: Hail, Virgin most holy, hail, thou from whom the mystic grape has sprung, hail, Gate of heaven, hail, Joy of all, hail, Gladness of Apostles, hail, Succour and Protectress of all upon earth, who praise thee.[3]

It is meet and right, O Blessed Virgin, that we should sing hymns in praise of thee, but in truth we cannot extol thee worthily, and

[1] *Liturgia Sancti Xysti, Papæ Romani.* Renaudot ii. 163.
[2] *Theotokia of the Græco Sclavonian Liturgy.* Office of SS. Peter and Paul.   [3] *Ibid.* No. 4.

therefore it is that we praise thee silently, honouring without words the ineffable mystery, which was operated, O blessed One, in thee.[1]

O holy Virgin, open to us those immortal arms which have borne the Creator, who in His mercy made Himself Flesh. And pray Him to deliver us from all temptations, from evil passions, and from every danger.[2]

O Virgin, most beloved of God, extinguish by the dew of thy mercy, the burning fires of our evil nature, and kindle the extinguished light of our hearts with the flame of thy golden and radiant lamp; O most Immaculate One![3]

Prayer to Mary Immaculate to obtain the Return of the Russian Church to Catholic Unity.

Full of confidence in thee, O Mother of God and Ever-Virgin, together with our separated brethren, we honour in thy con-

---

[1] *Theotokia of the Græco Sclavonian Liturgy.* Office of SS. Peter and Paul. No. 30.
[2] *Ibid.* No. 24.   [3] *Ibid.* No. 43.

ception the foundation of our Redemption, the source of grace and the stay of our hope. Listen favourably, O Mary, to the prayer which we offer up to thee for these our brethren, who, with us, address thee as "All-holy, Disposer of the gifts of God," and "that Blessed One by whom we obtain all good." Grant that, acknowledging at last the divine authority of Peter, whom they themselves designate the "Foundation of the Church and of the Apostles, Bearer of the Keys of the Kingdom of Heaven, indestructible basis of our faith," they may speedily be restored to the obedience of the Roman Pontiff, whom, in the person of the great St. Leo, they call their "Pastor, Inheritor of the Throne and Primacy of Peter, and Head of the Church." Amen.[1]

[1] This prayer is composed of passages taken from the Græco-Sclavonian Liturgy, given by Father Toudini, Barnabite. The Sovereign Pontiff has granted his especial Benediction to the *Association for Prayers* which has been founded by the Barnabites of Paris, (convent, 64, rue de Monceau) for the conversion of Russia.

The Greek Liturgy.

Immaculate Mother of God, none upon earth is innocent as thou, thou who hast conceived the true God, the Conqueror of death.

Thou art the spotless Vase, the Temple unprofaned, the sacred Ark, the Virginal Sanctuary, the Beauty of Jacob, the Choice of God. Strength and glory are born of thee, O Lady, for the salvation of all who were perishing, and thou wilt snatch from the gates of hell those who proclaim thee blessed. Our original transgression made us return to earth. Through thee, there is deliverance from corruption and death; thy hand, O Mary, has raised us from earth to heaven.[1]

The Judge of the living and the dead, Whom thou hast supernaturally clothed with the mantle of our flesh, this supreme Judge saves whom He will from the punishments of another life; but above all, those who honour,

[1] *Greek Liturgy:* Officium Exsequiarum. Cf. the *Euchologion* of Goar, p. 525.

love, and praise Him; and those who also love, honour, and praise thee, O Blessed Virgin Mary.[1]

Towards thee do I turn my heart, O Holy Virgin, who hast exercised thy maternal authority over the Son of God. None can refuse to praise thee, O purest One. Heal then the wounds of my soul. Conduct me through the dawn of penance to the fulness of thy light.[2]

The Armenian Liturgy.

Holy God, who rejoicest in the eternal happiness of Thy saints, Whom the Seraphim adore with a thrice-repeated *Sanctus*, Whom the Cherubim glorify, and Who art worshipped by all the celestial virtues. Nothing was, and Thou hast given being to all creatures. Thou hast made man after Thine own image and likeness; Thou hast adorned him with graces, and taught him how to seek wisdom. Man fell, but instead of despising him, Thou

---

[1] *Greek Liturgy:* Officium Funereum in Sacerdotem vita functum.

[2] *Greek Liturgy:* Canon funereus pro pueris vita functis.

gavest him redemption. We are unworthy, we are as nothing. Nevertheless, Thou didst suffer us to present ourselves before the holy and glorious altar where we are permitted to offer Thee acceptable adoration and praise. Sanctify our souls, our understandings, and our bodies, and grant us, Lord, during the whole course of our lives, to offer Thee a worship worthy of Thee; THROUGH THE INTERCESSION OF THE HOLY MOTHER OF GOD, and of all the Saints, whom Thou hast loved from the beginning of the world. To Thee, my God, be Holiness, to Thee, Glory, Power, and Honour, now and for ever. Amen.

The holy Church of God proclaims the incorruptibility of the Virgin Mary, Mother of God. She it is, who has given us the Bread of immortality and the Chalice of joy. Bless, therefore, the holy Virgin, praise her in spiritual songs. O Mary, pray for us.[1]

---

[1] Both from the Armenian Liturgy. *Codex mysterii Missæ Armenorum, sive liturgia Armena*, published at Rome in 1677.

The Mozarabic Liturgy.

Eternal God, supreme Father, behold us prostrate before the Clemency of Thy Divinity. Thou hast taken by the hand the most glorious Virgin Mary; and Thy Son, Who is also her Son, has conducted her after death to the immeasurable heights of heaven, amongst the splendid Legions of the Angels, amongst the Cohorts of the Prophets, in the midst of the glorious Company of the Apostles, the Choir of Virgins, and the holy Army of Martyrs. No man has ever been honoured by so exalted an Assumption, and no woman but Mary has ever been admitted to so great a glory; for she alone remained a virgin after childbirth; she alone divinely gave birth to the God of heaven and earth; she alone carried in her bosom the Word made Man. We pray Thee, we supplicate Thee, O Lord, that as Thou hast bestowed a gift so infinite upon the Virgin Mary, Thou wouldst in like manner grant to Thy Church throughout the world, strength to resist all attacks of her enemies, that by Thy aid she may remain unshaken in the faith, uncorrupt in morals. May she be holy in her priests, glorious in her religious orders, valiant in her martyrs, and immaculate in her virgins. To the poor and to the orphans grant abundance, to the married fruitfulness, to the widow continence. Guard tenderly the captives and the poor, raise the fallen, console the desolate, restrain the voluptuous.

In Thy Church and by Thy Church have pity upon all the despairing; be the Lord of the living, and the desired Rest of the faithful departed. Amen, amen.[1]

O Virgin Mother of God, whose Assumption to the celestial heights we celebrate, we beg of thee (unworthy sinners as we are)

[1] *Mozarabic Liturgy.* In Festo Assump. Sanctæ Mariæ Virginis.

that by the power of thy holy prayers, we may be one day raised to that place of beatitude where the glory of thy Assumption — this new miracle by which God was pleased to honour thee, O Mary—shines forth.

May thy admirable virginity intercede for us before Him, Who, after thy death, and when the course of thy earthly life was ended, transported thee from earth to heaven—and by thy intercession may our prayers be heard unceasingly before the throne of God.

Cleansed by thy means from all stain, may we merit to live in heaven above in the company of angels. Amen.[1]

THE ORIENTAL LITURGIES.

Jerusalem.

We supplicate Thee, O God, and before all we unweariedly commemorate before Thee her who is truly blessed: her whom all the nations of the earth unite in praising, even

[1] Same Source.

the holy and blessed Mother of God, Mary, ever Virgin.[1]

Liturgy of S. James.

May God be propitious to us, through the prayer and intercession of the Immaculate Virgin, the Holy Mother of God, Mary whom we beheld clothed with justice, and who is the second heaven.[2]

Alexandria.

Deign O Lord to be mindful of all those who since the beginning of the world have done that which is pleasing unto Thee: the holy Fathers, Patriarchs, Prophets, Apostles, all Preachers of the Truth; the Evangelists, Martyrs, Confessors, and all just souls who have spent their lives in the service of Christ. But above all, remember the most holy,

[1] *Liturgia Sancti Jacobi Apostoli*, according to the use of the Jacobites of Syria. We have divided the Oriental Liturgies into as many groups as they have principal centres.

[2] *Ordo generalis liturgiæ secundum ritum Syrorum Jacobitarum.* Cf. Renaudot, ii. 25.

glorious and Immaculate One, whom Thou hast filled with benedictions, Mary, our Lady; Mary, Mother of God; Mary, Ever-Virgin. Amen.[1]

The Liturgy of Antioch.

O my God, we commemorate before Thee all the Saints, whom we are about to name, and in order to secure their intercession, we introduce into Thy presence before all others Mary, the holy Mother of God; and next unto her, John the Baptist, the forerunner of our Lord; then the Deacon and first Martyr, Saint Stephen, and all the Army of Saints, Prophets, Apostles, Martyrs, Confessors, and all whose names are written in the Book of Life. Deign, in Thy divine tranquillity, to listen to the prayers of all these intercessors, and may Thy mercy incline Thee to grant their requests. Behold, we also, with them, offer to Thee our poor and imperfect prayers.

---

[1] *Liturgia Sancti Basilii Alexandrinæ*: Renaudot, i. 73. Cf. Liturgia Sancti Gregorii Alexandrinæ, and especially Liturgia Sancti Marci, and Liturgia Sancti Jacobi Apostoli.

We ask of Thee, O Lord, not to turn from us Thy divine Face, nor to withdraw Thyself from us in Thy anger, nor bruise us in Thy wrath; but may we be in the hands of Thy mercy, and may Thy superabundant goodness grant us pardon. Make to shine before us, as before Thy chosen people, the resplendent brightness of Thy Countenance, for in nothing dost Thou so delight as in the salvation of souls. To Thee belong all peace and salvation. Glory to Thee, with endless praises, glory to Thee, and to Thy only Son. Amen.[1]

The Liturgy of Constantinople.

O Virgin, at the very moment when Gabriel pronounced the words, *Ave Maria, gratia plena*, the God of all creation was incarnate within thee, as in a Sanctuary. The heavens are great, but thou wert then far greater, thou who wert bearing the Creator. Glory to Him, Who made His dwelling-place in thy bosom;

[1] *Liturgii Sancti Ignatii.* Renaudot, ii. 205.

glory to Him, Who was born of thee; glory to Him, Who by this blessed child-bearing has delivered the world.

And thou, who hast brought forth God, pray Him to save the souls of all. Amen.[1]

The Liturgy of Ethiopia.

All who are the ministers of thine altar, priest, deacon, clergy and Christian people, and I also thy poor unworthy servant, I also, miserable sinner, I pray with them to receive absolution from the mouth of the Blessed Trinity, Father, Son, and Holy Spirit, and I ask it, in the name of Mary, who is the second heaven. Hail, Virgin Mary; hail, Mother of God, thou who art the golden censer which hast carried the burning fire, which effaces and destroys all sin, for it is the Lord God, the Word Incarnate within thy bosom, Who is offered to the Father as an incense and a sacrifice most precious.

[1] *Liturgy of Saint Chrysostom.*

The Coptic Liturgy.

O Mary, the Holy Ghost the Comforter, even the Paraclete, descended upon thy Son in the waters of the Jordan, under the form of Noe's Dove.

And thou also, thou art the Dove which hast announced to us Peace, even that Peace divine which came down from heaven for men.

Thou also, O Virgin, art our Hope; thou art the spiritual Dove, and thou hast bestowed upon us the gift of Mercy, borne by thee in thy bosom.

The Liberator of our race is Jesus, even the Son of the Father; Who was born of thee, O Mary.[1]

[1] *Coptic Liturgy: Ordo ad faciendum catechumenum et Christianum.* Coptice editus, Assemani, Codd. liturg. i. 141. Cardinal Pitra, who published this text in the First Volume of his *Jus Ecclesiasticum Græcorum*, p. 644, adds, that this prayer is *Athanasianæ odore vetustatis respersa.*"

THE EARLY AND MEDIÆVAL FATHERS OF THE CHURCH.

First Century.

There exists a document which is by many learned critics assigned to the Apostolic age. It consists of a letter written by the priests and deacons of Achaia, in which they narrate the acts of the martyrdom of S. Andrew the Apostle. . . . In this letter S. Andrew, speaking of OUR LORD, is represented as saying that "*He was born of a blameless Virgin.*"[1]

There is, says Father Harper, another document, which is considered by some to be the work of an Apostle. . . . . . It is at all events an important witness to the Apostolic tradition. In the Liturgy that is called after the name of S. James the Apostle, we find the following words in four

---
[1] *Gallandas*, T. 1, quoted by Fr. Harper in his work, *Peace through the Truth.*

several parts of the Mass: "The most holy, immaculate, most glorious Mother of God, our Lady and Ever-Virgin Mary." "All blameless and Mother of our God, more to be honoured than the Cherubim, and more glorious beyond comparison than the Seraphim."

Second Century.

We give the testimony of three great doctors of this century.

Saint Justin Martyr.

(A.D. 120-169.)

We know that Jesus Christ, before all creatures, proceeded from His Father by His power and will, and by means of the Virgin became Man, that by that way also it might have an undoing. For Eve, being a virgin and undefiled, conceiving the word that was from the serpent, brought forth disobedience and death; but the Virgin Mary, taking faith and joy, when the angel told her the good tidings, that the Spirit of the Lord should come upon her, and the power of the Highest overshadow her, and therefore the Holy One that was born of her was Son of God, answered, Be it to me according to thy word.[1]

Tertullian.

(A.D. 160-240.)

God recovered His image and likeness which the Devil had seized, by a rival operation. For into Eve, as yet a virgin, had crept the word which was the framer of death. Equally into a virgin was to be introduced the Word of God, which was the builder up of life; that, what by that sex had gone into perdition, by the same sex might be brought back to salvation. Eve had believed the serpent; Mary believed Gabriel, the fault which the one committed by believing, the other by believing has blotted out."[2]

Saint Irenæus.

"With a fitness, Mary the Virgin is found obedient, saying, Behold thy handmaid, O Lord, be it according to Thy word. But Eve

[1] Tryph. 100.   [2] De Carne Christi, 17.

was disobedient, for she obeyed not, while she was yet a virgin. As she having indeed Adam for a husband, but as yet being a virgin, becoming disobedient, became the cause of death both to herself and to the whole human race; so also Mary, having the predestined man, and being yet a virgin, being obedient, became both to herself and to the whole human race the cause of salvation.[1]

And again: as Eve by the speech of an angel was seduced, so as to flee God, transgressing His word, so also Mary received the good tidings by means of the angel's speech, so as to bear God within her, being obedient to His word."

S. Justin represents Palestine; Tertullian, Africa and Rome, Asia Minor and Gaul; or rather he represents S. John the Evangelist, for he had been taught by S. Polycarp who was the intimate associate, as of S. John, so also of the other Apostles.

[1] Adv. Hœr. iii. 22-24.   [2] *Ibid.* v. 19.

Third Century.

Saint Dionysius of Alexandria.

In a letter written by this Saint to the heresiarch Paul of Samosata, he speaks of Our Lady as "Christ's Tabernacle not made with hands;" and says that "Christ was conceived in the womb of the Blessed Virgin Mary, the Holy Ghost descending upon her, and as He alone knew the order of His conception and birth, preserving the Mother incorruptible and blessed from head to foot; a Virginal Paradise."

These expressions have a sort of synodical authority, this letter being written on the part of the Antiochene Fathers, and the expression of their doctrine,

Saint Hippolytus, Bishop of Porto,

Who was a pupil of Clement of Alexandria and coeval with Origen, has these words:

"And the Ark of incorruptible wood was

the Saviour. . . But the Lord was without sin, made as regards his human nature of incorruptible wood, *i. e.*, of the Virgin and the Holy Ghost, covered over within and without, as it were, with the most pure gold of God the Word."

Saint Gregory Thaumaturgus.

Present at the first Council of Antioch, A.D. 264.

"'*Hail, full of grace!*' no longer shall the Devil be against thee; For where the enemy in times past inflicted a wound, there first does the Physician now apply the remedy of salvation. Whence death proceeded, there life shall find entrance. By a woman woes flowed forth; and by a woman blessings are showered down. Hail, full of Grace! Blush not that a woman has been the cause of damnation; for thou shalt be the Mother of the Judge and the Redeemer. Hail Immaculate spouse and mother of a widowed world! Hail, thou who didst drown in thy womb the death of mother Eve."

"All the celestial Power salute thee, the Holy Virgin, by my mouth. And what is more, He who is Lord of all has chosen thee, the holy and all-adorned one, from among all creatures; and by thy holy and chaste, pure and immaculate womb, the bright shining pearl comes forth for the salvation of the whole world, since thou hast been made the holy one, and more glorious, more pure, and more saintly, than all the rest of human kind, having a mind whiter than snow, and thy soul more purified than the finest gold."[1]

[1] This homily has been variously ascribed, now to the wonder-working S. Gregory, now to S. John Chrysostom, now again to Macarius of Philadelphia. All seem to be agreed that it is a learned document of these earliest ages of the Church. Fr. Harper, *Peace through the Truth;* p. 346, and p. 402.

Hom. 2a in Annunc. For the authenticity, same remark as above, Fr. Harper, p. 402.

Fourth Century.

Saint Ephrem Syrus.

(Died in 379.)

Ordained priest by S. Basil, one of the four doctors of the Greek Church. His praises are celebrated by S. Gregory of Nyssa, S. Chrysostom, S. Bazil, Theodoret, S. Jerome, and others, who called him "the master of the world;" and the "Euphrates of the Church;" and who tell us that his writings were publicly read in many churches next after the divine Scriptures.

"My Lady, most holy Mother of God, full of grace, blessed Mother of God, most pleasing to God, Receptacle of the Divinity of thy only begotten Son, fiery Throne far more glorious than the four-formed (*of Ezechiel*) of the Immortal and Invisible Father; all-Pure, all-Immaculate, wholly without spot, all-Unpolluted, all-Blameless, all-Praiseworthy, all-Incorrupt, wholly most blessed, all-Inviolate, all-Venerable, all-Honourable, wholly to be blessed and praised and honoured and desired, Virgin in soul and body and mind. Throne of the King who sitteth above the Cherubim, Heavenly gate through which we hasten from earth to heaven; Bride of God by whom we are reconciled, unexpected Miracle, inexplicable Utterance, Manifestation of the hidden mystery of God, invincible Defence, powerful Aid, living Fountain, exhaustless Ocean of Divine and unutterable graces and gifts, Height more sublime than that of the heavenly Powers, unfathomable Depth of hidden counsels, common Glory of nature, Exuberance of all things noble, Queen of all after the Trinity, the other Paraclete after the Paraclete; and, after the Mediator, Mediatrix of the whole world. Chariot of the intellectual Sun—that true light which lighteneth every man coming into the world, Bearing Him Who beareth all things by the Word; the Immaculate Vesture of Him Who clothes Himself with light as with a garment; Bridge of the whole World that leadeth us to the highest heaven, Higher and far more glorious beyond all comparison than Cherubim and Seraphim, Brightness of the angels, Safety of men, Key that opens heaven to us, Mother and Handmaid of that Star which knows no setting, Brightness of the true and mystical Day, Abyss of the unsearchable goodness of God, chariot divine and famous; Book written by the hand of God, by which the handwriting of Adam has been destroyed; Mountain of God, holy Mountain in which it hath pleased God to dwell; Root of Jesse, City of God, of which, says David, glorious things are spoken; Release from sorrow, Freedom from captivity, Deification of mortals, Beautiful Nature and removed from all possibility of blame, which springs forth from the frankincense of virginity, and fills the world with its perfume. Gate of Ezechiel looking towards the East, Masterpiece of the tremendous economy of grace, Lovely dwelling-place of the divine

Abasement, Reconciliation of the world, our Propitiation and our Refuge. Most desirable of all glorious gifts, flame-bearing sword-hilt which Isaias beheld. Mountains shaded with virtues which Habbakuk foresaw, Mountain of Daniel from which the stone was cut out without hands, sealed Book which no one may read, invisible Confidence of those who conquer, Firmness of Kings, Glory of priests, Remission of offences, Appeaser of the just Judge. . . . Delight after God of my soul, heaven-falling Rain to my parched heart. . . . My Lady, my Joy, my Splendour, my sleepless Advocacy with God, and since thou art the Mother of Him, Who alone is good and merciful, receive my miserable soul and deign to place it by thy mediation and defence at the right hand of thy only Son, and in the repose of His Elect and of His Saints. . . . .

"Wherefore also considering it as His own glory to yield to thy intercessions, He fulfils thy petitions as though it were an obligation.

Mother of my God, above all measure fondest of names. . . . . I confide in thee who did most truly bring forth according to the flesh the true God; to Whom is due all glory, honour, and adoration, with the unoriginated Father and His all-holy and good and life-giving Spirit, now and ever throughout all ages. Amen."[1]

Fourth Century.
Saint Basil of Seleucia.

(One of the Fathers present at the Council of Chalcedon.)

He addresses the Blessed Virgin in this wise, "O sacred Womb which received God, in which the handwriting of sin was torn to pieces. What gifts sufficiently worthy of her can we offer; of Whom all earthly things are unworthy. Amaranthine Paradise of chastity,

---

[1] S. Ephrem Syrus, *Precatio ad Deiparam*. This is very much longer in the original, which is throughout a hymn, as it were, in praise of Mary. *Sermo de sanctissimæ Dei genitricis Mariæ laudibus*, edition of Vossius, Antwerp, 1619, ii. 541. See also the eloquent prayer by the same Father in the Parisian Breviary in the Office for the Commemoration of the Vow of Louis XIII.

Mediatrix between God and man, Temple truly worthy of God; O all-holy Virgin, of whom, he who says all that is venerable and glorious errs not from the truth, but fails in duly exalting thy merit."

Saint Ephipanius.

(A.D. 310.)

O Virgin, sacred Treasure of the Church, Virgin whom we can call both Priestess and Altar, because thou hast prepared for us the table, and hast given us the Bread of Life, even Christ, for the remission of sin. What more can I say? Urged by the desire to praise thee, O Mother of God, and held back by my insufficiency, I will again say that thou art the Heaven and the Throne, at the same time the Cross, whose sacred arms have borne the Saviour. The angels accused Eve; thee O Mary, they glorify, who hast lifted up fallen Eve, and hast raised to heaven Adam driven from Paradise. By thee, indeed, O Holy Virgin, the wall of separation has been thrown down, the peace of heaven has been bestowed upon the world, men have become angels; the Cross has shone upon the whole earth, death is conquered and hell despoiled. By thee have the idols been overthrown and the Divine Doctrine propagated; and, finally, by thee have we known the only Son of God, Whom thou, O Virgin, hast brought forth, even Jesus Christ our Saviour, Whom men and angels adore. We believe in the Father Eternal, the Son Eternal, and the Holy Ghost Eternal; and we glorify the indivisible and consubstantial Trinity, for ever and ever.[1]

Fifth Century.

Saint Cyril, Patriarch of Alexandria.

Hail, Mary, Mother of God, Treasure worthy of Veneration, belonging to the whole Universe. Lamp of inextinguishable light,

[1] S. Epiphanius, Bishop of Salamina in Cyprus, 310-403. *Adversus hæreses*, lib. iii., v. ii., p. 18. Translated by Aug. Nicolas; in "*La Vièrge Marie vivant dans l'Eglise,*" ii. 160, 161.

Crown of Virginity, Sceptre of Orthodoxy, indestructible Temple, Abode of Him Whom no place can contain; Virgin and Mother. . . . . Hail, thou who didst bear the Uncontainable; thou by whom the Trinity is glorified, by whom the precious Cross is made known and adored in all the world ; by whom the heavens exult, by whom Angels and Archangels rejoice, by whom devils are put to flight, by whom the Tempter, the Evil One, is hurled from the heights of heaven ; by whom the fallen creature is received up into heaven; by whom the whole Creation, fettered in the chains of an insane idolatry, has come to a knowledge of the truth, and Baptism is given to them that believe ; by whom the Oil of Gladness, by whom Churches have been founded everywhere, and all nations are brought to penance! And what shall I say more ? By whom the only begotten Son of God has appeared all bright and glorious to poor humanity seated in darkness, and in the shadow of death ; by whom prophets prophesied; by whom apostles preached to all nations the doctrine of salvation. By whom the dead are raised to life, by whom kings reign through the grace of the Holy Trinity. What man is there who may enumerate the multitudinous Graces of Mary? That Virgin's Womb! O Miracle! The wonder strikes me dumb with amazement.[1]

Saint Ambrose.

(Died, 397.)

O Mary, we will keep our eyes steadfastly fixed upon thy life, that we may there contemplate the true portrait of virginity, and behold, shining as in a mirror, the rays of purity, and the beauty of virtue. On this model are impressed the features of the loftiest perfection; after this pattern ought virgins to form their life, and learn therefrom what they have to correct in their conver-

---

[1] Discourse of S. Cyril of Alexandria at the first Session of the Council of Ephesus, A.D. 431. See Labbe, ii. 583-586.

sation and imitate in their life. Thou, O Mary, wert ever a virgin, not only in body, but in mind. Thy guilelessness rendered thee incapable of the least disguise or of the slightest deceit. Thou wert humble of heart, grave in thy words, wise in thy designs: not given to much speaking, but diligent in thy study of the sacred books. Never didst thou place thy confidence in uncertain riches, but in the prayers of the poor. Always wert thou profitably employed, and discreet in thy discourse; permitting no other witness of thy inmost heart but God alone.

Far from giving pain, it was thy pleasure to do good to every one; rendering to thy "superiors" all honour, and never being envious of thine "equals"; fleeing vain glory, acting in all things according to reason, and ardently delighting in good.

Thy look was full of sweetness; thy bearing of humility; and thy actions of modesty: thy whole exterior being so ordered that thy countenance reflected the image of thy soul, and thy unvarying demeanour was a complete example of every virtue.

So wide was the embrace of thy charity, that thou knewest not where to place its limit. If we may speak of the slightness of thy nourishment, thou didst refuse thyself the most necessary things, prolonging thy fasts through several days. Thy sleep was no more than absolute need demanded, and whilst thy body slumbered, thy soul was watching: yes, even the moments of thy repose were for thee a time of religion and of piety.

Never wert thou less sensible of loneliness than when alone; and how indeed couldst thou be lonely, having by thy side the holy Books, the Archangels, and the Prophets.

Need I marvel that the Evangelist S. John should have revealed unto us the most lofty and sublime mysteries of religion, having dwelt with her who was their channel and their sanctuary? Ave Maria.[1]

[1] *De Virginibus*, lib. ii., cap. ii. See also the French

Saint Augustine.

(A.D. 430.)

Thou, O Mary, hast perfectly fulfilled the Will of the Heavenly Father; thy greatest honour and blessedness is, not to have been the Mother, but the Disciple of Christ. Blessed art thou to have listened to the Word of God, and to have kept it within thy heart. Thou didst harbour the Truth of Christ in thy understanding, even more than His humanity within thy womb.

Woman incomparable, thou art corporally and spiritually Mother and Virgin. Mother of our Head, who is the Saviour, thou art also in very truth the Mother of all the members of Christ, even of ourselves, because by thy charity thou hast co-operated in the birth of the faithful into the Church. . . . . It is by

translation by the Rev. Father Joseph Duranti de Bonrecueil; Paris, 1729. The last paragraph is extracted from the *De Institutione Virginis*, cap. v., § 35. In the latter book S. Ambrose peremptorily refutes those who attack the perpetual virginity of Mary.

thee, O Mother of the Lord, that the dignity of virginity was established upon the earth, even by thee, O Mary, who wast worthy to bear a Son, without ceasing to be a Virgin. For the honour of the Saviour Jesus, I will not endure to hear thee mentioned, O Holy Mary, in connection with sin. Thou art the Beauty and the Dignity of the earth, O Virgin, and thou hast been ever the type of the holy Church. By one woman came death, and life by one. This last art thou, O Mother of God. Ave Maria.

SIXTH CENTURY.

Saint Anastasius the Sinaïte.

And who, tell me I pray, whether of men or devils, will dare to say that she, who is of the same essence with God as regards the flesh, is not after the image and likeness of Him Who was born of her? For how is she Mother of such a Son, if she bear not in herself whole and unbroken the image of her Offspring?

SEVENTH CENTURY.

From the Litanies of St. Ildefonsus, Archbishop of Toledo.

O Light of nations, Field where, in the sunlight, blossoms the Eternal Flower. Fair and fruit-laden Olive-tree; Virginal Country, the Possession of God; true Evangelist; living Sacrifice, bright Pledge of our immortality; cause of the richness of the Incarnation; Restorer of universal life, and Salvation of the universe.

SEVENTH AND EIGHTH CENTURIES.

St. Andrew of Crete.

(For the Feast of the Assumption.)

Arise: rise upwards into the peace of heaven, O Virgin, and appease the Creator in favour of His creation. Whilst thou wert here below, a little portion only of our earth had the honour of possessing thee, but now that thou hast been borne from earth to heaven, the entire Universe claims thee as the universal Propitiatrix, O thou who hast bestowed life, and who, yet more, by thy Son, art the life of all the living, and again yet more, the cause of life.[1]

As connecting links between the early Doctors and the Saints of the Middle Ages, we have, in the Eighth century, S. Fortunatus, who wrote the well-known hymn, *Qui terra, pontus, sidera;* and S. Aldhelm, who speaks of our Lady as "a Turtle dove, all pure and spotless." In the Ninth century Ratramnus, who calls her "the Gate of Light," and S. Paschasius Radbertus, who addresses her as the "Illuminatrix of the world." To the Tenth century we owe the *Ave Maris Stella.*

[1] St. Andrew of Crete, Seventh to Eighth Century. Trans. Auguste Nicolas.

Saints of the Middle Ages.

ELEVENTH CENTURY.

Saint Peter Damian.

It is our joy to think upon thee O Mary, Palace of the Eternal King, and City of God. Thou art the Sunrise and the Dawn of Light.

Thou art the Myrtle and the Rose amongst the flowers of Paradise, thou art the Beauty of heaven, the Deliverer of captives, and the Dread of demons.

Thou art the Anchor which has held our poor lost vessel in safety, the Treasure which has procured our ransom, the Salt of our earth, and the End of our night; Thou art the Sunday of our hearts, and the Magnet towards which our souls are drawn; Draw thou our souls into the Rest of heaven.

TWELFTH CENTURY.

Saint Anselm, Archbishop of Canterbury.

Temple of Grace, Habitation of Divine glory

and wisdom, O thou to whom the Lord God was pleased to confide all the secrets of the eternal plan, thou who didst sanctify the world upon which thou didst bring blessing; thou art the Queen of life and the means of the great Reconciliation.

Hail to thee, who dost win, ravish, and absorb all intelligences; Hail to thee, who art the Alleluia and the heavenly song of all Christian lips.

Thou art the dismay of the spirits of darkness over whom thou hast victoriously triumphed; everlasting Glory of angels and of men; Rest of the heart.

Hail, Arm ever stretched forth over us for our defence; Patroness and living Protection of sinners, Pilot of mankind, sweet Voice, reclaiming and cheering those who are tempted to despair; Help of virgins, Mother of orphans; Joy of all who suffer.

Hail thou Height to which thought cannot attain; fair Star brightening every darkness; Sun of radiant splendour, peaceful solitude;

Eternal Flower of the heavenly garden; Pearl of the skies; Wall of defence, ever affording us a refreshing shade; Inexhaustible Stream; Stream of grace and of mercy.

Thou art as the mind and soul of all Christians, thou art the model of Divine Grace; the commencement of true life, and the Mother of our Hope.

Thou art the contriver of Mercy, the Way of the soul to Paradise; the Gate of heaven.

Mary, pray for us.[1]

TWELFTH CENTURY.

Saint Bernard.

Thou, O Blessed Virgin, art the ground of our hope, and the representative of the time of mercy. Thou hast been, *O Inventrix Gratiæ*, the commencement of all good, and the origin of all consolation.

* * * * * * *

---

[1] St. Anselm: Cf. the Prayer of the same Saint, beginning:—*Maria, tu illa Maria, tu illa maxima beatarum Mariarum;* Bibl. Maz. 814. Bibl. Nat. 1196 (of the MSS. in both Libraries).

Thou art the Royal Way of our Saviour; the Lord God was, as it were, a poor traveller wandering upon our earth, and thou art the House wherein He found a welcome. Thou art the Court, thou the Castle, thou the Sanctuary of the great God; thou art His Sceptre, His Diadem, and His Throne. Thou art the anti-type of the valiant woman, and the Repository of the secrets of the Godhead.

No word is so sweet to utter as thy name. Thou art the purest Snow, whiter than all other snow. Thou art the Flower-garden of God, the Urn of gold, the heavenly Plant, the Violet of humility; the priceless Pearl, the munificent Present of God to man. Thou art that Firmament, in which God hung the Sun, thou art the Image and Reflection of this Sun divine. Thou art the abundant River of Goodness, freshening and purifying the earth. Thou art the centre of the Universe, and in thyself alone a resplendent World. Thou art the Science of all sciences, *tu es negotium sæculorum*; O Mary, who hast repaired the past and prepared the future of mankind, *Ora pro nobis!*[1]

THIRTEENTH CENTURY.

Prayer of St. Bonaventure.

(A.D. 1274.)

O my most sweet Advocate, Virgin Mother of the beloved Spouse of my soul, where wert thou, when for the love of me Jesus suffered so bitter a Passion? Wert thou not at the foot of the Cross? Yes, truly thou wert there, and still much more, for thou wert crucified in spirit on that Cross with thy Son. Nor was there any difference in these two crucifixions, save that He was crucified in His Body,

---

[1] The foregoing extract from the prayers of S. Bernard is taken from the *Index Marianus* of the Patrology of Migne.

Amongst the other Saints and Doctors of this century, whose prayers and hymns to Mary Immaculate remain to us, we have only space to mention Richard of S. Victor, S. Hugh, S. Amadeus of Lausanne, the Venerable Rupert, Honorious of Autun, Philippe de Harveng, and Pierre de Celles. In this century also lived Adam of S. Victor, who wrote, besides many other hymns and poems, the *Ante Thorum Virginalem.* See MS. 577, Bibl. Nat.

and thou in thy soul. And although the Wounds of His Flesh were separate, they were in some sort re-united in one in thy heart, that heart so full of sorrow and of love. That heart, O my sweet Lady, was truly crowned with thorns, transfixed with three rough nails, given to drink of gall and vinegar, covered with blood, insulted, lacerated, and transpierced. The holy Gospel makes use of this last word in speaking of the sword of anguish which should pierce through thy soul because of thy beloved Child. O my sweet Lady, why wouldst thou die, and die for me? Did not the death of the Son suffice, but must the Mother also be crucified? O wherefore was it, Lady most prudent, that thou didst not remain alone within thine own chamber? Wherefore camest thou to the hill of Calvary? Was it according to thy custom, or fitting for thee, to appear in a place of so great tumult and of so much shame? Wherefore could naught restrain thee, neither thy Virgin modesty, nor the fear natural to woman, nor the horror of so fearful a crime, nor the confusion of seeing thy Son on the Cross, nor the thought of thy reputation, nor the fear of being called the Mother of an executed criminal, nor the infamous character of the place, nor the shrinking from weeping thus bitterly in public, nor the multitude of thine enemies, nor the malice of the Jews who might crucify thee with thy Son? Alas! my sweetest Mother, wilt thou not speedily return to thy home, lest with thy Son I may also lose thee? Ah, who then should console me for the death of Jesus? Leave not my soul all lonely and uncomforted; let me not die thus. But O, all sorrowful Mother, full well I see that thou wilt not hearken unto me, nor give heed to my entreaties, being so bowed down with woe that thy whole heart and understanding are utterly absorbed in the Passion of thy Son.

But humbly, I implore thee, O my sweet Advocate, effectually to unite and fix my affections to the precious Wounds of Jesus my Lord, in which I desire to abide; and thou wilt at least have the consolation of being no more alone in thy love.

I ask of thee neither gold, nor silver, nor worldly pleasures, nor honours, nor riches; wounds and sorrows alone I ask of thee; refuse them not, my Mother; and pray for me![1]

[1] *L'Esquillon d'amour divine, lequel fist Bonne aventure.* Bibl. Nat. Fr. 927, Fifteenth Century. It is a translation from the *Stimulus Amoris.*

EARLY ENGLISH HYMNS TO THE BLESSED VIRGIN.

THE following Early English Hymns to the Blessed Virgin, we have ventured to copy from the *Month* for June–July, 1873. They were "selected from the *Old English Miscellany*, published in 1872, by the Early English Text Society, which took them from MSS. of the thirteenth century in the British Museum and other libraries. They have been arranged in modern garb, with as little interference as possible with the quaint Old English in which they were written." They necessarily suggest one reflection—"the proof they afford of the perfect identity in devotional thought and practice between the thirteenth and nineteenth centuries in the Catholic Church."

The Annunciation of the Virgin Mary.

From heaven to earth God greeting He sent
By a holy archangel—to Mary he went,
Full mild was that Maid, with all beauties besprent.
Then Gabriel greeting her, thus sayeth he:
O Maiden most blessed, while Maiden thou be
A child shall be born and engender'd of thee;
  Believe me, Mary.
Answered him Mary, in accent most mild,
How comes it to pass that I can be with child,
For with knowledge of man I have ne'er been defiled.
  In dread was that Maid.

  *   *   *   *   *   *   *   *

My heart thy sweet tidings right gladsome have made,
God's handmaid I own me, and well have I sped;
His will be accomplished, e'en as thou hast said.
Now pray we our Lord wheresoe'er we may be,
Who sent the archangel, sweet Maiden, to thee,
For love of His Mother, so gentle, that He
May bring us to bliss that lasts endlessly.

MARY VENERATED IN ALL AGES.

The Five Joys of the Virgin.

Here begin the Five Blisses of our Lady Saint Mary.

1 Lady, for that bliss of thine,
   The bliss that first thy bliss begun,
When thou couldst say on word Divine
   That Jesus was to be thy Son.
     Through such a world as this
     In sins our race we run:
     Oh, help us not to miss
     The life that is to come.

2 Mother, happy wast thou then,
   When thou sawest heaven's King
Born of thee, but not with pain,
   That shaped us and everything.
     Shield us from our foe,
     And give us thy blessing,
     And keep us evermo'
     From every wrong-doing.

3 Lady, if thou wert right
   To be so glad and blithe,
When Christ put forth His might
   And rose from death to life,

That all the world did dight,
  Yet child of woman is.
Then let Him wash us white
  With those five Wounds of His.

4 When from the Mount of Olivet
    Thy Son was rising up the sky,
  Thy eyes were sweetly on Him set,
    For he was to thy heart anigh.
  And there, too, He has made thy seat
    In one high place for thee designed,
  Whom Angels like to come and greet—
    Thou art so winning and so kind.

5 Last, the King thy bosom bore,
    Fetched thee up to heaven, to get thee
  The bliss that had been lost before,
    And beside Himself He set thee.
      Of old thou wert His choice,
        And fairly did He greet thee:
      Then how didst thou rejoice
        When angels came to meet thee!

Mother of Mercy, Maiden kind,
  I pray thee as my power is,
Let the world not make us blind;—
  The world is full of enemies.

Oh, that thou help us at life's end,
    Thou that God and Man didst bear,—
And us all to heaven send
    When this world fails us, is my prayer.

Hear, Jesus, what Thy Mother says,
    That is so beautiful and bright,
That is Queen, most sure it is,
    Of heaven and earth by truest right.
Make us clean of all our sin,
    And give our eyes the endless light;
Mean us for heaven, and bring us in;
    Lord, have the will, Thou hast the might.

An Orison of our Lady.

On her I rest my life along,
    Of whom I will the praises sing:
Her I will herald men among;
    She did for us deliv'rance bring,
From pain of hell so sharp and strong;
    She brought us bliss so sweet and long—
All through her holy childbearing.
I pray her grant unto the song
    I now indite, a good ending,
        Though we do wrong.

Thou art our health, and life, and light,
   Thou helpest all the human race,
By thee we are full richly dight,
   'Tis thou bestowest joy and peace.
Thou broughtest day, and Eve brought night;
   She brought us woe, thou bringest right;
She brought us sin, thou bringest grace:
   Oh, look to me, thou Lady bright,
When I shall quit my earthly place,
     As well thou might.

This world shall all to ruin go,
   With sorrow and affliction sore;
And all this life we shall forego,
   Nor is it well to grieve therefore.
This world is not without our foe,
   For which I think to let it go,
And square my deeds, by God's wise lore:
   Earth's pleasure is not worth a sloe,
My God, Thy mercy I implore
     For evermore.

A fool too long I've borne to be,
   My folly turns to guilty fear:
I've loved to have delight and glee,
   And proud and dainty robes to wear:
Delusion all I plainly see.
   Therefore I purpose sin to flee,

And all my past besotted cheer.
  Look, gentle Lady, pray I thee;
Uphold and cherish, teach and rear
    Poor wayward me.

For guilt I cry me welladay,
  Sinful I am, and sad and wretched;
Lady, be thou my timely stay.
  Ere to the grave me death hath fetched,
Repent I will without delay.
  Then let me live and mend my way,
Lest by the devil I be catched:
  I sorrow for my sinful play:
I reck not of this world so gay:
    Mercy, I pray.

A Song to the Virgin.

Of one that is so fair and bright
    Velut maris stella,
Brighter than the day is light,
    Parens et puella.
I cry to thee, see thou to me,
Lady, pray thy Son for me,
    Tam pia,
That I may come to thee,
    Maria.

In sorrow counsel thou art best,
    Felix fecundata;
Of the weary thou art rest
    Mater honorata:
Pray to Him in mildest mood
That for us shed all His blood
    In cruce,
That we may come to Him
    In luce.

All this world was sore forlorn,
    Eva peccatrice,
Till our Lord therein was born
    De te genitrice.
With glad *Ave* sped away
Murky night, and comes the day
    Salutis;
The well—it springeth out of thee,
    Virtutis.

Lady, flower of everything,
    Rosa sine spina,
Thou bearest Jesus, heavenly King,
    Gratia divina.
Of all, thou bringest forth the prize,
O Lady, Queen of Paradise
    Electa,

Maiden mild—a Mother
> *Es effecta.*

Well He wots He is thy Son
> *Ventre quem portasti;*
Thee He will deny no boon
> *Parvum Quem portasti!*
So kindly and so good He is,
He hath brought us unto bliss
> *Superni,*
That hath hidden the foul pit
> *Inferni.*

A Prayer to the Virgin.

O, blessed art thou, Lady, full of heaven's best bliss,
Sweet Mother of all mildness,—Flower of Paradise!
Pray Jesus Christ thy Son, who the true Guide only is,
That wretched me, where'er I be, in ne land He miss.

I will to thee, fair Lady, mine orison begin:
O Mother, teach me sweetly thy dear Son's love to win;

For sigh I must, nor wot I to keep my sorrow in,
Till thou in gentle mercy shall bring me out of sin.

Oft I thy dear pity seek, oft on thy great name call,—
My flesh is foul, this world is false, O help me lest I fall;
Lady, shield and keep me free from all the pains of hell,
And bring me to the blessedness the which no tongue may tell.

They make me sad, O Lady, the works that I have-done:
I cry full oft, oh, hear me — thy name I call upon—
For if I have not help from thee, other there is none
To help; help me well thou mightest; thou helpest many a one.

O, blessed be thou, Lady, who art so fair and bright,
My hope is in thee only,—in thee by day and night—
O, help, then, in thy mildness, full well thou hast the might,

That ne'er for friend's friendship I lose eternal light.

Queen so bright and beautiful, thy Son's ruth I implore;
Of the sins that I have done it rueth me full sore;
Thee oft have I forsaken, but, Lady, never more—
For thy sake—will I hearken to Satan's crafty lore.

O, blessed art thou, Lady, that art so kind and bland,
Pray Jesus Christ thy Son to me His dearest grace to send,
Where'er I be, that ere my way hence from earth I wend,
I may win in Paradise the bliss withouten end.

Bright Queen of Stars, and beauteous, O do thou light me here;
In this false and fickle world so me direct and steer,
That at my ending day I no fiend may have to fear.
O Jesus, with Thy sweet Blood Thou boughtest me full dear.

Jesus, holy Mary's Son, O, hear me from Thy throne;
To cry to Thee I dare not, to her I make my moan;
Vouchsafe, then, that for her sweet sake I cleansèd be so clean,
That at day of doom I miss not Thy fair face serene.

Parchemin, encre ne cire,
Ne porroit durer ne suffire,
Por voy que l'on vosist ton sen, ta bonteit dire,
Et seuxent tous cès escrire
Qui furent seront et sont neis.[1]

Our little book cannot be more properly concluded than in the words by which, on the 8th of December, 1854, the Vicar of Jesus Christ, our own Pius IX., in the presence of the vast concourse of Catholic Bishops who thronged the Basilica of St. Peter, solemnly

---

[1] Neither parchment, ink, nor wax, could last or suffice to show all that one would of thy wisdom or tell of thy goodness, nor all those to write it, who have been, shall be, or are, born.—*Bibl. de l'Arsenal*, T. L. 319, 13th century. Cf. the Song of Pièrre de Carbiac, Troubadour of the same century, beginning, "*Donna dels Angels regina.*"—Rochequde, p. 302.

defined the Immaculate Conception of Mary to be an article of faith :—

"In honour of the most Holy and Undivided Trinity, for the glory and ornament of the Virgin Mother of God, for the exaltation of the Catholic Faith and the spread of the Christian religion, by the authority of our Lord Jesus Christ, of the blessed Apostles Peter and Paul, and by our own, we pronounce and define, that the doctrine, which maintains that the most blessed Virgin Mary, in the first moment of her conception, was, by a singular grace and privilege of Almighty God, in regard of the merits of Christ Jesus, the Saviour of the human race, preserved free from the stain of original sin, has been revealed by God, and is, therefore, to be firmly and constantly believed by all the faithful."

AVE MARIA,

GRATIA PLENA.

BY THE SAME AUTHOR.

THE LIFE OF PAUL SEIGNERET,

SEMINARIST OF SAINT SULPICE;

Shot at Belleville, Paris, May 26th, 1871.

Fcap 8vo, 1s.; stronger bound, 1s. 6d.; gilt, 2s.

Preface.—"In perusing the following account of Paul Seigneret, the reader may, perhaps, be inclined to ask why a life so simple, and, until the approach of its close, so devoid of anything remarkable, was written.

"The answer is, because in that life there was an integrity and consistency which turned every circumstance into a means of preparation for its end. It is the noviciate of a saint which is presented for contemplation; the story of one who 'being made perfect in a short time, fulfilled a long time,' and whose spirit of self-devotion, whether for life or death, together with his generous love of suffering, so fitted him for his early crown."

OPINIONS OF THE PRESS.

The Universe.—"This is an affecting and well-told narrative of the childhood and youth and heroic fate of that brave young Sulpician, who was brutally murdered by the Communists, at Belleville, during the cowardly reign of the Rochefort party after the horrors of the reign of Paris. It will necessarily be a great favourite, especially with our pure-minded, high-spirited young people."

Weekly Register.—"Should find its way into every Catholic household. We commend it to parents with sons under their care, and especially do we recommend it to those who are charged with the education and training of our Catholic youth, to whom the fervent piety and devotion which were the ever-prevailing characteristics in the life of this young servant of God, furnish an example well worthy of their imitation."

Tablet.—"An interesting account of the life and death of one of the many victims of the Paris Commune. Though only twenty-six, and not yet in Priest's orders, Paul Seigneret was remarkable for the simplicity and the heroism of both his natural and religious character."

R. Washbourne, 18 Paternoster Row, London.

BY THE SAME AUTHOR.

ROSALIE; Or, THE MEMOIRS OF A FRENCH CHILD.

WRITTEN BY HERSELF.

Translated from Mémoires d'une petite fille, par Mdlle. JULIE GOURAUD.

Fcap 8vo, 1s.; stronger bound, 1s. 6d.; gilt, 2s.

OPINIONS OF THE PRESS.

UNIVERSE.—" A really elegant translation of a pretty French book for the amusement and teaching of children. The tenth chapter is beautiful."

TABLET.—" It is prettily told, and in a natural manner. Rosalie does not make too much of her virtues, and is properly penitent for her faults, which are numerous. The account of her illness and First Communion is very well related. We can recommend the book for the reading of children."

WATERFORD NEWS.—" The story is simple but beautiful, and any child who is able to read could understand it easily. The lessons inculcated tend to improve the youthful mind. We cannot too strongly recommend this work, and we will only further add that it ought to be in the possession of every reader."

ILLUSTRATED CATHOLIC WORLD.—"This is one of those nicely-written stories for children which we now and then come across. It is not only prettily told, but that air of artificiality which so often mars works of this class is wholly absent. The volume is a charming present for a child, and we trust that mamma will not forget to gladden the hearts of her little ones by putting them in possession of it."

CHURCH HERALD.—" A charmingly-written autobiography of a little French girl, with the prettiest glimpses of French home-life among the upper classes, and some very natural descriptions of scenery. Rosalie's parents were evidently devout Roman Catholics."

R. Washbourne, 18 Paternoster Row, London.

R. WASHBOURNE'S CATALOGUE.

OCTOBER 1874.

New Books.

Life of Sister Mary Cherubina Clare of S. Francis, Translated from the Italian, with Preface by Lady Herbert. Cr. 8vo. with Photograph, 3s. 6d.

Paradise of God; or Virtues of the Sacred Heart. 4s.

Rome and her Captors. *In the press.*

Regina Sæculorum. *In the press.*

Stories of the Saints for Children. By M. F. S., author of "Tom's Crucifix, and other Tales," "Catherine Hamilton," &c. Fcap. 8vo. 2 vols., each 3s. 6d., gilt, 4s. 6d.

Oratorian Lives of the Saints. 2nd Series. *See page* 18.

S. John of God. *In the press.*

Sketch of the Life and Letters of the Countess Adelstan. An abridged translation from the French of the Rev. Père Marquigny, S.J., by E. A. M., author of "Rosalie, or the Memoirs of a French Child," "Life of Paul Seigneret, &c." 2s. 6d.

Life of B. Giovanni Colombini. By Feo Belcari. Translated from the editions of 1541 and 1832. with a Photograph. Cr. 8vo. 3s. 6d.

First Communion Picture. Tastefully printed in gold and colours. Price 1s., or 10s. a dozen, *net.*

"Just what has long been wanted, a really good picture, with Tablet for First Communion and Confirmation."—*Tablet.*

*** *Though this Catalogue does not contain the books of other Publishers, R. W. can supply all of them, no matter by whom they are published.*

R. Washbourne, 18 Paternoster Row, London.

Protestantism and Liberty. By Professor Ozanam. Translated by W. C. Robinson. 8vo. 1s.

The Supernatural Life. Translated from the French of Mgr. Mermillod, with a Preface by Lady Herbert. Cr. 8vo. 5s.

"Among the Catholic prelates on the Continent, no name stands higher than that of Dr. Mermillod, the exiled Bishop of Geneva, whose eloquence struck so forcibly the English pilgrims at Paray-le-Monial last year... The object of these conferences was to stir up the female portion of creation to higher and holier lives, in the hope of so influencing their husbands, their brothers, and other relatives, and so to lend a helping hand to the right side in that struggle which, as Lady Herbert so eloquently and so truly remarks, 'was formerly confined to certain places and certain minds, but is now going on all over the world—the struggle between God and the devil; between faith and unbelief; between those who still revere the word of God, and the entire negation of all divine revelation.'"—*Register.*

The Jesuits, and other Essays. By Willis Nevin. Fcap. 8vo. 2s. 6d.

"If any one wishes to read in brief all that can be said about and in favour of the sons of Ignatius Loyola, by all means let him get this little work, where he will find everything ready 'at his fingers' ends.'"—*Register.* "They are in the rough but earnest style, and perhaps are not the worse for being decidedly plain. Altogether, a Protestant, inclined to make rash statements upon Catholic subjects, will find these tracts a very awkward stumbling block in the pathway of his silliness."—*Universe.* "It displays considerable vigour of thought, and no small literary power. This small book is a work of promise from one who knows both sides of those questions."—*Union Review.*

On Contemporary Prophecies. By Mgr. Dupanloup. Translated by Rev. Dr. Redmond. 8vo. 1s.

Photographs (10), illustrating the history of the Miraculous Hosts, called the Blessed Sacrament of the Miracle. Price 2s. 6d. the set.

Catherine Hamilton. By the author of "Tom's Crucifix," "Stories of the Saints for Children," &c. Fcap. 8vo. 2s. 6d.; gilt, 3s.

"A short, simple, and well-told story, illustrative of the power of grace to correct bad temper in a wayward girl. For Catholic parents who are possessed with such children, we know of no better book than 'Catherine Hamilton.'"—*Register.* "We have no doubt this will prove a very attractive book to the little folks, and would be glad to see it widely circulated."—*American Catholic World.*

Novena of Meditations in Honour of S. Joseph, according to the method of S. Ignatius; preceded by a new exercise for hearing Mass according to the intentions of the souls in Purgatory. 18mo. 1s. 6d.

The Village Lily. Fcap. 8vo. 1s.; gilt, 1s. 6d.

Düsseldorf Society for the Distribution of Good, Religious Pictures. R.˙ Washbourne is now Sole Agent for Great Britain and Ireland. Yearly Subscription is 8s. 6d. *Catalogue post free.*

Düsseldorf Gallery. 8vo. half morocco, 31s. 6d. This volume contains 127 Engravings handsomely bound in half morocco, full gilt. Cash 25s.

Düsseldorf Gallery. 4to. half morocco, £6. This superb work contains 331 Pictures. Handsomely bound in half morocco, full gilt. Cash £5.

"We confidently believe that no wealthy Catholic could possibly see the volume which we have examined and admired without ordering 'The Düsseldorf Gallery' for the adornment of his drawing-room table... As lovers of art, we rejoice to see what has been done, and we can only desire with all possible heartiness, that such an enterprise as this may meet with the success it deserves."—*Tablet.* "The most beautiful Catholic gift-book that was ever sent forth from the house of a Catholic publisher."—*Register.*

Dramas, Comedies, Farces.

He would be a Lord. From the French of "Le Bourgeois Gentilhomme." Three Acts. (Boys.) 2s.

St. Louis in Chains. Drama in Five Acts, for boys. 2s.
"Well suited for acting in Catholic schools and colleges."—*Tablet.*

The Expiation. A Drama in Three Acts, for boys. 2s.
"Has its scenes laid in the days of the Crusades."—*Register.*

Shandy Maguire. A Farce for boys in Two Acts. 1s.

The Reverse of the Medal. A Drama in Four Acts, for young ladies. 6d.

Ernscliff Hall: or, Two Days Spent with a Great-Aunt. A Drama in Three Acts, for young ladies. 6d.

Filiola. A Drama in Four Acts, for young ladies. 6d.

The Convent Martyr, or Callista. By Dr. Newman. Dramatized by Dr. Husenbeth. 1s.

Garden of the Soul. (WASHBOURNE'S EDITION.) *With Imprimatur of the Archbishop of Westminster.* This edition has over all others the following advantages :—1. Complete order in its arrangements. 2. Introduction of Devotions to Saint Joseph, Patron of the Church. 3. Introduction into the English Devotions for Mass to a very great extent of the Prayers from the Missal. 4. The full Form of Administration of all the Sacraments publicly administered in Church. 5. The insertion of Indulgences above Indulgenced Prayers. 6. Its large size of type. Embossed, 1s.; with rims, 1s. 6d.; with Epistles and Gospels, 1s. 6d.; with rims, 2s. French morocco, 2s.; with rims, 2s. 6d.; with E. and G., 2s. 6d.; with rims, 3s. French morocco extra gilt, 2s. 6d.; with rims, 3s.; with E. and G., 3s.; with rims, 3s. 6d. Calf or morocco, 4s.; with rims, 5s. 6d.; with E. and G., 4s. 6d.; with rims, 6s. Calf or morocco extra, 5s.; with rims, 6s. 6d.; with E. and G., 5s. 6d.; with rims, 7s. Velvet, with rims, 8s., 10s. 6d., and 13s.; with E. and G., 8s. 6d., 11s., and 13s. 6d. Russia, antique, with clasp, 12s. 6d.; with E. and G., 13s. Ivory, 15s., 21s., 25s., and 30s.; with E. and G., 15s. 6d., 21s. 6d., 25s. 6d., and 30s. 6d. Antique bindings, with corners and clasps: morocco, 28s., with E. and G., 28s. 6d.; russia, 30s., with E. and G., 30s. 6d.

"This is one of the best editions we have seen of one of the best of all our Prayer-books. It is well printed in clear large type, on good paper."—*Catholic Opinion.* "A very complete arrangement of this which is emphatically the Prayer-book of every Catholic household. It is as cheap as it is good, and we heartily recommend it."—*Universe.* "Two striking features are the admirable order displayed throughout the book and the insertion of the Indulgences, in small type above Indulgenced Prayers."—*Weekly Register.*

The Epistles and Gospels in cloth, 6d., roan, 1s. 6d.

The Little Garden. Cloth, 6d., with rims, 1s.; embossed, 9d., with rims, 1s. 3d.; roan, 1s., with rims, 1s. 6d.; french morocco, 1s. 6d., with rims, 2s.; french morocco, extra gilt, 2s., with rims, 2s. 6d.; imitation ivory, with rims, 3s.; calf or morocco, 3s., with rims, 4s.; calf or morocco, extra gilt, 4s., with rims, 5s.; velvet, with rims, 5s., 8s. 6d., 10s. 6d.; russia, with clasp, 8s.; ivory, with rims, 10s. 6d., 13s., 15s., 17s. 6d.; antique binding, with clasps: morocco, 17s. 6d., russia, 20s.; with oxydized silver or gilt mountings, in morocco case, 30s.

A Few Words from Lady Mildred's Housekeeper. 2d.
"If any of our lady readers wish to give to their servants some hints as to the necessity of laying up some part of their wages instead of spending their money in dressing above their station, let them get 'A Few Words from Lady Mildred's Housekeeper,' and present it for the use of the servants' hall or downstairs department. The good advice of an experienced upper servant on such subjects ought not to fall on unwilling ears."—*Register*.

Religious Reading.

"Vitis Mystica;" or, the True Vine. A Treatise on the Passion of Our Lord. Translated, with Preface, by the Rev. W. R. Bernard Brownlow. With Frontispiece. 18mo. 4s., red edges, 4s. 6d.
"It is a pity that such a beautiful treatise should for so many centuries have remained untranslated into our tongue."—*Tablet*. "It will be found very acceptable spiritual food."—*Church Herald*. "We heartily recommend it for its unction and deep sense of the beauties of nature."—*The Month*. "Full of deep spiritual lore." —*Register*. "Every chapter of this little volume affords abundant matter for meditation."—*Universe*. "An excellent translation of a beautiful treatise."—*Dublin Review*.

Ebba; or, the Supernatural Power of the Blessed Sacrament. In French. 12mo. 1s. 6d.; cloth gilt, 2s. 6d.
"The author has caught very well many of the difficulties which bar the way to the Church in this country...We may venture to hope that the work will also bear fruit on the Continent."—*The Month*. "There are thoughts in the work which we value highly."—*Dublin Review*. "It is a clever and trenchant work... Written in a lively and piquant style."—*Register*. "The tone of the book is kind and fervent."—*Church Herald*. "The book is exceedingly well written, and will do good to all who read it."—*Universe*.

Holy Places; their Sanctity and Authenticity. By the Rev. Fr. Philpin. With Maps. Crown 8vo. 6s.

"It displays an amount of patient research not often to be met with."—*Universe.* "Dean Stanley and other sinners in controversy are treated with great gentleness. They are indeed thoroughly exposed and refuted."—*Register.* "Fr. Philpin has a particularly nervous and fresh style of handling his subject, with an occasional picturesqueness of epithet or simile."—*Tablet.* "We do not question his learning and industry, and yet we cannot think them to have been uselessly expended on this work."—*Spectator.* "... Fr. Philpin there weighs the comparative value of extraordinary, ordinary, and natural evidence, and gives an admirable summary of the witness of the early centuries regarding the holy places of Jerusalem, with archæological and architectural proofs. It is a complete treatise of the subject."—*The Month.* "The author treats his subject with a thorough system, and a competent knowledge. It is a book of singular attractiveness and considerable merit."—*Church Herald.* "Fr. Philpin's very interesting book appears most opportunely, and at a time when pilgrimages have been revived."—*Dublin Review.*

The Consoler; or, Pious Readings addressed to the Sick and to all who are afflicted. By the Rev. P. J. Lambilotte, S.J. Translated by the Right Rev. Abbot Burder, O. Cist. Fcp. 8vo. 4s. 6d., red edges, 5s.

"As 'The Consoler' has the merit of being written in plain and simple language, and while deeply spiritual contains no higher flights into the regions of mysticism where poor and ignorant readers would be unable to follow, it is very specially adapted for one of the subjects which its writer had in view, namely, its introduction into hospitals."—*Tablet.* "A work replete with wise comfort for every affliction."—*Universe.* "A spiritual treatise of great beauty and value."—*Church Herald.*

The Souls in Purgatory. Translated from the French, by the Right Rev. Abbot Burder, O. Cist. 32mo. 3d.

"It will be found most useful as an aid to the cultivation of this especial devotion."—*Register.*

Flowers of Christian Wisdom. By Lucien Henry. With a Preface by the Right Hon. Lady Herbert of Lea. 18mo. 2s.; red edges, 2s. 6d.

"A compilation of some of the most beautiful thoughts and passages in the works of the Fathers, the great schoolmen, and eminent modern Churchmen, and will probably secure a good circulation."—*Church Times.* "It is a compilation of gems of thought, carefully selected."—*Tablet.* "It is a small but exquisite bouquet, like that which S. Francis of Sales has prepared for *Philothea*."—*Universe.*

The Happiness of Heaven. By a Father of the Society of Jesus. Fcap. 8vo. 4s.

God our Father. By the same Author. Fcap. 8vo. 4s.

"Both of these books we can highly recommend."—*Register.*

The Light of the Holy Spirit in the World. By the Rev. Canon Hedley, O.S.B. 1s.; cloth, 1s. 6d.

A General History of the Catholic Church: from the commencement of the Christian Era until the present time. By the Abbé Darras. 4 vols., large 8vo. cloth, 48s.

The Book of Perpetual Adoration; or, the Love of Jesus in the most Holy Sacrament of the Altar. By Mgr. Boudon. Edited by the Rev. J. Redman, D.D. Fcap. 8vo. 3s.; red edges, 3s. 6d.

"This new translation is one of Boudon's most beautiful works, ... and merits that welcome in no ordinary degree."—*Tablet.* "The devotions at the end will be very acceptable aids in visiting the Blessed Sacrament, and there are two excellent methods for assisting at Mass."—*The Month.* "It has been pronounced by a learned and pious French priest to be 'the most beautiful of all books' written in honour of the Blessed Sacrament." -*The Nation.*

Spiritual Works of Louis of Blois, Abbot of Liesse. Edited by the Rev. John Edward Bowden, of the Oratory. Fcap. 8vo. 3s. 6d; red edges, 4s.

"No more important or welcome addition could have been made to our English ascetical literature than this little book. It is a model of good translation."—*Dublin Review.* "This handy little volume will certainly become a favourite."—*Tablet.* "Elegant and flowing."—*Register.* "Most useful of meditations."—*Catholic Opinion.*

Heaven Opened by the Practice of Frequent Confession and Communion. By the Abbé Favre. Translated from the French, carefully revised by a Father of the Society of Jesus. Third Edition. Fcap. 8vo. 3s. 6d.; red edges, 4s. Cheap edit. 2s.

"This beautiful little book of devotion. We may recommend it to the clergy as well as to the laity."—*Tablet.* "It is filled with quotations from the Holy Scriptures, the Fathers, and the Councils of the Church, and thus will be found of material assistance to the clergy, as a storehouse of doctrinal and ascetical authorities on the two great sacraments of Holy Eucharist and Penance."—*Register.*

The Spiritual Life. — Conferences delivered to the *Enfants de Marie* by Père Ravignan. Cr. 8vo. 5s.

"Père Ravignan's words are as applicable to the ladies of London as to those of Paris. They could not have a better book for their spiritual reading."—*Tablet.* "These discourses appear to be admirably suited to English Catholics at the present moment."—*Westminster Gazette.* "A depth of eloquence and power of exhortation which few living preachers can rival."—*Church Review.*

Lenten Thoughts. Drawn from the Gospel for each day in Lent. By the Bishop of Northampton. 1s. 6d.; stronger bound, 2s.; red edges, 2s. 6d.

"A beautiful little volume of Meditations."—*Universe.* "Will be found a useful manual."—*Tablet.* "An admirable little book."—*Nation.* "Clear and practical."—*The Month.* "A very beautiful and simple little book."—*Church Herald.*

Contemplations on the Most Holy Sacrament of the Altar, drawn from the Sacred Scriptures. 18mo. cloth, 2s.; cloth extra, red edges, 2s. 6d.

"This is a welcome addition to our books of Scriptural devotion. It contains thirty-four excellent subjects of reflection before the Blessed Sacrament, or for making a spiritual visit to the Blessed Sacrament at home; for the use of the sick."—*Dublin Review.*

Good Thoughts for Priests and People; or Short Meditations for Every Day in the Year. By Rev. T. Noethen. 12mo. 8s.

One Hundred Pious Reflections. Extracted from Alban Butler's "Lives of the Saints." 18mo. cloth, red edges, 2s.; cheap edition, 1s.

"A happy idea. The author of 'The Lives of the Saints' had a way of breathing into his language the unction and force which carries the truth of the Gospel into the heart."—*Letter to the Editor from* THE RIGHT REV. DR. ULLATHORNE, BISHOP OF BIRMINGHAM. "Well selected, sufficiently short, and printed in good bold type."—*Tablet.* "Good, sound, practical."—*Church Herald.*

The Imitation of Christ. With reflections. 32mo. 1s. Persian calf, 3s. 6d. Also an Edition with ornamental borders. Fcap. cloth, red edges, 3s. 6d.

Following of Christ. Small pocket edition, with initial letters. 1s. 6d.; roan, 2s; French morocco, 2s. 6d.; calf or morocco, 4s. 6d.; calf or morocco extra gilt, 5s. 6d.; ivory, 15s. and 16s.; morocco antique, 17s. 6d.; russia antique, 20s.

R. Washbourne, 18 Paternoster Row, London.

Conversion of the Teutonic Race. By Mrs. Hope, author of "Early Martyrs." Edited by the Rev. Father Dalgairns. 2 vols. crown 8vo. 12s.

I. Conversion of the Franks and the English, 6s.

II. S. Boniface and the Conversion of Germany, 6s.

"It is good in itself, possessing considerable literary merit; is forms one of the few Catholic books brought out in this country which are not translations or adaptations."—*Dublin Review.* "It is a great thing to find a writer of a book of this class so clearly grasping, and so boldly setting forth truths, which, familiar as they are to scholars, are still utterly unknown by most of the writers of our smaller literature."—*Saturday Review.* "A very valuable work . . . . Mrs. Hope has compiled an original history, which gives constant evidence of great erudition, and sound historical judgment."—*Month.* "This is a most taking book: it is solid history and romance in one."—*Catholic Opinion.* "It is carefully, and in many parts beautifully written."—*Universe.*

Cistercian Order: its Mission and Spirit. Comprising the Life of S. Robert of Newminster, and the Life of S. Robert of Knaresborough. By the author of "Cistercian Legends." Crown 8vo. 3s. 6d.

Cistercian Legends of the 13th Century. Translated from the Latin by the Rev. Henry Collins. 3s.

"Interesting records of Cistercian sanctity and cloistral experience."—*Dublin Review.* "A casket of jewels.."—*Weekly Register.* "Most beautiful legends, full of deep spiritual reading."—*Tablet.* "Well translated, and beautifully got up."—*Month.* "A compilation of anecdotes, full of heavenly wisdom."—*Catholic Opinion.*

The Directorium Asceticum; or, Guide to the Spiritual Life. By Scaramelli. Translated and Edited at St. Beuno's College. 4 vols. crown 8vo. 24s.

Maxims of the Kingdom of Heaven. New and enlarged Edition. 5s.; red edges, 5s. 6d.; calf or morocco, 10s. 6d.

"The selections on every subject are numerous, and the order and arrangement of the chapters will greatly facilitate meditation and reference."—*Freeman's Journal.* "We are glad to see that this admirable devotional work, of which we have before spoken in warm praise, has reached a second issue."—*Weekly Register.* "It has an Introduction by J. H. N., and bears the Imprimatur of the Archbishop of Westminster. We need say no more in its praise."—*Tablet.* "A most beautiful little book."—*Catholic Opinion.* "This priceless volume."—*Universe.* "Most suitable for meditation and reference."—*Dublin Review.*

The Oxford Undergraduate of Twenty Years Ago: his Religion, his Studies, his Antics. By a Bachelor of Arts. [Author of "The Comedy of Convocation."] 2s. 6d. ; cloth, 3s. 6d.

"The writing is full of brilliancy and point."—*Tablet.* "Time has not dimmed the author's recollection, and has no doubt served to sharpen his sense of undergraduate humour and his reading of undergraduate character."—*Examiner.* "It will deservedly attract attention, not only by the briskness and liveliness of its style, but also by the accuracy of the picture which it probably gives of an individual experience."—*The Month.* "Whoever takes this book in hand will read it through and through with the keenest pleasure and with great benefit."—*Universe.*

The Infallibility of the Pope. A Lecture. By the Author of "The Oxford Undergraduate," "Comedy of Convocation," &c. 8vo. 1s.

"A splendid lecture, by one who thoroughly understands his subject, and in addition is possessed of a rare power of language in which to put before others what he himself knows so well."—*Universe.* "There are few writers so well able to make things plain and intelligible as the author of 'The Comedy of Convocation.'. . . The lecture is a model of argument and style."—*Register.*

Comedy of Convocation in the English Church. Edited by Archdeacon Chasuble, D.D. 2s. 6d.

"Give me leave to be merry on a merry subject."—*S. Greg. Naz.*

The Harmony of Anglicanism. Report of a Conference on Church Defence. [By T. W. M. Marshall, Esq.] 8vo. 2s. 6d.

"'Church Defence' is characterized by the same caustic irony, the same good-natured satire, the same logical acuteness which distinguished its predecessor, the 'Comedy of Convocation.'. . . A more scathing bit of irony we have seldom met with."—*Tablet.* "Clever, humorous, witty, learned, written by a keen but sarcastic observer of the Establishment, it is calculated to make defenders wince as much as it is to make all others smile."—*Nonconformist.*

Consoling Thoughts of St. Francis de Sales. By Père Huguet. 18mo., 2s.

Holy Readings. Short Selections from well-known Authors. By J. R. Digby Beste, Esq. 32mo. cloth, 2s.; cloth, red edges, 2s. 6d.; roan, 3s.; morocco, 6s. [See "Catholic Hours," p. 23.]

Benedictine Almanack. Yearly. Price 1d.

St. Peter; his Name and his Office as set forth in Holy Scripture. By T. W. Allies. *Second Edition.* Revised. Crown 8vo. 5s.
"A standard work. There is no single book in English, on the Catholic side, which contains the Scriptural argument about St. Peter and the Papacy so clearly or conclusively put."—*Month.*
"An admirable volume."—*The Universe.* "This valuable work."—*Weekly Register.* "A second edition, with a new and very touching preface."—*Dublin Review.*

The Roman Question. By Dr. Husenbeth. 1s.

The Life of Pleasure. Translated from the French of Mgr. Dechamps. Fcap. 8vo. 1s. 6d.

Instructions for the Sacrament of Confirmation. 6d.

Sure Way to Heaven: a little Manual for Confession and Holy Communion. 32mo. cloth, 6d.

Compendium of the History of the Catholic Church. By Rev. T. Noethen. 12mo. 8s.

History of the Catholic Church, for schools. By Rev. T. Noethen. 12mo. 5s. 6d.

Commonitory of S. Vincent of Lerins. Translated. 12mo. 1s. 3d.

Anti-Janus. Translated from the German of Dr. Hergenröther, by Professor Robertson. 4s.

Catholic Calendar and Guide to the Services of the Church. Yearly. Price 6d.

Catholic Directory for Scotland. 1s.

Dr. Pusey's Eirenicon considered in Relation to Catholic Unity. By H. N. Oxenham. 2s. 6d.

Sancti Alphonsi Doctoris Officium Parvum—Novena and Little Office in honour of St. Alphonsus. Fcap. 8vo. 1s.; cloth, 2s.; cloth extra, 3s.

Synodi Dioeceseos Suthwarcensis ad ejusdem erectione anno 1850 ad finem anni 1868 habitæ. 8vo. cloth, 7s. 6d.; 1869-70, 1s.

Sweetness of Holy Living; or Honey culled from the Flower Garden of S. Francis of Sales. 1s. French morocco, 3s.
"In it will be found some excellent aids to devotion and meditation."—*Weekly Register.*

R. Washbourne, 18 Paternoster Row, London.

Men and Women of the English Reformation, from the days of Wolsey to the death of Cranmer. By S. H. Burke, M.A. 2 vols. 13s. Vol. ii., 6s. 6d.

"It contains a great amount of curious and useful information, gathered together with evident care."—*Dublin Review.* "Interesting and valuable."—*Tablet.* "It is, in truth, the only dispassionate record of a much contested epoch we have ever read."—*Cosmopolitan.* "It is so forcibly, but truthfully written, that it should be in the hands of every seeker after truth."—*Catholic Opinion.*—"On all hands admitted to be one of the most valuable historical works ever published."—*Nation.* "The author produces evidence that cannot be gainsayed."—*Universe.* "Full of interest, and very temperately written."—*Church Review.* "Able, fairly impartial, and likely to be of considerable value to the student of history. Replete with information."—*Church Times.* "The book supplies many hitherto unknown facts of the times of which it is a history."—*Church Opinion.* "A clever and well-written historical statement of facts concerning the chief actors of our so-called Reformation."—*The Month.*

Père Lacordaire's Conferences. God, 6s. Jesus Christ, 6s. God and Man, 6s.

A Devout Paraphrase on the Seven Penitential Psalms; or, a Practical Guide to Repentance. By the Rev. Fr. Blyth. To which is added:—Necessity of Purifying the Soul, by St. Francis of Sales. 18mo., 1s. 6d.; red edges, 2s.; cheap edition, 1s.

"A new edition of a book well known to our grandfathers. The work is full of devotion and of the spirit of prayer."—*Universe.* "A very excellent work, and ought to be in the hands of every Catholic."—*Waterford News.*

A New Miracle at Rome; through the Intercession of Blessed John Berchmans. 2d.

Cure of Blindness; through the Intercession of Our Lady and St. Ignatius. 2d.

BY THE POOR CLARES OF KENMARE.

Woman's Work in Modern Society. 7s. 6d.
A Nun's Advice to her Girls. 2s. 6d.
Daily Steps to Heaven. Fcap. 8vo. 4s. 6d.
Book of the Blessed Ones. 4s. 6d.
Jesus and Jerusalem; or, the Way Home. 4s. 6d.
The Spouse of Christ. Crown 8vo. 7s. 6d.
The Ecclesiastical Year. Fcap. 4s. 6d.; calf, 6s. 6d.

Sermons, Lectures, &c. By Rev. M. B. Buckley. 6s.
A Homely Discourse ; Mary Magdalen. Cr. 8vo. 6d.
Extemporaneous Speaking. By Rev. T. J. Potter. 5s.
Pastor and People. By Rev. T. J. Potter. 6s.
Meditations on the Veni Sancte Spiritus. 1s.
Eight Short Sermon Essays. By Dr. Redmond. 1s.
One Hundred Short Sermons. By Rev. H. T. Thomas. 8vo. 12s.
Catholic Sermons. By Father Burke, O.P., and others. 2s.
Non Possumus ; or, the Temporal Sovereignty of the Popes. By the Rev. Father Lockhart. 1s.
Secession or Schism. By Fr. Lockhart. 6d.
Who is the Anti-Christ of Prophecy? By the Rev. Fr. Lockhart. 1s.
The Communion of Saints. By the Rev. Father Lockhart. 1s. ; cloth, 1s. 6d.
The Church of England and its Defenders. By the Rev. W. R. Bernard Brownlow. 8vo. 1st Letter, 6d. ; 2nd Letter, 1s.
Lectures on the Life, Writings, and Times of Edmund Burke. By Professor Robertson. 5s.
Professor Robertson's Lectures on Modern History and Biography. Crown 8vo. cloth, 6s.
The Knight of the Faith. By the Rev. Dr. Laing.
1. A Favourite Fallacy about Private Judgment and Inquiry. 1d.
2. Catholic not Roman Catholic. 4d.
3. Rationale of the Mass. 1s.
4. Challenge to the Churches of England, Scotland, and all Protestant Denominations. 1d.
5. Absurd Protestant Opinions concerning *Intention*, and Spelling Book of Christian Philosophy. 4d.
6. Whence the Monarch's right to rule. 2s. 6d.
7. Protestantism against the Natural Moral Law. 1d.
8. What is Christianity ? 6d.

Diary of a Confessor of the Faith. 12mo. 1s.
Sursum, 1s. Homeward, 2s. Both by Rev. Fr. Rawes.
Sermon at the Month's Mind of the Most Rev. Dr. Spalding, Archbishop of Baltimore. 1s.
Commentary on the Psalms. By Bellarmin. 4to. 4s.
Monastic Legends. By E. G. K. Browne. 8vo. 6d.

BY DR. MANNING, ARCHBISHOP OF WESTMINSTER.

The Convocation in Crown and Council. 6d. net.
Confidence in God. Fcap. 1s.; cloth, 1s. 6d.
Temporal Sovereignty of the Popes. 1s.; cloth, 1s. 6d.
The Church, the Spirit, and the Word. 6d.

BY THE PASSIONIST FATHERS.

The School of Jesus Crucified. 3s. 6d.; morocco, 5s.
The Manual of the Cross and Passion. 32mo. 2s. 6d.
The Manual of the Seven Dolours. 32mo. 1s. 6d.
The Christian Armed. 32mo. 1s. 6d.; mor. 3s. 6d.
Guide to Sacred Eloquence. 2s.

Religious Instruction.

The Catechism, Illustrated with Passages from the Holy Scriptures. Arranged by the Rev. J. B. Bagshawe, with Imprimatur. Crown 8vo. 2s. 6d.

"I believe the Catechism to be one of the best possible books of controversy, to those, at least, who are inquiring with a real desire to find the truth."—*Extract from the Preface.*
"An excellent idea. The very thing of all others that is needed by many under instruction."—*Tablet.* "It is a book which will do incalculable good. Our priests will hail with pleasure so valuable a help to their weekly instructions in the Catechism, while in schools its value will be equally recognized."—*Weekly Register.*
"A work of great merit."—*Church Herald.* "We can hardly wish for anything better, either in intention or in performance."—*The Month.* "Very valuable."—*Dublin Review.*

A Dogmatic Catechism. By Frassinetti. Translated from the original Italian by the Oblate Fathers of St. Charles. With a Preface by His Grace the Archbishop of Westminster. Fcap. 8vo. 3s.

"We give a few extracts from Frassinetti's work, as samples of its excellent execution."—*Dublin Review.* "Needs no commendation."—*Month.* "It will be found useful, not only to catechists, but also for the instruction of converts from the middle class of society."—*Tablet.*

The Threshold of the Catholic Church. A course of Plain Instructions for those entering her Communion. By Rev. J. B. Bagshawe. Cr. 8vo. 4s.

"A scholarly, well-written book, full of information."—*Church Herald.* "An admirable book, which will be of infinite service to thousands."—*Universe.* "Plain, practical, and unpretentious, it exhausts so entirely the various subjects of instruction necessary for our converts, that few missionary priests will care to dispense with its assistance."—*Register.* "It has very special merits of its own. . It is the work, not only of a thoughtful writer and good theologian, but of a wise and experienced priest."—*Dublin Review.* "Its characteristic is the singular simplicity and clearness with which everything is explained. . . It will save priests hours and days of time."—*Tablet.* "There is much in it with which we thoroughly agree."—*Church Times.* "There was a great want of a manual of instruction for convents, and the want has now been supplied, and in the most satisfactory manner."—*The Month.*

The Catechism of Christian Doctrine. Approved for the use of the Faithful in all the Dioceses of England and Wales. Price 1d.; cloth, 2d.

A First Sequel to the Catechism. By the Rev. J. Nary. 32mo. 1d.

"It will recommend itself to teachers in Catholic schools as one peculiarly adapted to the use of such children as have mastered the Catechism, and yet have nothing else to fall back upon for higher religious instruction. It will be found a great assistance as well to teachers as to pupils who belong to the higher standards in our Catholic poor schools."—*Weekly Register.*

Catechism made Easy. A Familiar Explanation of "The Catechism of Christian Doctrine." By Rev. H. Gibson. Vol. I., 4s. Vol. II., 4s.

The Monitor of the Association of Prayer. Monthly, 1d. Volume, 2s. Notices, 6s. 1000. Prints, 7s. 6d. 1000. Zelator's Cards, 10s. 1000.

Protestant Principles Examined by the Written Word. Originally entitled, "The Protestant's Trial by the Written Word." *New edition.* 18mo. 1s.

"An excellent book."—*Church News.* "A good specimen of the concise controversial writing of English Catholics in the early part of the seventeenth century."—*Catholic Opinion.* "A little book which might be consulted profitably by any Catholic."—*Church Times.* "A clever little manual."—*Westminster Gazette.* "A useful little volume."—*The Month.* "An excellent little book."—*Weekly Register.* "A well-written and well-argued treatise."—*Tablet.*

R. Washbourne, 18 Paternoster Row, London.

Descriptive Guide to the Mass. By the Rev. Dr. Laing. 1s. ; extra cloth, 1s. 6d.
> "An attempt to exhibit the structure of the Mass. The logical relation of parts is ingeniously effected by an elaborate employment of differences of type, so that the classification, down to the minutest subdivision, may at once be caught by the eye."—*Tablet.*

The Necessity of Enquiry as to Religion. By Henry John Pye, M.A. 4d. ; for distribution, 20s. a hundred; cloth, 6d.
> "Mr. Pye is particularly plain and straightforward."—*Tablet.* "It is calculated to do much good. We recommend it to the clergy, and think it a most useful work to place in the hands of all who are under instruction."—*Westminster Gazette.* "A thoroughly searching little pamphlet."—*Universe.* "A clever little pamphlet. Each point is treated briefly and clearly."—*Catholic Opinion.*

A General Catechism of the Christian Doctrine. By the Right Rev. Dr. Poirier. 18mo. 9d.

The Grounds of Catholic Doctrine. By Dr. Challoner. Large type edition. 18mo. cloth, 4d.

Dr. Butler's *First* Catechism, ½d. *Second* Catechism, 1d. ; *Third* Catechism, 1½d.

Dr. Doyle's Catechism, 1½d.

Lessons on the Christian Doctrine, 1d.

Fleury's Historical Catechism. Large edition, 1½d.

Bible History for the use of Catholic Schools and Families. By the Rev. R. Gilmour. 2s.

Herder's Prints—Old and New Testament. 40 large coloured pictures. 12s.

Origin and Progress of Religious Orders, and Happiness of a Religious State. By Fr. Jerome Platus, S.J.; translated by Patrick Mannock. Fcap. 8vo. 2s. 6d.
> "The whole work is evidently calculated to impress any reader with the great advantages attached to a religious life."—*Register.*

Children of Mary in the World. 32mo. 1d.

The Christian Teacher. By Ven. de la Salle. 1s. 8d.

Christian Politeness. By the Ven. de la Salle. 1s.

Duties of a Christian. By the Ven. de la Salle. 2s.

The Monks of Iona and the Duke of Argyll. By the Rev. J. Stewart M'Corry, D.D. 8vo. 3s. 6d.

The Young Catholic's Guide to Confession and Holy Communion. By Dr. Kenny. *Third edition.* Paper, 4d.; cloth, 6d.; cloth, red edges, 9d.

"Admirably suited to the purpose for which it is intended."—*Weekly Register.* "One of the best we have seen. The instructions are clear, pointed, and devout, and the prayers simple, well constructed, and sufficiently brief. We recommend it."—*Church News.*

Practical Counsels for Holy Communion. By Mgr. de Ségur. Translated for children, 1s.

Pactical Counsels on Confession. By Mgr. de Ségur. Translated for children. 6d.

Auricular Confession. By Rev. Dr. Melia. 1s. 6d.

Explanation of the Epistles and Gospels, &c. By the Rev. Fr. Goffine. Illustrated. 7s.

Rules for a Christian Life. By S. Charles Borromeo. 2d.

Anglican Orders. By the Very Rev. Canon Williams. *Second Edition.* Crown 8vo. 3s. 6d.

The Rainy Day, and Guild of Our Lady. By the Rev. Fr. Richardson. 2d.

The Crusade, or Catholic Association for the Suppression of Drunkenness. By the Rev. Fr. Richardson. 1d.

Little by Little; or, the Penny Bank. By the Rev. Fr. Richardson. 1d.

Lives of Saints, &c.

Life of the Ven. Anna Maria Taigi. Translated from the French of Calixte, by A. V. Smith Sligo. 8vo. 5s.

"A most valuable book."—*Dublin Review.* "An edifying and delightful book of spiritual reading."—*Church Herald.* "We hope to see it meet with that success which works of the sort have a right to expect."—*Westminster Gazette.* "The translator's labour has been so ably performed that the book is wanting in few of the merits of an original work."—*Tablet.*

Butler's Lives of the Saints. 2 vols., 8vo., cloth, 28s.; or in cloth gilt, 34s.; or in 4 vols., 8vo., cloth, 32s.; or in cloth gilt, 48s.; or in leather gilt, 64s.

Life, Passion, Death, and Resurrection of Our Blessed Lord. Translated from Ribadeneira. 1s.

Oratorian Lives of the Saints. Second Series. Vol. I.—
S. Bernardine of Siena. Post 8vo. 5s.
Vol. II.—S. Philip Benizi. Post 8vo. 5s.
Vol. III.—S. Veronica Giuliani, and Blessed Battista Varani. Post 8vo. 5s.

1. It is proposed to publish a Second Series of the Lives of the Modern Saints, translated from foreign languages, and to bring out two or more volumes in the year. 2. The works translated from will be in most cases the Lives drawn up *for* or *from* the processes of canonization or beatification, as being more full, more authentic, and more replete with anecdote, thus enabling the reader to become better acquainted with the Saint's disposition and spirit; while the simple matter-of-fact style of the narrative is, from its unobtrusive character, more adapted for spiritual reading than the views and generalizations, and prologetic extenuations of more recent biographers. 3. The objects are those stated at the commencement of the First Series, viz., 1. To supply English Catholics with a cabinet-library of interesting as well as edifying reading, especially for families, schools, and religious refectories, which would for many reasons be particularly adapted for these times, and would with God's blessing act as a counter influence to the necessarily deadening and chilling effects which the neighbourhood of heresy and the consequent prevalence of earthly principles and low views of grace may have on the temper and habits of mind even of the faithful; 2. To present to our other countrymen a number of samples of the fruit which the system, doctrine, and moral discipline established by the holy and blessed Council of Trent have produced, and which will be to inquirers really in earnest about their souls, an argument more cogent than any that mere controversy can allege; and 3. To spread the honour and love of the ever-blessed Queen of Saints, by showing how greatly an intense devotion to her aided in forming those prodigies of heroic virtue with which the Holy Ghost has been pleased to adorn the Church since the schism of Luther, *more than in almost any previous times;* while the same motive will prevent the Series being confined to modern saints *exclusively*. 4. The work is published with the permission and approval of superiors. Every volume containing the Life of a person not yet canonized or beatified by the Church will be prefaced by a protest in conformity with the decree of Urban VIII., and in all Lives which introduce questions of mystical theology great care will be taken to publish nothing which has not had adequate sanction, or without the reader being informed of the nature and amount of the sanction.

Life of Fr. de Ravignan. Crown 8vo. 9s.
The Pilgrimage to Paray le Monial, with a brief notice of the Blessed Margaret Mary. 6d.
Patron Saints. By Eliza Allen Starr. Cr. 8vo. 10s.

Life of St. Boniface, and the Conversion of Germany. By Mrs. Hope. Edited, with a Preface, by the Rev. Father Dalgairns. Cr. 8vo. 6s.

"Every one knows the story of S. Boniface's martyrdom, but every one has not heard it so stirringly set forth as in her 22nd chapter by Mrs. Hope."—*Dublin Review.*

Louise Lateau: her Life, Stigmata, and Ecstasies. By Dr. Lefebvre. Translated from the French by T. S. Shepard. Fcap. 8vo. 2s.; cheap edition, 6d.

Venerable Mary Christina of Savoy. 6d.

Memoirs of a Guardian Angel. Fcap. 8vo. 4s.

Life of St. Patrick. 12mo. 1s.

Life of St. Bridget, and of other Saints of Ireland. 1s.

Insula Sanctorum: the Island of Saints. 1s.; cloth, 2s.

Life of Paul Seigneret, Seminarist of Saint-Sulpice. Fcap. 8vo., 1s.; cloth extra, 1s. 6d.; gilt, 2s.

"An affecting and well-told narrative... It will be a great favourite, especially with our pure-minded, high-spirited young people."—*Universe.* "Paul Seigneret was remarkable for the simplicity and the heroism of both his natural and his religious character."—*Tablet.* "We commend it to parents with sons under their care, and especially do we recommend it to those who are charged with the education and training of our Catholic youth."—*Register.*

A Daughter of St. Dominic. By Grace Ramsay. Fcap. 8vo. 1s. 6d.; cloth extra, 2s.

"A beautiful little work. The narrative is highly interesting."—*Dublin Review.* "It is full of courage and faith and Catholic heroism."—*Universe.* "One who has lived and died in our own day, who led the common life of every one else, but yet who learned how to supernaturalize this life in so extraordinary a way that we forget 'the doctor's daughter in a provincial town,' while reading Grace Ramsay's beautiful picture of the wonders effected by her ubiquitous charity, and still more by her fervent prayer."—*Tablet.* "The spirit of thorough devotion to Rome manifest in every page of this charming work will render it most attractive to Leaguers of St. Sebastian."—*The Crusader.*

The Glory of St. Vincent de Paul. By the Most Rev. Dr. Manning, Archbishop of Westminster. 1s.

DR. NEWMAN'S LIVES OF THE ENGLISH SAINTS.

Life of St. Augustine of Canterbury. 12mo. 3s. 6d.

Life of St. German. 12mo. cloth, 3s. 6d.

Life of Stephen Langton. 12mo. cloth, 2s. 6d.

Life of S. Edmund of Canterbury. From the French of the Rev. Father Massé, S. J. By George White. 1s., cloth 2s.

Life of Dr. Grant, first Bishop of Southwark. By Grace Ramsay. 8vo. 16s.

The Life of St. Francis of Assisi. Translated from the Italian of St. Bonaventure by Miss Lockhart. With a Preface by His Grace the Archbishop of Westminster. Fcap. 8vo. cloth, 2s. and 3s.; gilt, 4s.
" It is beautifully translated."—*Catholic Opinion.* " A most interesting and instructive volume."—*Tablet.* "This is a first-rate translation by one of the very few persons who have the art of translating as if they were writing an original work."—*Dublin Review.*

His Eminence Cardinal Wiseman; with full account of his Obsequies; Funeral Oration by Archbishop Manning, &c. 1s.; cloth, red edges, 1s. 6d.

Count de Montalembert. By George White. 6d.

Life of Mgr. Weedall. By Dr. Husenbeth. 3s. 6d.

Life of Pope Pius IX. 6d.

Life of Rev. Fr. Pallotti. By Rev. Dr. Melia. 4s.

Challoner's Memoirs of Missionary Priests. 8vo. 6s.

BY THE POOR CLARES OF KENMARE.

Life of Father Matthew. 2s. 6d.

Life and Revelations of St. Gertrude. Cr. 8vo. 7s. 6d.

Spirit of St. Gertrude. 18mo. 2s. 6d.

Life of St. Aloysius. 6d.; St. Joseph, 6d., cloth, 9d.; St. Patrick, 6d., cloth, 9d.

Life of St. Patrick. Illustrated by Doyle. 4to. 20s.

Our Lady.

The History of the Blessed Virgin. By the Abbé Orsini. Translated from the French by the Very Rev. F. C. Husenbeth, D.D. With eight Illustrations. Crown 8vo. 3s. 6d.

Manual of Devotions in Honour of Our Lady of Sorrows. Compiled by the Clergy at St. Patrick's Soho. 18mo. 1s.; cloth, red edges, 1s. 6d.

Miraculous Prayer—August Queen of Angels. 1s. per 100.

Devotion to Our Lady in North America. By the Rev. Xavier Donald Macleod. 8vo. 5s. *cash*.

"The work of an author than whom few more gifted writers have ever appeared among us. It is not merely a religious work, but it has all the charms of an entertaining book of travels. We can hardly find words to express our high admiration of it."—*Weekly Register*.

Life of the Ever-Blessed Virgin. Proposed as a Model to Christian Women. 1s.

Our Blessed Lady of Lourdes: a Faithful Narrative of the Apparitions of the Blessed Virgin Mary at the Rocks of Massabielle, near Lourdes, in the year 1858. By F. C. Husenbeth, D.D., V.G., and Provost of Northampton. 18mo. 6d.; cloth, 1s.; with Novena, 1s.; cloth, 1s. 6d. Novena, separately, 4d.; Litany, separately, 1d.

The Blessed Virgin's Root traced in the Tribe of Ephraim. By the Rev. Dr. Laing. 8vo. 10s. 6d.

Month of Mary for Interior Souls. By M. A. Macdaniel. 18mo. 2s.

Month of Mary, principally for the use of religious communities. 18mo. 1s. 6d.

Readings for the Feasts of Our Lady, and especially for the Month of May. By the Rev. A. P. Bethell. 18mo. 1s. 6d.; cheap edition, 1s.

A Devout Exercise in Honour of the Blessed Virgin Mary. From the Psalter and Prayers of S. Bonaventure. In Latin and English, with Indulgences applicable to the Holy Souls. 32mo. 1s.

The Definition of the Immaculate Conception. 6d.

The Little Office of the Immaculate Conception. In Latin and English. By the Very Rev. Dr. Husenbeth. 32mo. 4d.; cloth, 6d.; roan, 1s.; calf or morocco, 2s. 6d.

Our Lady's Lament, and the Lamentation of St. Mary Magdalene. 2s.

Life of Our Lady in Verse. 2s.

The Virgin Mary. By Dr. Melia. 8vo. 11s. 3d. cash.

Archconfraternity of Our Lady of Angels. 1s. per 100.

Litany of Our Lady of Angels. 1s. per 100.
Concise Portrait of the Blessed Virgin. 1s. per 100.
Origin of the Blue Scapular. 1d.

Prayer-Books.

Washbourne's Edition of the "Garden of the Soul," in medium-sized type (small type as a rule being avoided). For prices see page 4.

The Little Garden. 6d., and upwards. *See page* 5.

The Lily of St. Joseph; a little Manual of Prayers and Hymns for Mass. Price 2d.; cloth, 3d.; or with gilt lettering, 4d.; more strongly bound, 6d.; or with gilt edges, 8d.; roan, 1s.; French morocco, 1s. 6d.; calf, or morocco, 2s.; gilt, 2s. 6d.

"It supplies a want which has long been felt; a prayer-book for children, which is not a childish book, a handy book for boys and girls, and for men and women too, if they wish for a short, easy-to-read, and devotional prayer-book."—*Catholic Opinion.* "A very complete prayer-book. It will be found very useful for children and for travellers."—*Weekly Register.* "A neat little compilation, which will be specially useful to our Catholic School-children. The hymns it contains are some of Fr. Faber's best."—*Universe.*

Life of Our Lord Commemorated in the Mass; a Method of Assisting at the Holy Sacrifice. By the Rev. E. G. Bagshawe, of the Oratory. 32mo. 3d.; cloth, 4d.; roan, 1s.; French morocco, 1s. 6d.; calf or morocco, 2s. 6d.

Path to Paradise. 36 full page Illustrations. Cloth, 3d. With 50 Illustrations, cloth, 4d.

Manual of Catholic Devotion. Small, for the waistcoat pocket. 6d.; roan, 1s.; calf or morocco, 2s.

Ursuline Manual. Persian calf, 7s. 6d.; morocco, 10s.

Crown of Jesus. Persian calf, 6s.; morocco, 7s. 6d. and 8s. 6d., with rims, 10s. 6d.; morocco, extra gilt, 10s. 6d., with rims, 12s. 6d.; ivory, with rims, 21s., 25s., 27s. 6d. and 30s.

Burial of the Dead (Adults and Infants) in Latin and English. Royal 32mo. cloth, 6d.; roan, 1s. 6d.

"Being in a portable form, will be found useful by those who are called upon to assist at that solemn rite."—*Tablet.*

Devotions to the Sacred Heart. By the Rev. J. Joy Dean. Fcap. 8vo. 3s.

Devotions to Sacred Heart of Jesus. By the Rt. Rev. Dr. Milner. *New Edition.* To which is added Devotions to the Immaculate Heart of Mary. 3d.; cloth, 6d.; gilt, 1s.

Pleadings of the Sacred Heart. 18mo. 1s.

Sacred Heart of Jesus offered to the Piety of the Young engaged in Study. By Rev. A. Deham, S.J. 6d.

"Complete little Manual of Devotion to the Sacred Heart, and as such will be valued by Catholics of every age and ,station."—*Tablet.*

Treasury of the Sacred Heart. With Epistles and Gospels. 18mo. cloth, 3s. 6d.; roan, 4s. 6d.

Little Treasury of Sacred Heart. 32mo. 2s., roan 2s. 6d.

Manual of Devotion to the Sacred Heart, from the Writings of Bl. Margaret Mary Alacoque. By Denys Casassayas. Translated. 3d.

Act of Consecration to the Sacred Heart. 1d.

Act of Reparation to the Sacred Heart. 1s. per 100.

The Little Prayer-Book for Ordinary Catholic Devotions. Cloth, 3d.

Garden of the Soul, in large type. Roan, gilt edges, 2s.; French morocco, 3s., clasp and rims, 4s. 6d.; French morocco, antique, 3s. 6d.; calf, 5s.; morocco, 6s. 6d.; roan, sprinkled edges, with Epistles and Gospels, 2s. All the other styles with Epistles and Gospels, 6d. extra.

Missal (complete). Persian calf, 8s. 6d.; morocco, 10s. 6d., with rims, 13s. 6d.; morocco, extra gilt, 12s. 6d., with rims, 15s. 6d.; morocco, with turn-over edges, 13s. 6d.; morocco antique, 15s.; russia antique, 20s.; ivory, with rims, 31s. 6d.

Catholic Hours : a Manual of Prayer, including Mass and Vespers. By J. R. Digby Beste, Esq. 32mo. cloth, 2s; red edges, 2s. 6d.; roan, 3s.; morocco, 6s.

In Suffragiis Sanctorum. Commem S. Josephi. Commem S. Georgii. Set of five for 4d.

Manual of Catholic Piety. Edition with green border. French mor., 2s. 6d.; mor., 4s.

Occasional Prayers for Festivals. By Rev. T. Barge. 32mo. 4d. and 6d.; gilt, 1s.

Illustrated Manual of Prayers. 32mo., 3d.; cloth, 4d.

Key of Heaven. Very large type, 1s. Leather 2s. 6d. gilt, 3s.

Catholic Piety. 32mo. 6d.; roan, 1s.; with Epistles and Gospels, roan, 1s.; French morocco, 1s. 6d., with rims and clasp, 2s.; imitation ivory, rims and clasp, 2s. 6d.; velvet rims and clasps, 3s. 6d.

Key of Heaven. Same size and prices.

Catholic Piety, or Key of Heaven, with Epistles and Gospels. Large 32mo, French morocco, 2s.; with rims, 2s. 6d.; extra gilt, 3s.; with rims, 3s. 6d.

Novena to St. Joseph. Translated by M. A. Macdaniel. To which is added a Pastoral of the late Right Rev. Dr. Grant. 32mo. 4d.; cloth, 6d.

"All seasons are fitting in which to make Novenas to St. Joseph, for which reason this little work will be found very serviceable at any time."—*Weekly Register.*

A New Year's Gift to our Heavenly Father; or, Dedication of the First Hours of the Year, Quarter, Month, or Week to God. 4d.

Devotions for Mass. Very large type, 2d.

Memorare Mass. By the Poor Clares of Kenmare, 2d.

Fourteen Stations of the Holy Way of the Cross. By St. Liguori. Large type edition, 1d.

A Union of our life with the Passion of our Lord, by a daily offering. 1s. per 100.

Prayer for one's Confessor. 1s. per 100.

Litany of Resignation. 1s. per 100.

Intentions for Indulgences. 6d. per 100.

Prayers for the Dying. 1s. per 100.

Indulgenced Prayers for the Rosary of the Holy Souls. 1d. each, 6d. a dozen, 3s. per 100.

Indulgenced Prayers for Souls in Purgatory. 1s. per 100.

Devotions to St. Joseph. 1s. per 100.

Devotion to St. Joseph as Patron of the Church. 1d.

Catholic Psalmist: or, Manual of Sacred Music, containing Vespers, Chants, Hymns, Litanies, &c., with the Gregorian Chants for High Mass, Holy Week, &c. Compiled by C. B. Lyons, 4s.
The Complete Hymn Book, containing 136 Hymns for Missions, Month of Mary. Price 1d.
Douai Bible. 2s. 6d.; calf or morocco, 6s.; gilt, 7s.
Church Hymns. By J. R. Digby Beste, Esq. 6d.
Catholic Choir Manual: containing Vespers for all the Sundays and Festivals of the year, Hymns and Litanies, &c. Compiled by C. B. Lyons. 1s.
The Rosary for the Souls in Purgatory, *with Indulgenced Prayer*. 6d. and 9d. each. Medals separately, 1d. each, 9s. gross. Prayers separately, 1d. each, 3s. per 100.

Rome, &c.

Two Years in the Pontifical Zouaves. By Joseph Powell, Z.P. With 4 Engravings by Sergeant Collingridge, Z.P. 8vo. 3s. 6d.

"It affords us much pleasure, and deserves the notice of the Catholic public."—*Tablet.* "Familiar names meet the eye on every page, and as few Catholic circles in either country have not had a friend or relative at one time or another serving in the Pontifical Zouaves, the history of the formation of the corps, of the gallant youths, their sufferings, and their troubles, will be valued as something more than a contribution to modern Roman history."—*Freeman's Journal.*

The Victories of Rome. By the Rev. Fr. Kenelm Digby Beste. Second edition. 1s.
The Roman Question. By F. C. Husenbeth, D.D. 1s.
Defence of the Roman Church against Fr. Gratry. By Dom Gueranger. 6d.
Personal Recollections of Rome. By W. J. Jacob, Esq., late of the Pontifical Zouaves. 8vo. 1s. 6d.
Henri V. (Comte de Chambord), September 29, 1873. By W. H. Walsh. With a Portrait. 8vo. 1s. 6d.
The Rule of the Pope-King. By Rev. Fr. Martin. 6d.
The Years of Peter. By an Ex-Papal Zouave. 1d.
The Catechism of the Council. By a D.C.L. 2d.

Tales, or Books for the Library.

Tom's Crucifix, and other Tales. By M. F. S. 3s.

"Eight simple stories for the use of teachers of Christian doctrine."—*Universe.* "This is a volume of short, plain, and simple stories, written with the view of illustrating the Catholic religion practically by putting Catholic practices in an interesting light before the mental eyes of children.... The whole of the tales in the volume before us are exceedingly well written."—*Register.*

Simple Tales. Square 16mo. cloth antique, 2s. 6d.

"Contains five pretty stories of a true Catholic tone, interspersed with some short pieces of poetry. . . Are very affecting, and told in such a way as to engage the attention of any child."—*Register.* "This is a little book which we can recommend with great confidence as a present for young readers. The tales are simple, beautiful, and pathetic."—*Catholic Opinion.* "It belongs to a class of books of which the want is generally much felt by Catholic parents."—*Dublin Review.* "Beautifully written. 'Little Terence' is a gem of a Tale."—*Tablet.*

Fairy Tales for Little Children. By Madeleine Howley Meehan. Fcap. 1s.; cloth extra, 1s. 6d.; gilt, 2s.

"Full of imagination and dreams, and at the same time with excellent point and practical aim, within the reach of the intelligence of infants."—*Universe.* "Pleasing, simple stories, combining instruction with amusement."—*Register.* "A pretty little story-book for pretty little children."—*Tablet.*

Terry O'Flinn's Examination of Conscience. By the Very Rev. Dr. Tandy. Fcap. 8vo. 1s. 6d.; extra gilt, 2s.; cheap edition, 1s.

"The writer possesses considerable literary power."—*Register.* "The idea is well sustained throughout, and when the reader comes to the end of the book he finds the mystery solved, and that it was all nothing but a 'dhrame.'"—*Church Times.*

The Adventures of a Protestant in Search of a Religion: being the Story of a late Student of Divinity at Bunyan Baptist College; a Nonconformist Minister, who seceded to the Catholic Church. By Iota. 5s.; cheap edition, 3s.

"Will well repay its perusal."—*Universe.* "This precious volume."—*Baptist.* "No one will deny 'Iota' the merit of entire originality."—*Civilian.* "A valuable addition to every Catholic library."—*Tablet.* "There is much cleverness in it."—*Nonconformist.* "Malicious and wicked."—*English Independent.*

A Wasted Life. By Rosa Baughan. 8vo. 3s. 6d.

Rosalie ; or, the Memoirs of a French Child. Written by herself. Fcap. 8vo., 1s. and 1s. 6d.; extra gilt, 2s.

"It is prettily told, and in a natural manner. The account of Rosalie's illness and First Communion is very well related. We can recommend the book for the reading of children."—*Tablet.* "The tenth chapter is beautiful."—*Universe.*

The Story of Marie and other Tales. Fcap. 8vo., 2s.; cloth extra, 2s. 6d.; gilt, 3s.; or separately:—The Story of Marie, 2d.; Nelly Blane, and A Contrast, 2d.; A Conversion and a Death-Bed, 2d.; Herbert Montagu, 2d. ; Jane Murphy, The Dying Gipsy, and The Nameless Grave, 2d.; The Beggars, and True and False Riches, 2d.; Pat and his Friend, 2d.

"A very nice little collection of stories, thoroughly Catholic in their teaching."—*Tablet.* "A series of short pretty stories, told with much simplicity."—*Universe.* "A number of short pretty stories, replete with religious teaching, told in simple language."—*Weekly Register.*

Margarethe Verflassen. Translated from the German by Mrs. Smith Sligo. Fcap. 8vo. 3s. ; gilt, 3s. 6d.

"A portrait of a very holy and noble soul, whose life was passed in constant practical acts of the love of God."—*Weekly Register.* "It is the picture of a true woman's life, well fitted up with the practice of ascetic devotion and loving unwearied activity about all the works of mercy."—*Tablet.*

The Last of the Catholic O'Malleys. A Tale. By M. Taunton. 18mo. cloth, 1s. 6d.; extra, 2s.

"A sad and stirring tale, simply written, and sure to secure for itself readers."—*Tablet.* "Deeply interesting. It is well adapted for parochial and school libraries."—*Weekly Register.* "A very pleasing tale."—*The Month.*

Eagle and Dove. From the French of Mademoiselle Zénaïde Fleuriot. By Emily Bowles. Cr. 8vo., 5s.

"We recommend our readers to peruse this well-written story."—*Register.* "One of the very best stories we have ever dipped into."—*Church Times.* "Admirable in tone and purpose."—*Church Herald.* "A real gain. It possesses merits far above the pretty fictions got up by English writers."—*Dublin Review.* "There is an air of truth and sobriety about this little volume, nor is there any attempt at sensation."—*Tablet.*

Rupert Aubray. By the Rev. T. J. Potter. 3s.

Farleyes of Farleye. By the same author. 2s. 6d.

Sir Humphrey's Trial. By the same author. 2s. 6d.

Chats about the Rosary; or, Aunt Margaret's Little Neighbours. Fcap. 8vo. 3s.

"There is scarcely any devotion so calculated as the Rosary to keep up a taste for piety in little children, and we must be grateful for any help in applying its lessons to the daily life of those who already love it in their unconscious tribute to its value and beauty."—*Month*. "We do not know of a better book for reading aloud to children, it will teach them to understand and to love the Rosary."—*Tablet*. "A graceful little book, in fifteen chapters, on the Rosary, illustrative of each of the mysteries, and connecting each with the practice of some particular virtue."—*Catholic Opinion*.

Cistercian Legends of the 13th Century. Translated from the Latin by the Rev. Henry Collins. 3s.

Cloister Legends: or, Convents and Monasteries in the Olden Time. *Second Edition.* Cr. 8vo. 4s.

The People's Martyr, a Legend of Canterbury. 4s.

Keighley Hall and other Tales. By Elizabeth King. 18mo. 6d.; cloth, 1s.; gilt, 1s. 6d.; or, separately, Keighley Hall, Clouds and Sunshine, The Maltese Cross, 3d. each.

Sir Ælfric and other Tales. By the Rev. G. Bampfield. 18mo. 6d.; cloth, 1s.; gilt, 1s. 6d.

Ned Rusheen. By the Poor Clares. Crown 8vo. 6s.

The Prussian Spy. A Novel. By V. Valmont. 4s.

Adolphus; or, the Good Son. 18mo. gilt, 6d.

Nicholas; or, the Reward of a Good Action. 6d.

The Lost Children of Mount St. Bernard. 18mo. gilt, 6d.

A Broken Chain. 18mo. gilt, 6d.

The Baker's Boy; or, the Results of Industry. 6d.

"All prettily got up, artistically illustrated, and pleasantly-written. Better books for gifts and rewards we do not know."—*Weekly Register*. "We can thoroughly recommend them."—*Tablet*.

The Truce of God: a Tale of the Eleventh Century. By G. H. Miles. 4s.

Tales and Sketches. By Charles Fleet. 8vo. cloth, 2s. and 2s. 6d.; cloth, gilt, 3s. 6d.

"Pleasingly-written, and containing some valuable hints. There is a good deal of nice feeling in these short stories."—*Tablet*.

The Convent Prize Book. By the author of "Geraldine." Fcap. 8vo. 2s. 6d.; gilt, 3s. 6d.

The Journey of Sophia and Eulalie to the Palace of True Happiness. Translated by the Rev. Father Ambrose, Mount St. Bernard's. Fcap. 8vo. 3s. 6d. ; cheap edition, 2s. 6d.
The Fisherman's Daughter. By Conscience. 4s.
The Amulet. By Hendrick Conscience. 4s.
Count Hugo of Graenhove. By Conscience. 4s.
The Village Innkeeper. By Conscience. 4s.
Happiness of being Rich. By Conscience. 4s.
Florence O'Neill. By A. M. Stewart. 4s. 6d. and 6s.
Limerick Veteran. By the same. 4s. 6d. and 6s.
The Three Elizabeths. By the same. 3s. 6d. and 4s. 6d.
Alone in the World. By the same. 3s. 6d. and 4s. 6d.
Festival Tales. By J. F. Waller. 5s.
Shakespeare's Plays and Tragedies. Abridged and Revised for the use of Schools. By Rosa Baughan. 8vo. 7s. 6d.
Poems. By H. N. Oxenham. *Third Edition.* 3s. 6d.

Miscellaneous and Educational.

History of Modern Europe. With a Preface by the Right Rev. Dr. Weathers. 12mo. cloth, 5s. ; gilt, 6s. ; roan, 5s. 6d.
 " A work of especial importance for the way in which it deals with the early part of the present Pontificate."—*Weekly Register.*
Culpepper. An entirely New Edition of Brook's Family Herbal. 150 engravings, drawn and coloured from living specimens. Crown 8vo., 5s. 6d.
The Continental Fish Cook; or, a Few Hints on Maigre Dinners. By M. J. N. de Frederic. 18mo. 1s.
 "This is an admirable collection of recipes, which many housekeepers will welcome for use. We strongly recommend our lady readers at once to procure it."—*Church Herald.* "It will give to all mistresses of households very valuable hints on maigre dinners, and we feel sure they will be glad to know of the existence of such a manual."—*Register.* "There are 103 recipes, all of which have been practically tested ; they combine variety, wholesomeness, and economy."—*Universe.* "It is an unpretending little work, but nevertheless containing many recipes, enabling housekeepers to provide an excellent variety of dishes, such as may lawfully be eaten in times of fasting and abstinence."—*Church Times.*

University Education, under the Guidance of the Church ; or, Monastic Studies. By a Monk of St. Augustine's, Ramsgate. 8vo. 2s. 6d.

"An admirable pamphlet. Its contents are above praise. We trust that it will be widely circulated."—*Weekly Register.* "The author is evidently a scholar, a well-read man, and a person of experience and wide reading. His essay, consequently, is worth both studying and preserving."—*Church Herald.*

Elements of Philosophy, comprising Logic, and General Principles of Metaphysics. By Rev. W. H. Hill, S.J. Second edition, 8vo. 6s.

"This work is from the pen of one who has devoted many years to the study and teaching of philosophy. It is elementary, and must be concise; yet it treats the important points of philosophy so clearly, and contains so many principles of wide application, that it cannot fail to be especially useful in a country where sound philosophical doctrine is perhaps more needed than in any other."

History of England. By W. Mylius. 12mo. 3s. 6d.

Catechism of the History of England. Cloth, 1s.

History of Ireland. By T. Young. 18mo. cloth, 2s. 6d.

The Illustrated History of Ireland. By the Nun of Kenmare. Illustrated by Doyle. 8vo. 11s.

The Patriots' History of Ireland. By the Poor Clares of Kenmare. 18mo. cloth, 2s. ; cloth gilt, 2s. 6d.

A Chronological Sketch of the Kings of England and France. With Anecdotes for the use of Children. By H. Murray Lane. 2s. 6d. ; or separately, England, 1s. 6d., France, 1s. 6d.

"Admirably adapted for teaching young children the elements of English and French history."—*Tablet.* "A very useful little publication."—*Weekly Register.* "An admirably arranged little work for the use of children."—*Universe.*

The Catholic Alphabet of Scripture Subjects. Price, on a sheet, plain, 1s. ; coloured, 2s. ; mounted on linen, to fold in a case, 3s. 6d. ; varnished, on linen, on rollers, 4s.

"This will be hailed with joy by all young children in Catholic schools, and we should gladly see it placed conspicuously before the eyes of our little ones."—*Catholic Opinion.* "Will be very welcome in the infant school."—*Weekly Register.*

Bell's Modern Reader and Speaker. Cloth, 3s. 6d.

R. Washbourne, 18 Paternoster Row, London.

General. Questions in History, Chronology, Geography, the Arts, &c. By A. M. Stewart. 4s. 6d.
Extracts from the Fathers and other Writers of the Church. 12mo. cloth, 4s. 6d.
Brickley's Standard Table Book, ½d.
Washbourne's Multiplication Table on a sheet, 3s. per 100. Specimen sent for 1d. stamp.

Music (*Net*).

BY HERR WILHELM SCHULTHES.

Veni Domine. Motett for Four Voices. 2s.; vocal arrangement, 6d.
Cor Jesu, Salus in Te Sperantium. 2s.; with harp accompaniment, 2s. 6d.; abridged edition, 3d.
Mass of the Holy Child Jesus, and Ave Maria for unison and congregational singing, with organ accompaniment. 3s.
  The Vocal Part. 4d.; or in cloth, 6d.
The Ave Maria of this Mass can be had for Four Voices, with the Ingressus Angelus. 1s. 3d.
Recordare. Oratio Jeremiæ Prophetæ. 1s.
Ne projicias me a facie Tua. Motett for Four Voices. (T.B.) 1s. 3d.
Benediction Service, with 36 Litanies. 6s.
Oratory Hymns. 2 vols., 8s.
Regina Cœli. Motett for Four Voices. 3s.; vocal arrangement, 1s.
Twelve Latin Hymns, for Vespers, &c. 2s.

Litanies. By Rev. J. McCarthy. 1s. 3d.
Six Litany Chants. By F. Leslie. 6d.
Ave Maria. By T. Haydn Waud. 1s. 6d.
Fr. Faber's Hymns. Various, 9d. each.
Portfolio. With a patent metallic back. 3s.

A **separate** Catalogue of FOREIGN Books, Educational Books, Books for the Library or for Prizes, supplied; also a Catalogue of School and General Stationery, a Catalogue of Secondhand Books, and a Catalogue of Crucifixes and other Religious Articles.

INDEX TO AUTHORS.

Author	PAGE	Author	PAGE
A'Kempis, Thomas	8	King, Miss	28
Allies, T. W., Esq.	11	Lacordaire, Père	12
Amherst, Bishop	8	Laing, Rev. Dr.	13, 16, 21
Bagshawe, Rev. Fr.	22	Lane, H. Murray, Esq.	30
Bagshawe, Rev. J. B.	14, 15	Lockhart, Rev. Fr.	13
Bampfield, Rev. G.	28	M'Corry, Rev. Dr.	17
Barge, Rev. T.	23	Macdaniel, Miss	21, 24
Beste, J. R. D., Esq.	10, 23, 25	Macleod, Rev. X. D.	21
Beste, Rev. K. D.	25	Manning, Most Rev. Dr.	13, 19
Bethell, Rev. A. P.	21	Marshall, T. W. M., Esq.	10
Blosius	7	Meehan, Madeleine Howley	26
Boudon, Mgr.	7	Milner, Bishop	23
Bowles, Emily	27	Nary, Rev. I.	15
Bradbury, Rev. Fr.	29	Nevin, Willis	2
Brownlow, Rev. W. R. B.	5, 13	Newman, Dr.	19
Burder, Rt. Rev. Abbot	6	Oratorian Lives of the Saints	18
Burke, S. H., M.A.	12	Oxenham, H. N.	11, 29
Butler, Alban	8, 17	Ozanam, Professor	2
Challoner, Bishop	16	Passionist Fathers	13
Collins, Rev. Fr.	9	Philpin, Rev. Fr.	6
Conscience, Hendrick	29	Poirier, Bishop	16
Culpepper	29	Poor Clares of Kenmare	12, 20
Darras, Abbé	7	Powell, J., Esq.	25
Deham, Rev. A.	23	Pye, H. J., Esq.	16
Dupanloup, Mgr.	2	Ravignan, Père	8
Fleuriot, Mdlle. Zénaïde	27	Redmond, Rev. Dr.	1, 13
Francis of Sales, St.	10, 11	Richardson, Rev. Fr.	17
Frassinetti	14	Robertson, Professor	11, 13
Gibson, Rev. H.	15	Scaramelli	9
Gilmour, Rev. R.	16	Schulthes, Herr	31
Goffine, Rev. Fr.	16	Shakespeare	29
Grace Ramsay	19	Ségur, Mgr. de	17
Grant, Bishop	11, 24	Shepard, T. S., Esq.	19
Gueranger	25	Sligo, A. V. Smith, Esq.	17
Hedley, Canon	7	Sligo, Mrs. Smith	27
Herbert, Lady	1, 2, 6	Stewart, A. M.	29
Hill, Rev. Fr.	30	Tame, C. E., Esq.	21
Hope, Mrs.	9	Tandy, Very Rev. Dr.	26
Husenbeth, Very Rev. Dr.	20, 21	Taunton, Mrs.	27
Kenny, Dr.	17	Williams, Canon	16

CONTENTS.

	PAGE		PAGE
New Books	1	Prayer-Books	22
Dramas, Comedies, Farces	3	Rome, &c.	25
Religious Reading	5	Tales, or Books for Library	26
Religious Instruction	14	Educational Works	29
Lives of Saints, &c.	17	Music	31
Our Lady, Works relating to	20		

R. WASHBOURNE, 18 PATERNOSTER ROW.

www.ingramcontent.com/pod-product-compliance
Lightning Source LLC
Chambersburg PA
CBHW020843160426
43192CB00007B/766